George Henry Moore, Samuel Sewall

Notes on the History of Slavery in Massachusetts

George Henry Moore, Samuel Sewall
Notes on the History of Slavery in Massachusetts
ISBN/EAN: 9783744732611

Printed in Europe, USA, Canada, Australia, Japan

Cover: Foto ©Suzi / pixelio.de

More available books at **www.hansebooks.com**

NOTES

ON THE

HISTORY OF SLAVERY

IN

MASSACHUSETTS

BY

GEORGE H. MOORE

LIBRARIAN OF THE NEW-YORK HISTORICAL SOCIETY AND CORRESPONDING
MEMBER OF THE MASSACHUSETTS HISTORICAL SOCIETY

Quis nescit, primam esse historiæ legem, ne quid falsi
dicere audeat? deinde ne quid veri non audeat?
—*Cic. de Orat.*, II., 15.

NEW-YORK
D. APPLETON & CO. 443 & 445 BROADWAY
MDCCCLXVI

Entered, according to Act of Congreſs, in the year 1866, by
GEORGE H. MOORE,
In the Clerk's Office of the Diſtrict Court of the United States for the
Southern Diſtrict of New York.

Stereotyped by JOHN F. TROW & Co., 50 Greene Street, New York.

CONTENTS.

I. EARLY HISTORY OF SLAVERY IN MASSACHUSETTS. PURITAN THEORY AND PRACTICE OF SLAVERY. . 1—10

II. THE LAW OF SLAVERY IN MASSACHUSETTS. ITS ESTABLISHMENT AND MODIFICATION. SLAVERY HEREDITARY IN MASSACHUSETTS. RESOLVE IN 1646, TO RETURN STOLEN NEGROES TO AFRICA, NOT AN ACT HOSTILE TO SLAVERY. . . 10—30

III. SLAVERY OF INDIANS IN MASSACHUSETTS. ATTEMPT TO SELL CHILDREN OF QUAKERS. . . 30—48

IV. STATISTICS OF SLAVE-POPULATION. LEGISLATION CONCERNING SLAVES AND SLAVERY. TAXATION OF SLAVE-PROPERTY. THE SLAVE-TRADE. 48—72

V. EARLIEST ANTI-SLAVERY MOVEMENTS IN AMERICA, IN RHODE ISLAND AND PENNSYLVANIA. CHIEF-JUSTICE SEWALL. CHARACTER AND CONDITIONS OF SLAVERY IN MASSACHUSETTS. JAMES OTIS'S PROTEST AGAINST NEGRO-SLAVERY. JOHN ADAMS SHUDDERS AT HIS DOCTRINES. . . . . 72—111

VI. "THE FREEDOM SUITS." SLAVERY CHALLENGED. MOVEMENTS IN THE LEGISLATURE BETWEEN 1767 AND 1775. . . . . . 111—147

VII. THE DOCTRINE OF PRIZE IN NEGROES. ACTION OF MASSACHUSETTS IN 1776. NATIONAL LEGISLATION ON THE SUBJECT. HISTORY OF THE DOCTRINE. SOUTH CAROLINA SLAVES CAPTURED BY THE BRITISH, AND RECAPTURED BY MASSACHUSETTS VESSELS OF WAR. LEGIS-

LATIVE AND JUDICIAL PROCEEDINGS OF MASSA-
CHUSETTS. . . . . 148—176

VIII. PROGRESS OF PUBLIC OPINION ON SLAVERY IN MASSACHUSETTS DURING THE REVOLUTION. ATTEMPT TO ABOLISH SLAVERY IN 1777. SUBJECT REFERRED TO THE CONTINENTAL CONGRESS. THE CONSTITUTION OF 1778. CONTROVERSY ON NEGRO EQUALITY. STATUS OF FREE NEGROES. . . . . . . 176—200

IX. THE CONSTITUTION OF 1780. ALLEGED ABOLITION OF SLAVERY. THE QUESTION EXAMINED. JUDICIAL LEGISLATION IN 1781-83. THE JENNISON SLAVE-CASES. APPEAL OF SLAVE-OWNERS TO THE LEGISLATURE. . . . 200—223

X. ABOLITION OF THE SLAVE-TRADE. LEGISLATION AGAINST NEGROES. EXPULSION OF NEGROES FROM THE STATE. CONCLUSION. . . . 224—242

APPENDIX.

A. THE MILITARY EMPLOYMENT OF NEGROES IN MASSACHUSETTS. . . . . . . 243—246
B. ADDITIONAL NOTES, ETC. . . . . 246—250
C. JUDGE SAFFIN'S REPLY TO JUDGE SEWALL, 1701. . 251—256

NOTES ON THE HISTORY OF SLAVERY IN MASSACHUSETTS.

I.

WE find the earlieſt records of the hiſtory of ſlavery in Maſſachuſetts at the period of the Pequod War—a few years after the Puritan ſettlement of the colony. Prior to that time an occaſional offender againſt the laws was puniſhed by being ſold into ſlavery or adjudged to ſervitude; but the inſtitution firſt appears clearly and diſtinctly in the enſlaving of Indians captured in war. We may hereafter add a ſketch of the theories which were held to juſtify the bondage of the heathen, but at preſent limit ourſelves to the collection of facts to illuſtrate our general ſubject. And at the outſet we deſire to ſay that in this hiſtory there is nothing to comfort pro-ſlavery men anywhere. The ſtains which ſlavery has left on the proud eſcutcheon even of Maſſachuſetts, are quite as ſignificant of its hideous character as the satanic defiance of God and Humanity which accompanied the laying of the corner-stone of the Slave-holders' Confederacy.

The story of the extermination of the Pequods is well known. It was that warlike tribe who, in the early months of "that fatal year," 1637, were reported by Governor Winslow to Winthrop as follows:

"The Pecoats follow their fishing & planting as if they had no enemies. Their women of esteem & children are gone to Long Island with a strong gard at Pecoat. They professe there you shall finde them, and as they were there borne & bred, there their bones shall be buried, & rott in despight of the English. But if the Lord be on our side, their braggs will soon fall." *M. H. S. Coll.*, iv., vi., 164.

The extracts which follow explain themselves and hardly require comment.

Roger Williams, writing from Providence [in June, 1637] to John Winthrop, says: "I understand it would be very gratefvll to our neighbours that such Pequts as fall to them be not enslaved, like those which are taken in warr; but (as they say is their generall custome) be vsed kindly, haue howses & goods & fields given them: becaufe they voluntarily choose to come in to them, & if not receaved will [go] to the enemie or turne wild Irish themselues: but of this more as I shall vnderstand. . . ." *M. H. S. Coll.*, iv., vi., 195.

Again [probably in July, 1637]: "It having againe pleased the Most High to put into your hands another miserable droue of Adams degenerate feede, & our brethren by nature, I am bold (if I may not offend in it) to requeſt the keeping & bringing vp of one of the children. I haue fixed mine eye on this little one with the red about his neck, but I will not be peremptory in my choice, but will reſt in your loving pleaſure for him or any," &c. *M. H. S. Coll.*, IV., vi., 195-6.

Again [probably 18th September, 1637]: "Sir, concerning captiues (pardon my wonted boldneſs) the Scripture is full of myſterie & the Old Teſtament of types.

"If they have deſerued death 'tis sinn to spare:

"If they haue not deſerued death then what puniſhments? Whether perpetuall ſlaverie.

"I doubt not but the enemie may lawfully be weaknd & despoild of all comfort of wife & children &c., but I befeech you well weigh it after a due time of trayning vp to labour & reſtraint, they ought not to be ſet free: yet so as without danger of adioyning to the enemie." *M. H. S. Coll.*, IV., vi., 214.

Later in the ſame year [Nov. 1637] Roger Williams, who had promiſed certain fugitive ſlaves to intercede for them, " to write that they might be vſed kindly"—fulfilled his promiſe in a letter to Winthrop, in which, after ſtating their complaints of ill usage, &c., he adds:

"My humble deſire is that all that haue theſe poor wretches might be exhorted as to walke wiſely & iuſtly towards them, so to make mercy eminent, for in that attribute the Father of mercy moſt ſhines to Adams miserable ofspring." *M. H. S. Coll.*, IV., vi., 218, 219.

· Hugh Peter writes to John Winthrop from Salem

(in 1637) : "Mr. Endecot and my felfe falute you in the Lord Jefus, etc. Wee haue heard of a diuidence of women and children in the bay and would bee glad of a fhare, viz. : a young woman or girle and a boy if you thinke good. *I wrote to you for fome boyes for Bermudas, which I thinke is confiderable.*" *M. H. S. Coll.*, IV., vi., 95.

In this application of Hugh Peter we have a glimpse of the beginning of the Colonial Slave-Trade. He wanted "fome boyes for the Bermudas," which he thought was "confiderable."

It would feem to indicate that this difpofition of captive Indian boys was in accordance with custom and previous practice of the authorities. At any rate, it is certain that in the Pequod War they took many prifoners. Some of thefe, who had been "difposed of to particular perfons in the country," *Winthrop*, I., 232, ran away, and being brought in again were "branded on the fhoulder," *ib.* In July, 1637, Winthrop fays, "We had now flain and taken, in all, about feven hundred. We fent fifteen of the boys and two women to Bermuda, by Mr. Peirce ; but he, miffing it, carried them to Providence Ifle," *Winthrop*, I., 234. The learned editor of Winthrop's Journal, referring to the fact that this proceeding in that day was probably juftified by reference to the practice or inftitution of the Jews, very quaintly obferves, "Yet that cruel people never fent prifoners fo far." *Ib.*, *note*.

Governor Winthrop, writing to Governor Bradford of Plymouth, 28th July, 1637, an account of their fuccefs againft the Pequods—"ye Lords greate mercies towards us, in our prevailing againſt his & our enimies"—says:

"The priſoners were devided, ſome to thoſe of yᵉ river [the Connecticut Colony] and the reſt to us. Of theſe we ſend the male children to Bermuda, by Mr. William Peirce, & yᵉ women & maid children are diſpoſed aboute in yᵉ tounes. Ther have now been ſlaine and taken, in all, aboute 700." *M. H. S. Coll.*, IV., iii., 360. Compare the order for "diſpoſing of yᵉ Indian ſquaws," in *Mass. Records*, I., 201.

Bradford's note to the letter quoted above, ſays of their being ſent to Bermuda: "But yᵉʸ were carried to yᵉ Weſt Indeas."

Hubbard, the contemporary hiſtorian of the Indian Wars, ſays of theſe captives, "Of thoſe who were not ſo deſperate or ſullen to ſell their lives for nothing, but yielded in time, the male Children were ſent to the *Bermudas*, of the females ſome were diſtributed to the Engliſh Towns; ſome were diſpoſed of among the other *Indians*, to whom they were deadly enemies, as well as to ourſelves." *Narrative*, 1677, p. 130.

A ſubſequent entry in Winthrop's Journal gives us another glimpſe of the ſubject, Feb. 26, 1638.

"Mr. Peirce, in the Salem ſhip, the Deſire, returned from the Weſt Indies after ſeven months. He had been at Providence, and brought ſome cotton, and tobacco, and negroes, etc., from thence, and ſalt from Tertugos;" *Winthrop*, I., 254. He adds to this account that "Dry fiſh and ſtrong liquors are the only commodities for thoſe parts. He met there two men-of-war, ſet forth by the lords, etc., of Providence with letters of mart, who had taken divers prizes from the Spaniard and many negroes." Long afterwards Dr. Belknap said of the slave-trade, that the rum distilled in Massachusetts was "the mainspring of this traffick." *M. H. S. Coll.*, I., iv., 197.

Josselyn says, that "they sent the male children of the Pequets to the Bermudus." 258. *M. H. S. Coll.*, IV., iii., 360.[1]

This single cargo of women and children was probably not the only one sent, for the Company of Providence Island, in replying from London in 1638, July 3, to letters from the authorities in the island, direct special care to be taken of the "Cannibal negroes brought from New England." *Sainsbury's Calendar*, 1574–1660, 278.[2]

And in 1639, when the Company feared that the number of the negroes might become too great to be managed, the authorities thought they might be sold and sent to New England or Virginia. *Ib.*, 296.

The ship "Desire" was a vessel of one hundred and twenty tons, built at Marblehead in 1636, one of the earliest built in the Colony. *Winthrop*, I., 193.

In the Pequot War, some of the Narragansetts

---

[1] Governor Winthrop in his will (1639-41) left to his son Adam his island called the Governor's Garden, adding, "I give him also my Indians there and my boat and such household as is there."—*Winthrop's Journal*, II., 360., *App.*

[2] "We would have the Cannibal negroes brought from New England inquired after, whose they are, and speciall care taken of them." P. R. O. *Col. Ent. Bk.*, Vol. IV., p. 124. In the preface to the Colonial Calendar, p. xxv., Mr. Sainsbury explains why no answers to the Company's letters are in the State Paper Office. The Bahama Islands were governed absolutely by a Company in London, and unfortunately the letters *received by* the Company have not been preserved, or if so, it is not known where they now are. MS. *Letter.*

joined the English in its prosecution, and received a part of the prisoners as slaves, for their services. Miantunnomoh received eighty, Ninigret was to have twenty. Mather says of the principal engagement, "the captives that were taken were about one hundred and eighty, which were divided between the two Colonyes, and they intended to keep them as servants, but they could not endure the Yoke, for few of them continued any considerable time with their masters." *Drake*, 122, 146. *Mather's Relation*, quoted by *Drake*, 39. See also *Hartford Treaty*, Sept. 21, 1638, in *Drake*, 125. *Drake's Mather*, 150, 151.

Captain Stoughton, who assisted in the work of exterminating the Pequots, after his arrival in the enemy's country, wrote to the Governor of Massachusetts [Winthrop] as follows: " By this pinnace, you shall receive forty-eight or fifty women and children. . . . Concerning which, there is one, I formerly mentioned, that is the fairest and largest that I saw amongst them, to whom I have given a coate to cloathe her. It is my desire to have her for a servant, if it may stand with your good liking, else not. There is a little squaw that Steward Culacut desireth, to whom he hath given a coate. Lieut. Davenport also desireth one, to wit, a small one, that hath three strokes upon her stomach, thus: — ||| +. He desireth her, if it will stand with your liking. Sosomon, the Indian, desireth a young little squaw, which I know not." *MS. Letter* in Mass. Archives, quoted by *Drake*, 171.

An early traveller in New England has preserved for us the record of one of the earliest, if not, indeed, the very first attempt at breeding of slaves in America. The following paffage from Joffelyn's Account of Two Voyages to New England, publifhed at London in 1664, will explain itfelf:

"The Second of *October*, [1639] about 9 of the clock in the morning Mr. *Mavericks* Negro woman came to my chamber window, and in her own Countrey language and tune fang very loud and fhrill, going out to her, fhe ufed a great deal of refpect towards me, and willingly would have expreffed her grief in *Englifh;* but I apprehended it by her countenance and deportment, whereupon I repaired to my hoft, to learn of him the caufe, and refolved to intreat him in her behalf, for that I underftood before, that fhe had been a Queen in her own Countrey, and obferved a very humble and dutiful garb ufed towards her by another Negro who was her maid. *Mr. Maverick* was defirous to have a breed of Negroes, and therefore feeing fhe would not yield by perfuafions to company with a Negro young man he had in his houfe; he commanded him will'd fhe nill'd fhe to go to bed to her, which was no fooner done but fhe kickt him out again, this fhe took in high difdain beyond her flavery, and this was the caufe of her grief." *Joffelyn*, 28.

Joffelyn vifited New England twice, and fpent about ten years in this country, from 1638–39 and 1663 to 1671. In fpeaking of the people of Bofton he mentions that the people "are well accommodated with fervants .... of thefe fome are Englifh, others Negroes." *Ibid.*, 182.

Mr. Palfrey fays: "Before Winthrop's arrival there were two negro flaves in Maffachufetts, held by Mr. Maverick, on Noddle's Ifland." *Hiftory of New England*, II., 30, *note*. If there is any evidence to fuftain this ftatement, it is certainly not in the authority to which he refers. On the contrary, the inference is irrefiftible from all the authorities together, that the negroes of Mr. Maverick were a portion of thofe imported in the firft colonial flave-fhip, the Defire, of whofe voyage we have given the hiftory. It is not to be fuppofed that Mr. Maverick had waited ten years before taking the fteps towards improving his ftock of negroes, which are referred to by Joffelyn. Ten years' flavery on Noddle's Ifland would have made the negro-queen more familiar with the Englifh language, if not more compliant to the brutal cuftoms of flavery.

It will be obferved that this firft entrance into the flave-trade was not a private, individual fpeculation. It was the enterprife of the authorities of the Colony. And on the 13th March, 1639, it was ordered by the General Court "that 3*l* 8*s* should be paid Leiftenant Davenport for the prefent, for charge difburfed for the flaves, which, when they have earned it, hee is to repay it back againe." The marginal note is, " Lieft. Davenport to keep ye flaues." *Mafs. Rec.*, 1., 253.

Emanuel Downing, a lawyer of the Inner Temple, London, who married Lucy Winthrop, fifter of the elder Winthrop, came over to New England in 1638. The editors of the Winthrop papers fay of him, " There were few more active or efficient friends of the Maffachufetts Colony during its earlieft and moft critical period." His fon was the famous Sir George Downing, Englifh ambaffador at the Hague.

In a letter to his brother-in-law, "probably written during the fummer of 1645," is a moft luminous illuftration of the views of that day and generation on the subject of human flavery. He fays:

"A warr with the Narraganfett is verie confiderable to this plantation, ffor I doubt whither yt be not fynne in vs, hauing power in our hands, to fuffer them to maynteyne the worfhip of the devill, which their paw wawes often doe; 2lie, if upon a Juft warre the Lord fhould deliver them into our hands, we might eafily haue men, woemen and children enough to exchange for Moores, which wilbe more gayneful pilladge for vs than wee conceive, for I doe not fee how wee can thrive vntill wee gett into a ftock of slaves fufficient to doe all our buifines, for our children's children will hardly fee this great Continent filled with people, foe that our fervants will ftill defire freedom to plant for them felues, and not ftay but for verie great wages. And I fuppofe you know verie well how wee fhall maynteyne 20 Moores cheaper than one Englifhe fervant.

"The fhips that fhall bring Moores may come home laden with falt which may beare most of the chardge, if not all of yt. But I marvayle Conecticott fhould any wayes hafard a warre without your advife, which they cannot mayntayne without your helpe."
M. H. S. Coll., iv., vi., 65.

II.

WE come now to the era of pofitive legiflation on the fubject of human bondage in America. Mr.

Hurd, the ablest writer on this subject, says: "The involuntary servitude of Indians and negroes in the several colonies originated under a law not promulgated by legislation, and rested upon prevalent views of universal jurisprudence, or the *law of nations*, supported by the express or implied authority of the home Government." *Law of Freedom and Bondage*, § 216, I., 225.

Under this sanction slavery may very properly be said to have originated in all the colonies, but it was not long before it made its appearance on the statute-book in Massachusetts. The first statute establishing slavery in America is to be found in the famous CODE OF FUNDAMENTALS, or BODY OF LIBERTIES OF THE MASSACHUSETTS COLONY IN NEW-ENGLAND—the first code of laws of that colony, adopted in December, 1641. These liberties had been, after a long struggle between the magistrates and the people, extracted from the reluctant grasp of the former. "The people had [1639] long desired a body of laws, and thought their condition very unsafe, while so much power rested in the discretion of magistrates." *Winthrop*, I., 322. Never were the demands of a free people eluded by their public servants with more of the contortions as well as wisdom of the serpent. *Compare Gray in M. H. S.*, III., viii., 208.

The scantiness of the materials for the particular history of this renowned code is such as to forbid the attempt to trace with certainty to its origin the law in question. It is, however, obvious that it was made to provide for slavery as an existing, substantial fact, if not to restrain the application of those higher—

law doctrines, which the magistrates must have sometimes found inconvenient in administration. The preamble to the Body of Liberties itself might have been construed into some vague recognition of rights in individual members of society superior to legislative power—although it was promulgated by the possessors of the most arbitrary authority in the then actual holders of legislative and executive power. *Compare Hurd's Law of Freedom and Bondage*, 1., 198. Had they only learned to reason as some of the modern writers of Massachusetts history have done on this subject, the poor Indians and Negroes of that day might have compelled additional legislation if they could not vindicate their rights to freedom in the general court. For the first article of the Declaration of Rights in 1780, is only a new edition of " the glittering and sounding generalities " which prefaced the Body of Liberties in 1641. Under the latter, human slavery existed for nearly a century and a half without serious challenge, while under the former it is said to have been abolished by inference by a public opinion which still continued to tolerate the slave-trade.

But to the law and the testimony. The ninety-first article of the Body of Liberties appears as follows, under the head of

" *Liberties of Forreiners and Strangers.*

" 91. There shall never be any bond slaverie, villinage or captivitie amongst us unles it be lawfull captives taken in just warres, and such strangers as willingly selle themselves or are sold to us. And these shall have all the liberties and Christian usages which the law of God eſtabliſhed in Iſraell concerning ſuch perſons doeth morally require. This exempts none from ſervitude who ſhall be Judged thereto by Authoritie." *M. H. S. Coll.*, III., viii., 231.

Theſe laws were not printed, but were publiſhed in manuſcript[1] under the ſuperintendence of a committee in which Deputy-Governor Endicott was aſſociated with Mr. Downing and Mr. Hauthorne, and, Governor Winthrop ſays, "eſtabliſhed for three years, by that experience to have them fully amended and eſtabliſhed to be perpetual." *Maſs. Records*, I., 344, 346. *Winthrop's Journal*, II., 55. By the ninety-eighth and laſt ſection of this code, it was decreed as follows:

"98. Laſtly becauſe our dutie and deſire is to do nothing ſuddainlie which fundamentally concerne us, we decree that theſe rites and liberties, ſhall be Audably read and deliberately weighed at every Generall Court that ſhall be held, within three yeares next inſueing, And ſuch of them as ſhall not be altered or repealed they ſhall ſtand ſo ratified, That no man ſhall infringe them without due puniſhment.

"And if any Generall Court within theſe next thre yeares ſhall faile or forget to reade and conſider them as aboveſaid, The Governor and Deputy Governor for the time being, and every Aſſiſtant preſent at ſuch Courts, ſhall forfeite 20 ſh. a man, and everie Deputie 10 ſh. a man for each neglect, which ſhall be

---

[1] There is no reaſon to doubt the authenticity of the ancient MS. which was the foundation of the very able and inſtructive paper of the late Mr. Francis C. Gray on "*The Early Laws of Maſſachuſetts,*" as a part of which the Body of Liberties was printed in 1843.

paid out of their proper eftate, and not by the Country or the Townes which choofe them, and whenfoever there fhall arife any queftion in any Court amonge the Affiftants and Affociates thereof about the explanation of thefe Rites and liberties, The Generall Court onely fhall have power to interprett them." *M. H. S. Coll.*, III., viii., 236, 237.

It is not to be doubted that at the following feffions of the General Court, "the lawes were read over," in accordance with this decree. And before the expiration of the three years, committees were appointed to revife the Body of Liberties, and orders relating to it were paffed every year afterward until 1648, when the laws were firft printed. *Gray's Reports*, IX., 513.[1]

Of this firft printed edition of the laws it is fuppofed that no copy is now in exiftence. *Ibid.* This is much to be regretted, as a comparifon might poffibly throw fome light on the change in the law of flavery, which appears in all the fubfequent editions. Although hitherto entirely unnoticed, we regard it as highly important; for it takes away the foundation of a grievous charge againft that God-fearing and law-abiding people. For, if "no perfon was ever born into legal flavery in Maffachufetts," there was a moft fhocking chronic violation of law in that Colony and Province for more than a century, hardly to be reconciled with their hiftorical reputation.

[1] In the elaborate, learned, and moft valuable note of Mr. Gray, here referred to, the reader will find references to all the original authorities, which it is needlefs to repeat in this place. We have been unable to verify his reference to *Mafs. Records*, II., 2, for proceedings of the General Court on the 20th May, 1642, in the common copies of that volume.

In the second printed edition, that of 1660, the law appears as follows, under the title

"*BOND-SLAVERY.*

IT is Ordered by this Court & Authority thereof; That there shall never be any bond-slavery villenage or captivity amongst us, unles it be Lawfull captives, taken in just warrs, [*or such*] as [*shall*] willingly sell themselves, or are sold to us, and such shall have the liberties, & Christian usuage, which the Law of God established in Israel, Concerning such persons, doth morally require, provided this exempts none from servitude, who shall be judged thereto by Authority. [1641.]" *Mass. Laws, Ed.* 1660, *p.* 5.

The words italicized in brackets appear among the manuscript corrections of the copy which (formerly the property of Mr. Secretary Rawson, who was himself apparently the Editor of the volume) is now preserved in the Library of the American Antiquarian Society at Worcester, in Massachusetts. It is plain, however, that the printed text required correction, and—although no better authority can possibly be demanded than that of the Editor himself—it is confirmed by the subsequent edition of 1672, in which the same error, having been repeated in the text, is made the occasion of a correction in the printed table of errata. There is a want of accuracy even in this correction itself; but the intention is so obvious that it cannot be mistaken. *Mass. Laws, Ed.* 1672, *pp.* 10, 170.

To prevent any possible doubt which may still linger in the mind of any reader at the end of the demonstration through which we ourselves first arrived at this refult, we will add the following record—evidence afterwards difcovered—which it will puzzle the moft aftute critic to make "void and of none effect."

In May, 1670, on the laft day of the month, a committee was appointed by the General Court "to pervfe all our lawes now in force, to collect & drawe vp any literall errors or mifplacing of words or fentences therein, or any libertjes infringed, and to make a convenient table for the ready finding of all things therein, that fo they may be fitted ffor the preffe, & the fame to prefent to the next feffion of this Court, to be further confidered off & approved by the Court." *Mafs. Records*, iv., ii., 453.

At the following feffion of the Court, the committee prefented their report accordingly, and on the 12th October, 1670, the following order was made:

"The Court, having pervfed & confidered of the returne of the comittee, to whom the revejw of the lawes was referred, &c., by the Generall Court in May laft, as to the litterall erratars, &c., do order that in *   *   *   *   *

"Page 5, lj : 3, tit. Bondflauery, read 'or fuch as fhall willingly,' &c." *Mafs. Records*, iv., ii., 467.

As the circumftances under which all thefe laws and liberties were originally compofed and after long difcuffion, minute examination, and repeated revifions, finally fettled and eftablifhed, forbid the fuppofition that flavery came in an unbidden or unwelcome gueft —fo is it equally impoffible to admit that this alteration of the fpecial law of flavery by the omiffion of so important and fignificant a word could have been accidental or without motive.

If under the original law the children of enflaved captives and ftrangers might poffibly have claimed exemption from that fervitude to which the recognized common law of nations affigned them from their birth; this amendment, by ftriking out the word "ftrangers," removed the neceffity for alienage or foreign birth as a qualification for flavery, and took off the prohibition againft the children of flaves being "born into legal flavery in Maffachufetts."

It is true there is little probability that in thofe days the natural rights of thefe little heathen, born in a Chriftian land, would have been much regarded, or that the owners of flave parents would have had much difficulty in quieting the title by having the increafe of their chattels duly "judged" to fervitude by authoritie," in accordance with the civil law; ftill there might have been color for the claim to freedom, which this amendment effectually barred. And this was in accordance, too, with the law of Mofes—the children of flaves remained flaves, being the clafs defcribed as "born in the houfe."

This Maffachufetts law of flavery was not a regulation of the ftatus of indentured fervants. "Bondflavery" was not the name of their fervice, neither is it placed among the "*Liberties of fervants,*" but thofe of "*Forreiners and ftrangers.*" And in all the editions of the laws, this diftinction is maintained; "*Bondflavery*" being invariably a feparate title. White fervants for a term of years would hardly be defignated as ftrangers,[1] and a careful ftudy of the whole fubject

---

[1] John Cotton, in his letter to Cromwell, July 28, 1651, fays: "the Scots, whom God delivered into your hands at Dunbarre, and whereof

justifies at least the doubt whether the *privileges* of
servants belonged to slaves at all.

The law must be interpreted in the light of contemporaneous facts of history. At the time it was
made (1641), what had its authors to provide for?
1. Indian slaves — their captives taken in war.
2. Negro slaves — their own importations of
"strangers" obtained by purchase or exchange.
3. Criminals — condemned to slavery as a punishment for offences.

In this light, and only in this light, is their legislation intelligible and consistent. It is very true that
the code of which this law is a part "exhibits throughout the hand of the practised lawyer, familiar with the
principles and securities of English Liberty;" but
who had ever heard, at that time, of the "common-
law rights" of Indians and negroes, or anybody else
but Englishmen?

Thus stood the statute through the whole colonial
period, and it was never expressly repealed. Based on
the Mosaic code, it is an absolute recognition of
slavery as a legitimate status, and of the right of one
man to sell himself as well as that of another man to
buy him. It sanctions the slave-trade, and the perpetual bondage of Indians and negroes, their children
and their children's children, and entitles Massachusetts to precedence over any and all the other colonies

---

sundry were sent hither, we have been desirous (as we could) to make their yoke easy. * * * They have not been sold for slaves to perpetuall servitude, but for 6, or 7 or 8 yeares, as we do our owne." *Hutchinson's Coll.*, 235. He certainly did not mean " our owne " Indians and negroes.

in fimilar legiflation. It anticipates by many years anything of the fort to be found in the ftatutes of Virginia, or Maryland, or South Carolina, and nothing like it is to be found in the contemporary codes of her fifter colonies in New England. *Compare Hildreth*, I., 278.

Yet this very law has been gravely cited in a paper communicated to the Maffachufetts Hiftorical Society, and twice reprinted in its publications without challenge or correction, as an evidence that "fo far as it felt free to follow its own inclinations, uncontrolled by the action of the mother country, Maffachufetts was hoftile to flavery as an inftitution." *M. H. S. Coll.*, IV., iv., 334. *Proc.*, 1855-58, *p.* 189.

And with the ftatute before them, it has been perfiftently afferted and repeated by all forts of authorities, hiftorical and legal, up to that of the Chief Juftice of the Supreme Court of the Commonwealth, that "flavery to a certain extent feems to have crept in; not probably by force of any law, for none fuch is found or known to exift." *Commonwealth* vs. *Aves*, 18 *Pickering*, 208. *Shaw, C. J.*

The leading cafe in Maffachufetts is that of *Winchendon* vs. *Hatfield in error*, IV *Mafs. Reports*, 123. It relates to the fettlement of a negro pauper who had been a flave as early as 1757, and paffed through the hands of nine feparate owners before 1775. From the ninth he abfconded, and enlifted in the Maffachufetts Army among the eight-months' men, at Cambridge, in the beginning of the Revolutionary War. His term of fervice had not expired when he was again fold, in July, 1776, to another citizen of Maffachufetts, with whom he lived about five weeks, when he enlifted into the three-years' fervice, and his laft owner received the whole of his bounty and part of his wages.

EDOM LONDON, for fuch was the name of this revolutionary patriot, in 1806 was "poor," and "had become chargeable" to the town in which he refided. That town magnanimoufly ftruggled through all the Courts, from the Juftices Court up to the Supreme Court of the Commonwealth, to fhift the refponsibility for the maintenance and fupport of the old foldier from itfelf to one of the numerous other towns in which he had fojourned from time to time as the flave of his eleven mafters. The attempt was unfuccefsful; but it is worthy of notice, as Chief Juftice Parfons, in the decifion on the appeal, fettled feveral very important points concerning the laws of flavery in Maffachufetts. He said:

"Slavery was introduced into this country [Maffachufetts] foon after its firft fettlement, and was tolerated until the ratification of the prefent Conftitution [the Conftitution of 1780]. . . . The iffue of the female flave, according to the maxim of the Civil law, was the property of her mafter."

With regard to this latter point, Chief Juftice Dana, in directing a jury, in 1796, had ftated as the unanimous opinion of the Court, that a negro born in the State before the Conftitution of 1780, was born free, although born of a female flave.

Chief Juftice Parfons, however, candidly declared that "it is very certain that the general practice and common ufage had been oppofed to this opinion."

Chief Juſtice Parker, in 1816, cautiouſly confirmed this view of the ſubject by his predeceſſor. *Andover* vs. *Canton*, 13 *Maſs. Reports*, 551-552.

"The practice was . . . to conſider ſuch iſſue as ſlaves, and the property of the maſter of the parents, liable to be ſold and transferred like other chattels, and as aſſets in the hands of executors and adminiſtrators." He adds, "we think there is no doubt that, at any period of our hiſtory, the iſſue of a ſlave huſband and a free wife would have been declared free." [1]

"His children, if the iſſue of a marriage with a ſlave, would, immediately on their birth, become the property of his maſter, or of the maſter of the female ſlave."

Notwithſtanding all this, in Mr. Sumner's famous ſpeech in the Senate, June 28, 1854, he boldly aſſerted that "in all her annals, no perſon was ever born a ſlave on the ſoil of Maſſachuſetts," and "if, in point of fact, the iſſue of ſlaves was ſometimes held in bondage, it was never by ſanction of any ſtatute-law of Colony or Commonwealth."

And recent writers of hiſtory in Maſſachuſetts have aſſumed a ſimilar lofty and poſitive tone on this ſubject. Mr. Palfrey ſays: "In fact, no perſon was ever born into legal ſlavery in Maſſachuſetts." *Hiſt. N. E.*, II., 30, *note*. Neither Mr. Sumner nor Mr. Palfrey give any authorities for their ſtatements be-

---

[1] Kendall, who travelled through the northern parts of the United States in the years 1807 and 1808, referring to this ſubject, ſays: "While ſlavery was maintained in Maſſachuſetts, there was a particular temptation to negroes for taking Indian wives, the children of Indian women being acknowledged to be free." *Travels*, II., 179. See *Hiſt. Coll. Eſſex Inſtitute*, Vol. VII., p. 73. *Caſe of Priscilla, &c., againſt Simmons.*

yond the cafes in *Maffachufetts Reports*, IV., 128, 129; XVI., 73, and *Cufhing's Reports*, X., 410, which are alfo referred to by Mr. Juftice Gray in a ftill more recent and authoritative publication. The diftinguifhed ability of this gentleman, fo long recognized and acknowledged at the bar in Maffachufetts, will do ample honor to the bench to which he is fo juftly advanced. We entertain the higheft refpect for his attainments, his judgment, and his critical fagacity; but in this inftance we think he has fallen into a ferious error, which not even the great weight of his authority can eftablifh or perpetuate in hiftory.

In an elaborate hiftorical note to the cafe of *Oliver* vs. *Sale*, *Quincy's Reports*, 29, he fays:

"Previoufly to the adoption of the State Conftitution in 1780, negro flavery exifted to fome extent, and negroes held as flaves might be fold, but *all children of flaves were by law free.*"

So diftinct and pofitive an affertion fhould have been fortified by unequivocal authority. In this cafe Mr. Gray gives us two or three dozen feparate references. Thefe are numerous and conclufive enough as to the facts in the firft claufes of his ftatement—that negro flavery exifted in Maffachufetts, and that negro flaves might be fold; but for the laft and moft important part of it, that *all children of flaves were by law free*,[1] there is not an iota of evidence or author-

---

[1] In the cafe of *Newport* vs. *Billing*, which Mr. Gray believes to have been "the lateft inftance of a verdict for the mafter," it was found by the higheft court in Maffachufetts, on appeal from a fimilar decifion in the inferior court, "that the faid Amos [Newport] was not a freeman, as he alledged, but the proper flave of the faid Jofeph [Billing]. *Records*, 1768, *fol.* 284. As this feems to have been one of the fo-called "freedom

ity in the entire array, excepting the opinion of the Court in 1796, already referred to.

This "unanimous opinion of the Court," in 1796, which has been so often quoted to sustain the reputation of Massachusetts for early and consistent zeal against slavery, will hardly suffice to carry the weight assigned to it. In the first place, the facts proved to the jury in the case itself were set at naught by the Court in the statement of this opinion. We quote them, omitting the peculiar phraseology by which they are disguised in the report.

An action was brought by the inhabitants of Littleton, to recover the expense of maintaining a negro, against Tuttle, his former master. It was tried in Middlesex, October Term, 1796. The negro's name was Cato. His father, named Scipio, was a negro slave when Cato was born, the property of Nathan Chase, an inhabitant of Littleton. Cato's mother, named Violet, was a negro in the same condition, and the property of Joseph Harwood. Scipio and Violet were lawfully married, and had issue, Cato, born in Littleton, January 18th, 1773, a slave, the property of the said Harwood, as the owner of his mother. *Mass. Reports*, iv., 128, *note*.

But whatever may be inferred from these facts taken in connection with the "opinion" of the Court, in 1796, we ask the attention of the reader to another case a little later, before the same tribunal. In the case of *Perkins, Town Treasurer of Topsfield*, vs. *Emerson*, tried in Essex, the Court held that a certain negro

cases," it is to be regretted that Mr. Gray did not ascertain from the files whether "the said Amos" was a native of Massachusetts!

girl born in the Province in Wenham in 1759, was a flave belonging to Emerfon from 1765 to 1776, when fhe was freed. This decifion was in November, 1799. *Dane's Abridgment*, II., 412. Thus it appears that the Supreme Judicial Court of Maffachufetts inftructed a jury in 1796, by an unanimous opinion, that a negro born in the State before the Conftitution of 1780, was born free, although born of a female flave. Three years later, the fame Court and the fame judges (three out of four),[1] held a negro girl born in the province in 1759 to have been the lawful flave of a citizen of Maffachufetts from 1765 to 1776. In the latter cafe, too, the decifion of the Court was given on the queftion of law alone, as prefented upon an agreed ftatement of the facts. *MS. Copy of Court Records.*

A cafe in Connecticut prefents an illuftration of great importance. It is that of "a fugitive flave, and attempted refcue, in Hartford, 1703," of which an account is given in one of Mr. J. Hammond Trumbull's admirable articles on fome of the Connecticut Statutes. *Hiftorical Notes, etc.,* No. VI.

"The case laid before the Honorable General Affembly in October, 1704," after a ftatement of facts, etc., proceeds with reafons for the return of the fugitive, fome of which we quote.

---

[1] The judges prefent at thefe Terms refpectively were the following, viz.:

October Term, 1796, *in Middlesex:*
Francis Dana, *Chief Juftice.*
Robert Treat Paine,
Increafe Sumner,
Nathan Cufhing,
Thomas Dawes, jr., *Juftices.*

November Term, 1799, *in Effex:*
Francis Dana, *Chief Juftice.*
Robert Treat Paine,
Theophilus Bradbury,
Nathan Cufhing, *Juftices.*

"I. *According to the laws and constant practice of this colony and all other plantations*, (as well as by the civil law) *such persons as are born of negro bond-women are themselves* in like condition, that is, *born in servitude. Nor can there be any precedent in* this government, or *any of her Majesty's plantations, produced to the contrary*.[1] And though the law of this colony doth not say that such persons as are born of negro women and supposed to be mulattoes, shall be slaves, (which was needless, because of *the constant practice by which they are held as such*,) yet it saith expressly that 'no man shall put away or make free his negro *or mulatto* slave,' etc., which undeniably shows and declares an approbation of such servitude, and that mulattoes may be held as slaves within this government."

The value of this testimony on the subject is enhanced by the character and position of the witness. He was Gurdon Saltonstall, born in Massachusetts, the son of a magistrate, educated at Harvard College, and afterwards Governor of Connecticut,—"at that time the popular minister of the New London church, and nearly as distinguished at the bar as in the pulpit. The friend and confidential adviser of the governor (Winthrop), who was one of his parishioners, his influence was already felt in the Colonial Councils, and he was largely entrusted with the management of public affairs. In general scholarship, and in the extent of his professional studies, both in divinity and law, he had probably no superior in the colony: as an advo-

---

[1] Lay, in his tract "*All Slave-Keepers Apostates*," *p.* 11., enumerating the hardships of the institution, says, "Nor doth this satisfy, but their children also are kept in slavery, *ad infinitum* ; . . . "

cate, according to the teftimony of his contemporaries, he had no equal." *J. Hammond Trumbull's Hiftorical Notes. Backus*, II., 35. *Trumbull's Connecticut, Vol.* I. (1797), 417. Mr. Trumbull alfo mentions a queftion raifed in 1722, as to the ftatus of the children of Indian captive-flaves, in a memorial to the Legiflature, from which it is apparent that no doubt was entertained as to the legal flavery of children of negroes or imported Indians from beyond feas.

Ample evidence is given elfewhere in these notes of the fact, that the children of flaves were actually held and taken to be flaves, the property of the owners of the mothers, liable to be fold and transferred like other chattels and as affets in the hands of executors and adminiftrators.[1] This fact comes out in many portions of this hiftory; there is no one thing more patent to the reader. The inftances are numerous, and it is needlefs to recapitulate them here; but it may be proper to refer to the facts that in the inftructions of the town of Leicefter to their representative in 1773, among the ways and means fuggefted for extinguifhing flavery, they propofed "that every negro child that fhall be born in faid government after the enacting fuch law fhould be free at the fame age that the children of white people are," and in the petition of the negro flaves for relief in

---

[1] "A bill of fale, or other formal inftrument, was not neceffary to transfer the property in a flave, which was a mere perfonal chattel, and might pafs, as other chattels, by delivery." *Milford* vs. *Bellingham*, 16 *Mafs. Reports*, 110. Governor Dudley's report to the Board of Trade on flaves and the flave-trade in Maffachufetts, etc., in 1708, ftated that "in Boston, there are 400 negro fervants, *one half of whom were born here.*" *Collections Amer. Stat. Affoc.*, I., 586.

1777 to the General Court of Maſſachuſetts, they humbly pray that "their children (who were born in this land of liberty) may not be held as ſlaves after they arrive at the age of twenty-one years." *Maſs. Archives. Revolutionary Reſolves, Vol.* VII., *p.* 132.

The Articles of Confederation of the United Colonies of New England, 19th May, 1643, which commence with the famous recital of their object in coming into thoſe parts of America, viz., "to advaunce the Kingdome of our Lord Jeſus Chriſt, and to enjoy the liberties of the Goſpell in puritie with peace," practically recognize the lawful exiſtence of ſlavery.

The fourth Article, which provides for the due adjuſtment of the expenſe or "charge of all juſt warrs whether offenſive or defenſive," concludes as follows :

"And that according to their different charge of eich Juriſdiccon and plantacon, the whole advantage of the warr (if it pleaſe God to bleſs their Endeavours) whether it be in lands, goods, or PERSONS, ſhall be proportionably devided among the ſaid Confederats." *Hazard*, II., 3. *Plymouth Records*, IX., 4. The ſame feature remained in the Conſtitution of the Confederacy to the end of its exiſtence.[1] See *Ratification of 1672. Plymouth Records*, X., 349.

The original of the Fugitive Slave Law proviſion in the Federal Conſtitution is to be traced to this

---

[1] The agreement between Leiſler of New York, and the Commiſſioners of Maſſachuſetts, Plymouth, and Connecticut, May 1, 1690, provided that "all plunder and *captives* (if any happen) ſhall be divided to yͤ officers and ſoldiers according to yͤ Cuſtome of Warr." *N. Y. Doc. Hiſt.*, II., 134, 157. Stoughton and Sewall were the Commiſſioners for Maſſachuſetts.

Confederacy, in which Massachusetts was the ruling colony. The Commissioners of the United Colonies found occasion to complain to the Dutch Governor in New Netherlands, in 1646, of the fact that the Dutch agent at Hartford had harbored a fugitive Indian woman-slave, of whom they say in their letter: "Such a servant is parte of her master's estate, and a more considerable parte than a beast." A provision for the rendition of fugitives, etc., was afterwards made by treaty between the Dutch and the English. *Plymouth Colony Records*, ix., 6, 64, 190.

Historians have generally supposed that the transactions in 1644–5, in which Thomas Keyser and one James Smith, the latter a member of the church of Boston, were implicated, "first brought upon the colonies the guilt of participating in the traffic in African slaves." *Bancroft*, i., 173–4.

The account which we have given of the voyage of the first colonial slave-ship, the Desire, shows this to have been an error, and that which we shall give of these transactions will expose another of quite as much importance.

Hildreth, in whose history the curious and instructive story of New England theocracy is narrated with scrupulous fidelity, gives so clear an account of this business as to require little alteration, and we quote him with slight additions, and references to the authorities, which he does not give in detail.

This affair has been magnified by too precipitate an admiration into a protest on the part of Massachusetts against slavery and the slave-trade. So far, however, from any such protest being made, the first code of laws in Maſſachuſetts eſtabliſhed ſlavery, as we have ſhown, and at the very birth of the foreign commerce of New England the African ſlave-trade became a regular buſineſs. The ſhips which took cargoes of ſtaves and fiſh to Madeira and the Canaries were accuſtomed to touch on the coaſt of Guinea to trade for negroes, who were carried generally to Barbadoes or the other Engliſh Iſlands in the Weſt Indies, the demand for them at home being ſmall.[1] In the caſe referred to, inſtead of buying negroes in the regular courſe of traffic, which, under the fundamental law of Maſſachuſetts already quoted, would have been perfectly legal,[2] the crew of a Boſton ſhip joined with ſome London veſſels on the coaſt, and, on pretence of ſome quarrel with the natives, landed a "murderer"—the expreſſive name of a ſmall piece of cannon—attacked a negro village on Sunday, killed many of the inhabitants, and made a few priſoners, two of whom fell to the ſhare of the Boſton ſhip. In the courſe of a lawſuit between the maſter, mate, and owners, all this ſtory came out, and one of the magiſtrates preſented a petition to the General Court, in which he charged the maſter and mate with a threefold offence,

---

[1] "One of our ſhips, which went to the Canaries with pipe-ſtaves in the beginning of November laſt, returned now [1645] and brought wine, and ſugar, and ſalt, and ſome tobacco, which ſhe had at Barbadoes, *in exchange for Africoes, which ſhe carried from the Iſle of Maio.*" *Winthrop's Journal*, II., 219.

[2] In awarding damages to Captain Smith againſt his aſſociate in this buſineſs, they would allow him nothing for the negroes; but the reaſon they give is worth quoting here:

"4. * * For the negars (*they being none of his, but ſtolen*) we thinke meete to alowe nothing." *Maſs. Records*, II., 129.

This was "the Court's opinion" "by both howſes." *Ib.*, III., 58.

murder, man-ſtealing, and Sabbath-breaking; the two firſt capital by the fundamental laws of Maſſachuſetts, and all of them "capital by the law of God." The magiſtrates doubted their authority to puniſh crimes committed on the coaſt of Africa; but they ordered the negroes to be ſent back, as having been procured not honeſtly by purchaſe, but unlawfully by kidnapping. *Hildreth,* I., 282. *Maſs. Records,* II., 67, 129, 136, 168, 176, 196; III., 46, 49, 58, 84. *Winthrop's Journal,* II., 243, 379.

In all the proceedings of the General Court on this occaſion, there is not a trace of anti-ſlavery opinion or ſentiment,[1] ſtill leſs of anti-ſlavery legiſlation; though both have been repeatedly claimed for the honor of the colony.

III

THE coloniſts of Maſſachuſetts aſſumed to themſelves "a right to treat the Indians on the footing of Canaanites or Amalekites," and praƈtically regarded them from the firſt as forlorn and wretched heathen, poſſeſſing few rights which were entitled to reſpeƈt. *Bancroft,* III., 408. *Bp. Berkeley's Works,* III., 247.

---

[1] It is poſſible that the petition referred to in the following extraƈt from the Records may have related to this ſubjeƈt; but it left no impreſſion which can be traced.

"29 May, 1644. Mr. Blackleach his petition about the Mores was conſented to, to be comitted to the elders, to enforme us of the mind of God herein, & then further to confider it." *Maſs. Records,* II., 67. Mr. John Blackleach, a merchant, was of Salem as early as 1634, and repreſentative in 1636. Some of his letters are printed in *M. H. S. Coll.,* IV., vii., 146-155.

Sermon before the Soc. for the Prop. of the Gospel, 1731, *p.* 19. Cotton Mather's speculations on their origin illustrate the temper of the times.

"We know not *When* or *How* these Indians first became Inhabitants of this mighty Continent, yet we may guess that probably the Devil decoy'd these miserable Salvages hither, in hopes that the Gospel of the Lord Jesus Christ would never come here to destroy or disturb his *Absolute Empire* over them." *Magnalia, Book* III., *Part* III.

The instructions from the Commissioners of the United Colonies to Major Gibbons, on being sent against the Narragansetts in 1645, further illustrates this spirit.

He was directed to have " due regard to the honour of God, who is both our sword and shield, and to the distance which is to be observed betwixt Christians and Barbarians, as well in warres as in other negociations." Of this Hutchinson says: "It was indeed strange that men, who professed to believe that God hath made of one blood all nations of men for to dwell on all the face of the earth, should upon every occasion take care to preserve this distinction. Perhaps nothing more effectually defeated the endeavors for Christianizing the Indians. It seems to have done more: to have sunk their spirits, led them to intemperance, and extirpated the whole race." *Hutchinson's Collection of Papers*, 151.

In 1646, the Commissioners of the United Colonies made a very remarkable order, practically authorizing, upon complaint of trespass by the Indians, the seizure of " any of that plantation of Indians that shall entertain, protect, or rescue the offender." The order further proceeds: "And, because it will be chargeable keeping Indians in prisone, and if they should escape, they are like to prove more insolent and dangerous after, that upon such seazure, the delinquent or satisfaction be againe demanded, of the Sagamore or plantation of Indians guilty or accessory as before, and if it be denied, that then the magistrates of the Jurisdiccon deliver up the Indians seased to the party or parties indamaged, either to serve, or to be shipped out and exchanged for Negroes as the cause will justly beare." *Plymouth Records*, ix., 71.

The Commissioners themselves were not blind to the severity of this proceeding, although they alleged that it was "just."

There are here two features of historical importance which the reader will not fail to notice, viz., the export for trade of Indians for Negroes, and the measure of "justice" in those days between the colonists and the natives.

It may be observed that in these notes we have not drawn the lines between the Plymouth Colony and that of the Massachusetts Bay. In this connection they may justly be regarded as one; indeed, they cannot be separated, for in these and similar proceedings, to quote a significant proverb of that day, "the Plymouth saddle was always on the Bay horse."

In 1658, June 29, certain persons were punished by fines by the County Courts at Salem and Ipswich for attending a Quaker meeting and otherwise "syding with the Quakers and absenting themselves from the publick ordinances." Among them were two children,

Daniel and Provided Southwick, son and daughter to Lawrence Southwick, who were fined ten pounds, but their fines not being paid, and the parties (as is stated in the proceedings) " pretending they have no estates, resolving not to worke and others likewise have been fyned and more like to be fyned"—the General Court were called upon in the following year, May 11, 1659, to decide what course should be taken for the satisfaction of the fines.

This they did, after due deliberation, by a resolution empowering the County Treasurers to sell the said persons to any of the English nation at Virginia or Barbadoes—in accordance with their law for the sale of poor and delinquent debtors. To accomplish this they wrested their own law from its just application, for the special law concerning fines did not permit them to go beyond imprisonment for non-payment. *Mass. Laws*, 1675, *p.* 51. *Felt's Salem*, II., 581. *Mass. Records*, IV., i., 366. *Mass. Laws*, 1675, *p.* 6. *Bishop's N. E. Judged*, 85. Hazard, II., 563.

The father and mother of these children, who had before suffered in their estate and persons, were at the same time banished on pain of death, and took refuge in Shelter Island, where they shortly afterwards died. *Mass. Records*, IV., i., 367. Hazard, II., 564. *Bishop*, 83. The Treasurer, on attempting to find passage for the children to Barbadoes, in execution of the order of sale, found " none willing to take or carry them." Thus the entire design failed, only through the reluctance of these shipmasters to aid in its consummation. *Bishop*, 190. *Sewel's Hist. of the Quakers*, I., 278.

Provided Southwick was subsequently in the same year, in company with several other Quaker ladies, "whipt with tenn stripes," and afterwards "committed to prison to be proceeded with as the law directs." *Mass. Records*, IV., i., 411.

The indignant Quaker historian, in recounting these things, says, "After such a manner ye have done to the *Servants* of the Lord, and for *speaking* to one another, . . . and for *meeting* together, ransacking *their Estates*, breaking open *their Houses*, carrying away *their Goods* and *Cattel*, till ye have left none, then their *wearing apparel*, and then (as in Plimouth government) *their Land;* and when ye have left *them nothing*, sell *them* for this which *ye* call *Debt*. Search the Records of former Ages, go through the Histories of the Generations that are past; read the Monuments of the Antients, and see if *ever* there were *such* a thing as this since the Earth was laid, and the Foundations thereof in the *Water*, and *out of the Water*. . . . O *ye* Rulers of Boston, ye Inhabitants of the *Massachusetts!* What shall I say unto *you?* Whereunto shall I liken *ye?* Indeed, I am at a stand, I have no Nation with *you* to compare, I have no People with *you* to parallel, I am at a loss with *you* in this point; I must say of *you*, as *Balaam* said of *Amalek* when his eyes were open, *Boston, the first of the Nations that came out thus to war against, to stop Israel in their way to Canaan from Egypt.*" *Bishop's N. E. Judged*, 90.

At the time of King Philip's War, the policy and practice of the Colony of Massachusetts, with regard to slavery, had been already long settled upon the basis of positive law. Accordingly the numerous "captives taken in war" were disposed of in the usual way. The notes which follow are mainly from the official records of the colony, and will be sufficient to show the general current of public opinion and action at that period.

In August, 1675, the Council at Plymouth ordered the sale of a company of Indians, "being men, weomen, and children, in number one hundred and twelve," with a few exceptions. The Treasurer made the sale "in the countryes behalfe." *Plymouth Records*, v., 173.

A little later the Council made a similar disposition of fifty-seven more (Indians) who "had come in a submissive way." These were condemned to perpetual servitude, and the Treasurer was ordered and appointed "to make sale of them, to and for the use of the collonie, as opportunity may present." *Ib.*, 174.

The accounts of the Colony of Massachusetts for receipts and expenditures during "the late War," as stated from 25th June, 1675, to the 23d September, 1676, give among the credits the following:

" By the following accounts received
    in or as silver, viz. :
"Captives; for 188 prisoners at war
    sold   397.13.00."

Plymouth Records, x., 401.

There is a peculiar significance in the phrase which occurs in the Records—"sent away by the Treasurer." It means sold into slavery. *Mass. Records*, v., 58.

The statistics of the traffic carried on by the Treasurers cannot be accurately afcertained from any fources now at command. But great numbers of Philip's people were fold as flaves in foreign countries. In the beginning of the war Captain Mofeley captured eighty, who were confined at Plymouth. In September following one hundred and feventy-eight were put on board a veffel commanded by Captain Sprague, who failed from Plymouth with them for Spain. *Drake*, 224.

Thefe proceedings were not without witneffes againft their injuftice and inhumanity. The Apoftle Eliot's earneft remonftrance is a glorious memorial of his fearlefs devotion to reafon and humanity—to which neither rulers nor people of Maffachufetts were then inclined to liften.

"To the Honorable the Governor and Council, fitting at Bofton this 13t. of the 6t, 75, the humble petition of John Eliot, Sheweth that the terror of felling away fuch Indians unto the Ilands for perpetual flaves, who fhall yield up y^{m}felves to your mercy, is like to be an effectual prolongation of the warre, and fuch an exafperation of them, as may produce we know not what evil confequences, upon all the land. Chrift hath faide, bleffed are the mercyfull for they fhall obtain mercy. This ufeage of them is worfe than death . . . it feemeth to me, that to fell them away for flaves is to hinder the inlargement of his [Chrift's] kingdom . . . to fell foules for money feemeth to me a dangerous merchandize. If they deferve to die, it is far better to be put to death under godly governors, who will take religious care, that meanes may be ufed, that they may die penitently. . . . Deut. 23: 15–16.

If a fugitive fervant from a Pagan Mafter might not be delivered to his mafter but be kept in Ifrael for the good of his foule, how much lefs lawful is it to fell away foules from under the light of the gofpel, into a condition, where theire foules will be utterly loft, fo far as appeareth unto man." *Plymouth Colony Records,* x., 451–2. *Compare Mather's Magnalia, Book* vii., 109 (753), *concerning the neglect to profelyte the Indians, etc.*

There is nothing to fhow that " the Council gave heed to the petition of Eliot," but a careful examination of the archives difclofed only a report of a Committee of the General Court, dated Nov. 5, 1675, and adopted by the Magiftrates and Deputies the fame day, by which feveral were to be fent away.[1] *MS. Letter.*

In 1676, November 4th, it was ordered that whereas there is an Acte or order made by the Councell of War bearing date July, 1676, prohibiting any male

---

[1] Eliot appears alfo to have been the firft in America to lift up his voice againft the treatment which Negroes received in New England. Towards the end of his life, Cotton Mather ftates, " He had long lamented it with a Bleeding and Burning Paffion, that the Englifh ufed their Negro's but as their Horfes or their *Oxen,* and that fo little care was taken about their immortal Souls; he look'd upon it as a Prodigy, that any wearing the *Name* of *Chriftians* fhould fo much have the *Heart* of *Devils* in them, as to prevent and hinder the Inftruction of the poor *Blackamores,* and confine the fouls of their miferable Slaves to a *Deftroying Ignorance,* meerly for fear of thereby lofing the Benefit of their Vaffalage; but now he made a motion to the *Englifh* within two or three Miles of him, that at fuch a time and Place they would fend their *Negro's* once a week to him : For he would then *Catechife* them, and *Enlighten* them, to the utmoft of his Power in the Things of their Everlafting Peace; however, he did not live to make much Progrefs in this Undertaking." *Mather's Magnalia, Book* iii., 207 (325). *Compare also p.* 209 (327).

Indian captive to abide in this Jurifdiction that is above fourteen years of age att the beginning of his or their captivity, and in cafe any fuch fhould continue in the Collonie after the time then prefixed they fhould be forfeit to the ufe of the Gov^t, this Court fees caufe to ratify and confirme that order and acte, and do therefore order; that all fuch as have any fuch Indian male captive that they fhall difpofe of them out of the Collonie by the firft of December next on paine of forfeiting every fuch Indian, or Indians to the ufe of the Collonie; and the Conftables of each town of this Jurifdiction are hereby ordered to take notice of any fuch Indian or Indians ftaying in any of the refpective towns of this Collonie after the time prefixed, and fhall forthwith bring them to the Treafurer to be difpofed of to the ufe of the Government as aforefaid. *Plymouth Records*, xi., 242.

There were a few, about five or fix, exceptions made to this order, in favor of certain Indians, who had been affured by Capt. Benjamin Church that they fhould not be fold to any foreign parts, upon good behavior, &c. *Ib.*, 242.

The Maffachufetts General Court made an order in 1677, 24 May, that the Indian children, youths or girls, whofe parents had been in hoftility with the Colony, or had lived among its enemies in the time of the war, and were taken by force, and given or fold to any of the inhabitants of this jurifdiction, fhould be at the difpofall of their mafters or their affignes, who were to inftruct them in Civility and Chriftian religion. *Mafs. Records*, v., 136. *Note the diftinction between friendly Indians whofe children were to be held until* 24 *years of age, both in this order and in Plymouth Records*, v., 207, 223.

The Court, in the following year (1678), found caufe to prohibit "all and every perfon and perfons within our jurifdiction or elfewhere, to buy any of the Indian children of any of thofe our captive falvages that were taken and became our lawfull prifoners in our late warrs with the Indians, without fpecial leave, liking and approbation of the government of this jurifdiction. *Ib.*, 253.

In the fucceeding year (1679), the following entry appears in the records:

"In reference unto feverall Indians bought by Jonathan Hatch of Capt. Church, the brothers of the woman, defireing fhee might be releafed, appeared in Court with the faid Jonathan Hatch, and came to compofition with her for the freedom of both her and her hufband, which are two of the three Indians above named; and her brothers payed on that accompt the fume of three pounds filver mony of New England, and have engaged to pay three pounds more in the fame fpecie, and then the faid man and woman are to be releafed; and for the third of the faid Indians, it being younge, the Court have ordered, that it fhall abide with the faid Jonathan Hatch untill it attains the age of 24 years, and then to be releafed for ever." *Plymouth Records*, VI., 15

It were well if the record were no worfe; but to all this is to be added the bafenefs of treachery and falfehood. Many of thefe prifoners furrendered, and ftill greater numbers came in voluntarily to fubmit, upon the promife that they and their wives and children should have their lives spared, and none of them transported out of the country. In one instance, narrated by the famous Captain Church himself, no less than "eight score persons" were "without any regard to the promises made them on their surrendering themselves, carried away to Plymouth, there sold and transported out of the country." *Church*, 23, 24, 41, 51, 57. Baylies, in his *Memoir of Plymouth Colony*, Part III., *pp.* 47, 48, gives some additional particulars of this affair.

"After the destruction of Dartmouth, the Plymouth forces were ordered there, and as the Dartmouth Indians had not been concerned in this outrage, a negotiation was commenced with them. By the persuasions of Ralph Earl, and the promises of Captain Eels, who commanded the Plymouth forces, they were induced to surrender themselves as prisoners, and were conducted to Plymouth. Notwithstanding the promises by which they had been allured to submit, notwithstanding the earnest, vehement, and indignant remonstrances of Eels, Church, and Earl, the government, to their eternal infamy, ordered the whole to be sold as slaves, and they were transported out of the country, being about one hundred and sixty in number. So indignant was Church at the commission of this vile act, that the government never forgave the warmth and the bitterness of his expressions, and the resentment that was then engendered induced them to withhold all command from this brave, skilful, honest, open-hearted and generous man, until the fear of utter destruction compelled them, subsequently, to entrust him with a high command. This mean and treacherous conduct alienated all the Indians who were doubting, and even those who were strongly predispofed to join the English."

Eafton, in his *Relation*, p. 21, says: "Philip being flead; about a 150 Indians came in to a Plimouth Garrifon volentarly. Plimouth authority fould all for Slafes (but about fix of them) to be carried out of the country."

Church's authority from Plymouth Colony to demand and receive certain fugitives (whether men, women, or children) from the authorities of Rhode Ifland government, Auguft 28, 1676, is printed in *Hough's Eafton's King Philip's War*, p. 188. He was "impowered to fell and difpofe of fuch of them, and foe many as he fhall fee caufe for, there: to the Inhabitants or others, for Term of Life, or for fhorter time, as there may be reafons. And his actinge, herein, fhall at all Times be owned and juftefied by the faid Collony."

Nor did the Chriftian Indians or Praying Indians efcape the relentlefs hoftility and cupidity of the whites. Befides other cruelties, inftances are not wanting in which fome of thefe were fold as flaves, and under accufations which turned out to be utterly falfe and without foundation. *Gookin's Hift. of the Chriftian Indians.*

Some of them are probably referred to by Eliot, in his letter to Boyle, Nov. 27, 1683, in which he fays, "I defire to take boldnefs to propofe a requeft. A veffel carried away a great number of our furprifed Indians, in the times of our wars, to fell them for flaves; but the nations, whither fhe went, would not buy them. Finally, fhe left them at Tangier; there they be, fo many as live, or are born there. An Englifhman, a mafon, came thence to Bofton, he told me they defired I would ufe fome means for their return home. I know not what to do in it; but now it is in my heart to move your honour, fo to meditate, that they may have leave to get home, either from thence hither, or from thence to England, and fo to get home. If the Lord fhall pleafe to move your charitable heart herein, I fhall be obliged in great thankfulnefs, and am perfuaded that Chrift will, at the great day, reckon it among your deeds of charity done unto them, for his name's fake." *M. H. S. Coll.*, III., 183.

Cotton Mather furnifhes another extract appropriate in this connection.

"Moreover, 'tis a Prophefy in Deut. 28, 68. *The Lord fhall bring thee into Egypt again with fhips, by the way whereof I fpake unto thee. Thou fhalt fee it no more again; and there fhall ye be fold unto your Enemies, and no Man fhall buy you.* This did our Eliot imagine accomplifhed, when the Captives taken by us in our late Wars upon them, were fent to be fold, in the Coafts lying not very remote from Egypt on the Mediterranean Sea, and fcarce any Chapmen would offer to take them off." *Mather's Magnalia*, Book III., Part III.

Mr. Everett, in one of the moft elaborate of his finifhed and beautiful orations, has narrated the ftory of two of the laft captives in that famous war, in a paffage of furpaffing eloquence which we venture to quote:

"Prefident Mather, in relating the encounter of

the 1st of August, 1676, the last but one of the war, says, 'Philip hardly escaped with his life also. He had fled and left his *peage* behind him, also his squaw and son were taken captive, and are now prisoners at Plymouth. Thus hath God brought that grand enemy into great misery before he quite destroy him. It must needs be bitter as death to him to lose his wife and only son (for the Indians are marvellous fond and affectionate towards their children) besides other relations, and almost all his subjects, and country also.'

"And what was the fate of Philip's wife and his son? This is a tale for husbands and wives, for parents and children. Young men and women, you cannot understand it. What was the fate of Philip's wife and child? She is a woman, he is a lad. They did not surely hang them. No, that would have been mercy. The boy is the grandson, his mother the daughter-in-law of good old Massasoit, the first and best friend the English ever had in New England. Perhaps—perhaps now Philip is slain, and his warriors scattered to the four winds, they will allow his wife and son to go back—the widow and the orphan —to finish their days and sorrows in their native wilderness. They are sold into slavery, West Indian slavery! an Indian princess and her child, sold from the cool breezes of Mount Hope, from the wild freedom of a New England forest, to gasp under the lash, beneath the blazing sun of the tropics! 'Bitter as death;' aye, bitter as hell! Is there anything,—I do not say in the range of humanity—is there anything animated, that would not struggle against this?"

Everett's Address at Bloody Brook, 1835; Church, 62, 63, 67, 68.

Well might the poet record his sympathy for their fate—

> " Ah! happier they, who in the strife
> For freedom fell, than o'er the main,
> Those who in galling slavery's chain
> Still bore the load of hated life,—
> Bowed to base tasks their generous pride,
> And scourged and broken-hearted, died!"

or in view of this phase of civilization and progress, sigh for that elder state, when all were

> " Free as nature first made man,
> Ere the base laws of servitude began,
> When wild in woods the noble savage ran."

In the prosecution of his admirable historical labors, Ebenezer Hazard, of Philadelphia, endeavored to ascertain what was done with the son of Philip. He wrote to the late Judge Davis, of Boston, who was unable, at that time, to give a satisfactory answer. Mr. Hazard died in 1817; but Judge Davis was afterwards enabled to furnish a very interesting account of the affair, derived from documents communicated to him by Nahum Mitchell, Esq.

From these documents he learned "that the question, whether the boy should be put to death, was seriously agitated, and the opinion of learned divines was requested on the subject. The Rev. Mr. Cotton, of Plymouth, and the Rev. Mr. Arnold, of Marshfield, gave the following answer:

"The question being propounded to us by our honored rulers, whether Philip's son be a child of death! Our anfwer, hereunto is, that we do acknowledge, that rule, Deut. 24: 16, to be morall, and therefore perpetually binding, viz., that in a particular act of wickednefs, though capitall, the crime of the parent doth not render his child a fubject to punifhment by the civill magiftrate; yet, upon ferious confideration, we humbly conceive that the children of notorious traitors, rebells, and murtherers, efpecially of fuch as have bin principal leaders and actors in fuch horrid villanies, and that againft a whole nation, yea the whole Ifrael of God, may be involved in the guilt of their parents, and may, *falva republica*, be adjudged to death, as to us feems evident by the fcripture inftances of *Saul, Achan, Haman*, the children of whom were cut off, by the fword of Juftice for the tranfgreffions of their parents, although concerning fome of thofe children, it be manifeft, that they were not capable of being co-acters therein. Samuel Arnold,

September 7th, 1670. John Cotton."

The Rev. Increafe Mather, of Bofton, offers thefe fentiments on the queftion, in a letter to Mr. Cotton, October 30, 1676.

"If it had not been out of my mind, when I was writing, I fhould have faid fomething about Philip's fon. It is neceffary that fome effectual courfe fhould be taken about him. He makes me think of Hadad, who was a little child when his father, (the Chief Sachem of the Edomites) was killed by Joab; and, had not others fled away with him, I am apt to think, that David would have taken a courfe, that Hadad fhould never have proved a fcourge to the next generation."

The Rev. James Keith, of Bridgewater, took a different view of the subject, and gave more benignant interpretations. In a letter to Mr. Cotton of the same date with Dr. Mather's, he says, "I long to hear what becomes of Philip's wife and his son. I know there is some difficulty in that psalm, 137, 8, 9, though I think it may be considered, whether there be not some specialty and somewhat extraordinary in it. That law, Deut. 24: 16, compared with the commended example of Amasias, 2 Chron. 25: 4, doth sway much with me, in the case under consideration. I hope God will direct those whom it doth concern to a good issue. Let us join our prayers, at the throne of grace, with all our might, that the Lord would so dispose of all public motions and affairs, that his Jerusalem in this wilderness may be the habitation of justice and the mountain of holiness; that so it may be, also, a quiet habitation, a tabernacle that shall not be taken down."

The question thus seriously agitated would not, in modern times, occur in any nation in Christendom. Principles of public law, sentiments of humanity, and the mild influence of the Gospel, in preference to a recurrence of the Jewish dispensation, so much regarded by our ancestors in their deliberations and decisions,[1] would forbid the thought of inflicting punishment on children for the offences of a parent. It is gratifying to learn, that, in this instance, the meditated severities were not carried into execution, but that the merciful

---

[1] In this discussion, however, both scripture rule and example were in favour of the prisoner. The case quoted by Mr. Keith from 2 Chronicles is directly in point. "But he slew not their children, but did as it is written in the law in the book of Moses," &c.

spirit manifested in Mr. Keith's suggestions prevailed. In a letter from Mr. Cotton to his brother Mather, on the 20th of March following, on another subject, there is this incidental remark: 'Philip's boy goes now to be sold.'" *Davis's Morton's Memorial, Appendix, pp. 353-5.*

In the winter of 1675-6, Major Waldron, a Commissioner, and Magistrate for a portion of territory claimed by Massachusetts (now included in that of Maine), issued general warrants for seizing every Indian known to be a manslayer, traitor, or conspirator. These precepts, which afforded every man a plausible pretext to seize suspected Indians, were obtained by several shipmasters for the most shameful purposes of kidnapping and slave-trading. One with his vessel lurked about the shores of Pemaquid, and notwithstanding warning and remonstrance, succeeded in kidnapping several of the natives, and, carrying them into foreign parts, sold them for slaves. Similar outrages were committed farther east upon the Indians about Cape Sable, "who never had been in the least manner guilty of any injury done to the English." Hubbard adds to his account of this affair, "the thing alleadged is too true as to matter of Fact, and the persons that did it, were lately committed to prison in order to their further tryal." If the careful research of Massachusetts antiquarians can discover any record of the trial, conviction and *just* punishment of these offenders, it will be an honorable addition to their history—far more creditable than the constant reiteration of the story of "the negro interpreter" in 1646, which has been so long in service, "to bear witness against y^o

haynos and crying finn of man-ftealing," in behalf of "The Gen'all Co'te" of Maffachufetts. *Hubbard's Narrative*, 1677, *pp.* 29, 30. *Williamfon's Maine*, I., 531.

After the death of King Philip, fome of the Indians from the weft and fouth of New England who had been engaged in the war, endeavored to conceal themfelves among their brethren of Penacook who had not joined in the war, and with them of Offapy and Pigwackett who had made peace.

By a "contrivance" (as Mather calls it) which favors ftrongly of treachery, four hundred of thefe Indians were taken prifoners, one half of whom were declared to have been acceffories in the late rebellion; and being "fent to Bofton, feven or eight of them, who were known to have killed any Englifhmen, were condemned and hanged; the reft were fold into flavery in foreign parts."

Some of thofe very Indians, who were thus seized and fold, afterwards made their way home, and found opportunity to fatisfy their revenge during the war with the French and Indians known as King William's War. *Belknap*, I., 143, 245. *Mather's Magnalia*, Book VII., 55 (699).

IV.

At firft, the number of flaves in Maffachufetts was comparatively fmall, and their increafe was not large until towards the clofe of the feventeenth century. Edward Randolph, in 1676, in an anfwer to feveral heads of inquiry, &c., stated that there were "not above 200 slaves in the colony, and those are brought from Guinea and Madagascar." He also mentioned that some ships had recently sailed to those parts from Massachusetts. *Hutchinson's Collection of Papers, pp.* 485, 495. Governor Andros reported that the slaves were not numerous in 1678—"not many servants, and but few slaves, proportionable with freemen." *N. Y. Col. Doc.*, III., 263.

In May, 1680, Governor Bradstreet answered certain Heads of Inquiry from the Lords of the Committee for Trade and Foreign Plantations. Among his statements are the following:

"There hath been no company of blacks or slaves brought into the country since the beginning of this plantation, for the space of fifty years, onely one small Vessell about two yeares since, after twenty months' voyage to Madagascar, brought hither betwixt forty and fifty Negroes, most women and children, sold here for 10*l.*, 15*l.* and 20*l.* apiece, which stood the merchant, in near 40*l.* apiece: Now and then, two or three Negroes are brought hither from Barbadoes and other of his Majestie's plantations, and sold here for about twenty pounds apiece. So that there may be within our Government about one hundred or one hundred and twenty. . . . . There are a very few blacks borne here, I think not above [five] or six at the most in a year, none baptized that I ever heard of. . ." *M. H. S. Coll.*, III., viii., 337.

The following century changed the record. Many "companies" of slaves were "brought into the country," and the institution flourished and waxed strong.

Judge Sewall referred to the "numeroufnefs" of the flaves in the province in 1700. Gov. Dudley's report to the Board of Trade, in 1708, gave four hundred as then in Bofton, one half of whom were born there; and in one hundred other towns and villages one hundred and fifty more—making a total of five hundred and fifty. He ftated that negroes were found unprofitable, and that the planters there preferred white fervants "who are ferviceable in war prefently, and after become planters." From January 24, 1698, to 25 December, 1707, two hundred negroes arrived in Maffachufetts.

Gov. Shute's information to the Lords of Trade, in 1720, Feb. 17, gave the number of flaves of Maffachufetts at 2,000, including a few Indians. He added that, during the fame year, thirty-feven male and fixteen female negroes were imported, with the remark, "No great difference for feven years laft paft." *Felt, Coll. Amer. Stat. Affoc.,* 1., 586.

In 1735, there were 2,600 negroes in the Province. In 1742, there were 1,514 in Bofton alone. *Douglafs,* 1., 531. Thefe are probably very imperfect eftimates, as it is well known that regular enumerations of the population were confidered very objectionable by the people of the Bay. Some recalled the numbering of Ifrael by David, and perhaps all were jealous of the poffible defigns of the Government in England in obtaining accurate information of their numbers and refources. It is a curious fact that the firft cenfus in Maffachufetts, was a cenfus of negro flaves.

In 1754, an account of property in the Province liable to taxation being required, Gov. Shirley fent a special meffage to the Houfe of Reprefentatives, in which he faid :

"There is one part of the Eftate, viz., the Negro Slaves, which I am at a lofs how to come at the knowledge of, without your affiftance." *Journal, p.* 119.

On the fame day, November 19, 1754, the Legislature made an order that the Affeffors of the feveral towns and diftricts within the Province, forthwith fend into the fecretary's office the exact number of the negro flaves, both males and females, fixteen years old and upwards, within their refpective towns and districts. *Ib.*[1]

This enumeration, as corrected by Mr. Felt, gives an aggregate of 4,489. The census of Negroes in 1764-5, according to the fame authority, makes their number 5,779, in 1776, 5,249; in 1784, 4,377, in 1786, 4,371; and in 1790 (by the United States census) 6,001.[2]

The royal inftructions to Andros, in 1688, as

---

[1] There is a curious illuftration of "the way of putting it" in Maffachufetts, in Mr. FELT's account of this "cenfus of flaves," in the *Collections of the American Statiftical Affociation, Vol.* I., *p.* 208. He fays that the General Court paffed this order "for the purpofe of having an accurate account of flaves in our Commonwealth, *as a fubject in which the people were becoming much interefted, relative to the caufe of liberty!*" There is not a particle of authority for this fuggeftion—fuch a motive for their action never exifted anywhere but in the imagination of the writer himfelf!

[2] It is to be regretted that we have no official authorities on the fubject of the changes in this clafs of population during the period from 1776 to 1784. There is a moft extraordinary, if not incredible, ftatement made by the Duke de la Rochefoucault Liancourt in his *Travels through the United States* . . . *in the years* 1795, 1796, *and* 1797, of which a tranflation was publifhed in London in 1799. In that work, Vol. II., page 166, he fays, "It is to be obferved, that, in 1778, the general cenfus of Maffachufetts included eighteen thoufand flaves, whereas the fubfequent cenfus of 1790 exhibits only fix thoufand blacks."

Governor of New England, required him to "pafs a law for the reftraining of inhuman feverity which may be ufed by ill mafters or overfeers towards the Chriftian fervants or flaves; wherein provifion is to be made that the wilful killing of Indians and Negroes be punifhed with death, and a fitt penalty impofed for the maiming of them." *N. Y. Col. Doc.*, III., 547. The reader will note the diftinction in thefe inftructions between the *Chriftian* fervants or flaves, and the *Indians and Negroes*. It points to a feature of flavery in Maffachufetts, at that time, which we propofe to notice in another portion of thefe notes.

The Law of 1698, Chapter 6, forbids trading or trucking with any "Indian, molato or negro fervant or flave, or other known diffolute, lewd, and diforderly perfons, of whom there is juft caufe of fufpicion." Such perfons were to be punifhed by whipping for fo trading with money or goods improperly obtained.

The Law of 1700, Chapter 13, was enacted to protect the Indians againft the exactions and oppreffion which fome of the Englifh exercifed towards them "by drawing them to confent to covenant or bind themfelves or children apprentices or fervants for an unreafonable term, on pretence of or to make fatisfaction for fome fmall debt contracted or damage done by them." Other fimilar acts were afterwards paffed in 1718 and 1725, the latter having a claufe to protect them againft kidnapping.

In 1701, the Reprefentatives of the town of Bofton were "defired to promote the encouraging the bringing of white fervants, and to put a period to Negroes being flaves." *Drake's Bofton,* 525. *M. H. S. Coll.,* II., viii., 184. We have no knowledge of the efforts made under this inftruction of the town of Bofton, but they failed to accomplifh anything. Indeed, the very next enactment concerning flavery was a ftep backward inftead of an advance towards reform—a meafure which turned out to be a permanent and effective barrier againft emancipation in Maffachufetts.

The Law of 1703, Chapter 2, was in reftraint of the " Manumiffion, Difcharge, or Setting free" of "Molatto or Negro flaves." Security was required againft the contingency of thefe perfons becoming a charge to the town, and "none were to be accounted free for whom fecurity is not given;" but were "to be the proper charge of their refpective mafters or miftreffes, in cafe they ftand in need of relief and fupport, notwithftanding any manumiffion or inftrument of freedom to them made or given," etc.[1] A practice was prevailing to manumit aged or infirm flaves, to relieve the mafter from the charge of fupporting them. To prevent this practice, the act was

---

[1] Jonathan Sewall, writing to John Adams, February 31, 1760, puts the following cafe:

"A man, by will, gives his negro his liberty, and leaves him a legacy. The executor confents that the negro fhall be free, but refufeth to give bond to the felectmen to indemnify the town againft any charge for his fupport, in cafe he fhould become poor, (without which, by the province law, he is not manumitted,) or to pay him the legacy.

Query. Can he recover the legacy, and how?

John Adams, in reply, after illuftrating in two cafes the legal principle that the intention of the teftator, to be collected from the words, is to be obferved in the conftruction of a will, applied it to the cafe prefented as follows, viz.:

"The teftator plainly intended that his negro fhould have his liberty and a legacy; therefore the law will prefume that he intended his executor fhould do all that without which he could have neither. That this in-

passed. *C. J. Parsons. Winchendon* vs. *Hatfield in error*, iv *Mass. Reports*, 130. This act was still in force as late as June, 1807, when it was reproduced in the revised laws, and continued until a much later period to govern the decisions of courts affecting the settlement of town paupers. An unsuccessful attempt to repeal it, will be found duly noticed in a subsequent portion of these notes.

The Law of 1703, Chapter 4, prohibited Indian, Negro and Molatto servants or slaves, to be abroad after nine o'clock, etc.

The Law of 1705, Chapter 6, "for the better preventing of a Spurious and Mixt Issue, &c.;" punishes Negroes and Molattoes for improper intercourse with whites, by selling them out of the Province. It also

---

demnification was not in the testator's mind, cannot be proved from the will any more than it could be proved, in the first case above, that the testator did not know a fee simple would pass a will without the word heirs; nor than, in the second case, that the devise of a trust, that might continue for ever, would convey a fee simple without the like words. I take it, therefore, that the executor of this will is, by implication, obliged to give bonds to the town treasurer, and, in his refusal, is a wrong doer; and I cannot think he ought to be allowed to take advantage of his own wrong, so much as to allege this want of an indemnification to evade an action of the case brought for the legacy by the negro himself.

But why may not the negro bring a special action of the case against the executor, setting forth the will, the devise of freedom and a legacy, and then the necessity of indemnification by the province law, and then a refusal to indemnify, and, of consequence, to set free and to pay the legacy?

Perhaps the negro is free at common law by the devise. Now, the province law seems to have been made only to oblige the master to maintain his manumitted slave, and not to declare a manumission in the master's lifetime, or at his death, void. Should a master give a negro his freedom, under his hand and seal, without giving bond to the town, and should afterwards repent and endeavor to recall the negro into servitude, would not that instrument be a sufficient discharge against the master?" *Adams' Works*, 1., 51, 55.

punishes any Negro or Molatto for striking a Christian, by whipping at the discretion of the Justices before whom he may be convicted. It also prohibits marriage of Christians with Negroes or Molattoes—and imposes a penalty of Fifty Pounds upon the persons joining them in marriage. It provides against unreasonable denial of marriage to Negroes with those of the same nation, by any Master—"any Law, Usage, or Custom, to the contrary notwithstanding."

This proviso against the unreasonable denial of marriage to negroes is very interesting. Legislation against the arbitrary exercise and abuse of authority proves its existence and the previous practice. It was as true then as it is now that the institution of slavery was inconsistent with the just rules of Christian morality.

In Pennsylvania, five years before, William Penn had proposed to his Council, " the necessitie of a law [among others] about ye marriages of negroes." The subject was referred to a committee of both houses of the legislature, and resulted in a Bill in the Assembly, "for regulating *Negroes* in their Morals and Marriages, etc.," which was twice read and rejected. *Penn. Col. Rec.*, I., 598. 606. *Votes of Assembly*, I., 120, 121. This proposition of Penn was in accordance with the views of George Fox, whose testimony in regard to the treatment of slaves, given at Barbadoes in 1671, is elsewhere referred to in these notes. In his "Gospel Family Order, being a short discourse concerning the Ordering of Families, both of Whites, Blacks, and Indians," he particularly enforced the necessity of looking after the marriages of the blacks, to see that there was some order and solemnity in the manner, and that the marriages should be recorded, and should be binding for life. See *The Friend, Vol.* XVII. 29, 4*to.,* Phil. 1843.

No Christian man or woman, Quaker or Puritan, could fail to be shocked at the looseness of all such ties and relations under the slave system. One solitary witness against slavery in Massachusetts in 1700, referred to the well known " Temptations Masters were under to connive at the Fornication of their Slaves, lest they should be obliged to find them Wives or pay their Fines." *Sewall,* 1700. The laws against the irregular commerce of the sexes were an awkward part of a system which established and protected slavery, and marriage (such as it was) saved the expense of constant fines to masters and mistresses for delinquent slaves.

But what protection was there for the married state or sanction of marital or parental rights and duties? This law did not and could not protect or sanction either, and must have been of little practical value to the slaves. Governed by the humor or interest of the master or mistress, their marriage was not a matter of choice with them, more than any other action of their life. Who was to judge whether the denial of a master or mistress was unreasonable or not? And what remedy had the slave in case of denial?[1] The owner of a valuable female slave was to

---

[1] The case of *The Inhabitants of Stockbridge* vs. *The Inhabitants of West Stockbridge*—regarding the settlement of a negro pauper (who had been a soldier in the American Army of the Revolution) presents a decision of the

consider what all the risks of health and life were to be, and whether the increase of stock would reimburse the loss of service.¹

The breeding of slaves was not regarded with favor.² Dr. Belknap says, that "negro children were considered an incumbrance in a family; and when weaned, were given away like puppies." *M. H. S. Coll.*, I., iv., 200. They were frequently publicly advertised "to be given away,"—sometimes with the additional inducement of a sum of money to any one who would take them off.

At the same time there is no room for doubt that there were public and legalized marriages among slaves in Massachusetts, subsequently to the passage of this act of 1705. Mr. Justice Gray states that, "the subsequent records of Boston and other towns show that their banns were published like those of white persons.³

Supreme Judicial Court of Massachusetts in 1817, not only recognizing the fact of the absolute legal continuance of slavery in that State in the years 1770 –1777; but settling a point of law which is interesting in this connection. At that time "*no contract made with the slave was binding on the master; for the slave could have maintained no action against him, had he failed to fulfil his promise* [a promise to emancipate] which was an undertaking merely voluntary on his part." *Mass. Reports*, XIV., 257.

¹ A Bill of Sale of a Negro Woman Servant in Boston in 1724, recites that "Whereas Scipio, of Boston aforesaid, Free Negro Man and Laborer, purposes Marriage to Margaret, the Negro Woman Servant of the said Dorcas Marshall [a Widow Lady of Boston] : Now to the Intent that the said Intended Marriage may take Effect, and that the said Scipio may Enjoy the said Margaret without any Interruption," etc., she is duly sold, with her apparel, for Fifty Pounds. *N. E. Hist. and Gen. Reg.*, XVIII., 78.

² So early as the poet Hesiod, married slaves, whether male or female, were esteemed inconvenient. *Works and Days*, line 406, also 602–3.

³ Mr. Charles C. Jones, of Georgia, in his work on the *Religious Instruction of the Negroes in the United States*, published at Savannah, in 1842, gives, pp. 34, 35, memoranda of four instances of the kind, which he ob-

In 1745, a negro flave obtained from the Governor and Council a divorce for his wife's adultery with a white man. In 1758, it was adjudged by the Superior Court of Judicature, that a child of a female flave 'never married according to any of the forms prescribed by the laws of this land,' by another flave, who 'had kept her company with her mafter's confent,' was not a baftard." *Quincy's Reports*, 30, *note*. This judgment indicates liberal views with regard to the law of marriage as applied to flaves, although we fufpect there was fpecial occafion for the exercife of charity and mercy which might deprive it of any authority as a leading cafe.

It is perfectly well known that it was practically fettled in Maffachufetts that baptifm was not emancipation—although there is no evidence in their ftatutes to fhow that the queftion was ever mooted in that colony, as it was in other colonies, where legiflation was found neceffary to eftablifh the doctrine.

Still it was in the power of mafters in Maffachufetts to deny baptifm to their flaves, as appears from the following extract, from Matthias Plant to the Secretary of the Society for the Propagation of the Gofpel, etc. Anfwers to Queries, from Newbury, October 25, 1727:

" 6. Negroe Slaves, one of them is defirous of baptifm, but denied by her Mafter, a woman of wonderful fenfe, and prudent in matters, of equal knowledge in Religion with moft of her fex, far exceeding any of her own nation that ever yet I heard of."

---

ferved in looking over the old record of "Entryes for Publications" (for marriages) within the town of Bofton, two in the year 1707, and two in 1710.

About baptism of slaves "borne in the house, or bought with monie," see letter of Davenport to the younger Winthrop, June 14, 1666, and postscript. *M. H. S. Coll.* III., x., 60. 62.

Mr. Palfrey gives it as his opinion, that "From the reverence entertained by the Fathers of New England for the nuptial tie, it is safe to infer that slave husbands and wives were never parted." *Hist. N. E.*, II., 30, *note*. The Fathers of New England also cherished a due regard for parental and filial duties and responsibilities, yet it is certain that slave mothers and children were separated. Resting upon "the law of God, established in Israel," the Puritan could have had no scruple about this matter—such a condition of marriage to the slave must have been regarded as an axiom as it was by the Hebrew. *Compare Exodus*, XXI., 4, 5, 6. Mr. Palfrey's inference is not warranted by the facts.

In 1786, the legislature of the State of Massachusetts passed an "Act for the orderly Solemnization of Marriage," by the seventh section whereof it was enacted "that no person authorized by this act to marry shall join in marriage any white person with any Negro, Indian or Mulatto, under penalty of fifty pounds; and all such marriages shall be absolutely null and void." The prohibition continued until 1843, when it was repealed by a special "act relating to marriage between individuals of certain races."

The statute of 1705 also provided an import duty of four pounds per head on every Negro brought into the Province from and after the 1st day of May, 1706, for the payment of which both the vessel and master were anfwerable. A penalty of double the amount of the duty on each one omitted was impofed for refufal or neglect to make the prefcribed entry of "Number, Names, and Sex, in the Impoft Office." A drawback was allowed upon exportation, and the like advantage was allowed to the purchafer of any Negro fold within the Province, in cafe of the death of his Negro within six weeks after importation or bringing into the Province.

Mr. Drake fays that, in 1727, "the traffic in flaves appears to have been more an object in Bofton than at any period before or fince." *Hift. of Bofton*, 574, and in the following year (1728) an additional "Act more effectually to fecure the Duty on the Importation of Negroes" was paffed, by which more ftringent regulations were adopted to prevent the smuggling of fuch property into the Province, and the drawback was allowed on all negroes dying within twelve months.

This act expired by its own limitation in 1735, but another of a fimilar character was paffed in 1739, which recognifed the old law of 1705 as being ftill in force.[1] It reduced the time for the drawback on the death of negroes to fix months after importation.

Free Negroes not being allowed to train in the

---

[1] "Dec. 7, 1737, Col. Royal petitions the General Court, that, having lately arrived from Antigua, he has with him feveral flaves for his own ufe, and not to fell, and therefore prays that the duty on them be remitted. The duty was £4 a-head. This petition was laid on the table, and refts there yet." *Brooks's Medford*, 435. The act of 1739 was for ten years, and therefore expired in 1749. We have found no repeal of the old law, but the proceedings concerning the act propofed in 1767 would feem to fhow all the old acts of Impoft to be expired or obfolete.

Militia, an act paffed in 1707, Chapter 2, required them to do fervice on the highways and in cleaning the ftreets, etc., as an equivalent. Thirty-three free negroes were mentioned in the minutes of the Selectmen of Bofton, in 1708, to whom, according to this law, two hundred and eighteen days of labor were affigned upon the highways and other public works. *Lyman's Report*, 1822. The fame act prohibited them to entertain any fervants of their own color in their houfes, without permiffion of the refpective mafters or miftreffes.

In 1712, an act was paffed prohibiting the importation or bringing into the Province any Indian fervants or flaves. The preamble recites the bad character of the Indians and other flaves, "being of a malicious, furley and revengeful fpirit; rude and infolent in their behaviour, and very ungovernable." A glimpfe of poffible future reform is to be caught in this act, for it recognizes the increafe of flaves as a "difcouragement to the importation of White Chriftian Servants." But its chief motive was in the peculiar circumftances of the Province "under the forrowful effects of the Rebellion and Hoftilities" of the Indians, and the fact that great numbers of Indian flaves were already held in bondage in the Province at the time.

This act had a fpecial reference to Southern Indians, the Tufcaroras and others, captives in war, chiefly from South Carolina. Governor Dudley afterwards entered into correfpondence with other colonial governors, about preventing the fale of Indians from that Province to the Northern colonies. Similar acts were paffed by Pennfylvania in 1712,

New Hampſhire in 1714, and Connecticut and Rhode Iſland in 1715.

Under the earlieſt laws of taxation in Maſſachuſetts, ſlaves muſt have been rated (if taxed at all) as polls, the owners paying for them as for other ſervants and children, "ſuch as take not wages." This continued until the period of the Province Charter, when, in the year 1692, "every male ſlave of ſixteen years old and upwards" was rated "at Twenty Pounds Eſtate." In 1694, "all Negro's, Molattoes and Indian Servants, as well male as female, of 16 years old and upwards, at the rate of 12*d.* per poll ſame as other polls." In 1695, "all Negro's, Molatto, and Indian Servants, males of 14 years of age and upward at the rate of 20*l.* eſtate, and Females at 14*l.* eſtate, unleſs diſabled by infirmity." They were ſubſequently in the ſame year rated "as other perſonal eſtate," which mode was continued in 1696, 1697, and 1698, in the latter year "according to the ſound judgment and diſcretion of the Aſſeſſors, *not excluding faculties.*"

This rating for "faculties" was a prominent feature in the early tax-laws of Maſſachuſetts, and was continued after the commencement of the preſent century.[1]

It was applied to white men in Maſſachuſetts from the beginning, being intended as a juſt valuation for thoſe who had arts, trades, and faculties, by the produce of which they were "more enabled to bear the publick charge than common laborers and Workmen,

---

[1] Mr. Felt ſays, in his memoranda, under the date of 1829, "the rating for faculties, long a prominent item in our former tax-acts, and not unfrequently made a ſubject of pleaſant remark, has been dropped, like other notions of ancient cuſtom." *Coll. Amer. Stat. Aſſoc.*, I., 502. *See also pp.* 297, 374.

as *Butchers, Bakers, Brewers, Victuallers, Smiths, Carpenters, Taylors, Shoomakers, Joyners, Barbers, Millers and Masons,* with all other manual persons and Artists." *Mass. Laws, Ed.* 1672, *p.* 24. The law of 1698, however, appears to have been the first, if not the only one, in which this feature was applied to the " Negroes, Molattoes and Indians " in bondage; and may be justly regarded as an indication of progress, for it was an admission that these unfortunate creatures had " faculties," valuable to their owners, if not to themselves.[1]

There was little variation in these laws during the entire colonial period—all Indian, Negro, and Mulatto. servants continuing to be rated as personal property—excepting that occasionally some of those who were servants for a term of years, but not for life, were numbered and rated as polls.

In 1716, an attempt was made to modify this feature of the legislation of Massachusetts. The following extract from Judge Sewall's Diary is copied from the original. Though quoted by Coffin, in his *History of Newbury,* 188, and Felt, in the *Coll. Amer.*

---

[1] The early records of the town of Boston preserve the fact that one Thomas Deane, in the year 1661, was prohibited from employing a negro in the manufacture of hoops under a penalty of twenty shillings, for what reason is not stated. *Lyman's Report,* 1822. Phillis Wheatley's was not the only instance, in Boston, of the negro's capacity for intellectual improvement. A worthy Englishman, Richard Dalton, Esq., a great admirer of the Greek classics, because of the tenderness of his eyes, taught his negro boy, Cæsar, to read to him distinctly any Greek writer, without understanding the meaning or interpretation. *Douglass,* ii., 345. In the *Boston Chronicle* for September 21, 1769, is advertised:—" To be sold, a Likely Little negroe boy, who *can speak the French language,* and very fit for a Valet."

Stat. Affociation, 1., 586, it is not correctly printed by either.

"1716. I effayed June 22, to prevent Indians and Negroes being rated with Horfes and Hogs; but could not prevail. Col. Thaxter bro't it back" [from the Deputies], "and gave as a reafon of y^r" [their] "Nonagreement, They were juft going to make a New Valuation."

This concife mention of Judge Sewall's benevolent "effay," indicates that he had firft propofed the matter in the Council, of which he was then a member; and that the Council agreeing, their decifion was fent down to the Houfe for their concurrence. But the Houfe non-concurred; and fignified by Colonel Thaxter, that they declined their affent to the refolve of the Council, for the reafon that "they were juft going to make a New Valuation;" and as in the preceding valuations of the property of their conftituents, Indian, Negro, and Mulatto flaves had been prominent articles, they muft keep on ftill in the old track; Indians, Negroes, and Mulattoes muft ftill be valued, as property, and for this fpecies of property their owners muft ftill be taxed. *MS. Letter of Rev. Samuel Sewall.*

In 1718, all Indian, Negro, and Mulatto fervants for life were eftimated as other Perfonal Eftate—viz: Each male fervant *for life* above fourteen years of age, at fifteen pounds value; each female fervant for life, above fourteen years of age, at ten pounds value. The affeffor might make abatement for caufe of age or infirmity. Indian, Negro, and Mulatto Male fervants *for a term of years* were to be numbered and rated as other Polls, and not as Perſonal Eſtate.[1] In 1726, the aſſeſſors were required to eſtimate Indian, Negro, and Mulatto ſervants proportionably as other Perſonal Eſtate, according to their ſound judgment and diſcretion. In 1727, the rule of 1718 was reſtored, but during one year only, for in 1728 the law was the ſame as that of 1726; and ſo it probably remained, including all ſuch ſervants, as well for term of years as for life, in the rateable eſtates. We have ſeen the ſupply bills for 1736, 1738, 1739, and 1740, in which this feature is the ſame.

And thus they continued to be rated with horſes, oxen, cows, goats, ſheep, and ſwine, until after the commencement of the War of the Revolution. We have not ſeen the law, but Mr. Felt ſtates that "in 1776 the colored polls were taxed the ſame as the white polls, and ſo continued to be." *Coll. Amer. Stat. Aſſoc.*, I., 475. See alſo pp. 203, 311, 345, 411.

In the inventory of Captain Paul White, in 1679, was "one negrow = 30*l*." In 1708, an Indian boy from South Carolina brought 35*l*. An Indian girl brought fifteen pounds, at Salem, in Auguſt, 1710. The higheſt price paid for any of a cargo brought into Boſton, by the ſloop Katherine, in 1727, was eighty pounds. The eſtate of Samuel Morgaridge, who died in 1754, included the following: "Item, three negroes 133*l*. 6*s*. 8*d*." *Coffin's Newbury*, 188, 336. *Coll. Eſſex Inſtitute*, I., 14. *Felt's Salem*, II., 416.

"The Guinea Trade," as it was called then, ſince known and branded by all civilized nations as piracy,

---

[1] Another act of the year 1718 forbade, under heavy penalties, Maſters of Ships to carry off "any *bought* or hired ſervant or apprentice."

whofe beginnings we have noticed, continued to flourifh under the aufpices of Maffachufetts merchants down through the entire colonial period, and long after the boafted Declaration of Rights in 1780 had terminated (?) the legal exiftence of flavery within the limits of that State. *Felt's Salem*, II., 230, 261, 265, 288, 292, 296. To gratify thofe who are curious to fee what the inftructions given by refpectable merchants in Maffachufetts to their flave captains were in the year 1785, we copy them from *Felt's Salem*, II., 289–90; probably the only fpecimen extant.[1]

"————, Nov. 12, 1785.
" Capt ————.

" Our brig,[2] of which you have the command, being cleared at the office, and being in every other refpect complete for fea ; our orders are, that you embrace the firft fair wind and make the beft of your way to the coaft of Africa, and there inveft your cargo in flaves. As flaves, like other articles, when brought to market, generally appear to the beft advantage ; therefore, too critical an infpection cannot be paid to them before purchafe ; to fee that no dangerous diftemper is lurking about them, to attend particularly to their age, to their countenance, to the ftraightnefs of their limbs, and, as far as poffible to the goodnefs or badnefs of their conftitution, &c. &c., will be very confiderable objects.

" Male or female flaves, whether full grown or not, we cannot particularly inftruct you about ; and on this head fhall only obferve, that prime male flaves generally fell beft in any market. No people require more kind and tender treatment to exhilarate their fpirits, than the Africans ; and, while on the one hand you are attentive to this, remember that on the other hand, too much circumfpection cannot be obferved by yourfelf and people, to prevent their taking the advantage

---

[1] *Brooks's Medford* preferves fimilar inftructions in 1759, and a fpecimen of the flave captain's day-book on the coaft of Africa, *pp.* 436–7.

[2] This veffel was probably the Brig Favorite. *Compare Felt's Salem,* II., 287 *and* 291.

of such treatment by insurrection, &c. When you consider that on the health of your slaves, almost your whole voyage depends; for all other risques, but mortality, seizures and bad debts, the underwriters are accountable for;—you will therefore particularly attend to smoking your vessel, washing her with vinegar, to the clarifying your water with lime or brimstone, and to cleanliness among your own people, as well as among the slaves.

" As the factors on the coast have no laws but of their own making, and of course such as suit their own convenience, they therefore, like the Israelites of old, do whatsoever is right in their own eyes; in consequence of which you ought to be very careful about receiving gold dust, and of putting your cargo into any but the best hands, or if it can be avoided, and the same dispatch made, into any hands at all, on any credit. If you find that any saving can be made by bartering rum for slops, and supplying your people with small stores, you will do it; or even if you cannot do it without a loss, it is better done than left undone; for shifts of clothes, particularly in warm climates, are very necessary. As our interest will be considerable, and as we shall make insurance thereon, if any accident should prevent your following the track here pointed out, let it be your first object to protest publicly, why, and for what reason you were obliged to deviate. You are to have four slaves upon every hundred, and four at the place of sale; the priviledge of eight hogsheads, and two pounds eight shillings per month; —these are all the compensations you are to expect for the voyage.

" Your first mate is to have four hogsheads privilege, and your second mate two, and wages as per agreement. No slaves are to be selected out as priviledged ones, but must rise or fall with the general sales of the cargo, and average accordingly. We shall expect to hear from you, by every opportunity to Europe, the West Indies, or any of these United States; and let your letters particularly inform us, what you have done, what you are then doing, and what you expect to do. We could wish to have as particular information as can be obtained, respecting the trade in all its branches on the coast; to know if in any future time, it is probable a load of N. E. Rum could be sold for bills of exchange on London, or any part of Europe; or, for gold dust; and what despatch in this case might be made.

" You will be careful to get this information from gentlemen of veracity, and know of them if any other articles would answer from this quarter. We should be glad to enter into a contract, if the terms would answer, with any good factor for rum, &c. If any such would write us upon the subject, and enclose a memorandum with the prices annexed, such letters and memorandums shall be duly attended to. We are in want of about five hundred weight of camwood, and one large elephant's tooth of about 80 lbs., which you will obtain. If small teeth can be bought from 15 to 30 lbs., so as to sell here without a loss, at three shillings, you may purchase 200 lbs. Should you meet with any curiosities on the coast, of a small value, you may expend 40 or 50 gallons of rum for them. Upon your return you will touch at St. Pierre's, Martinico, and call on Mr. John Mounreau for your further advise and destination. We submit the conducting of the voyage to your good judgment and prudent management, not doubting of your best endeavours to serve our interest in all cases; and conclude with committing you to the almighty Disposer of all events.

"We wish you health and prosperity,
"And are your friends and owners."

The slaves purchased in Africa were chiefly sold in the West Indies, or in the Southern colonies; but when these markets were glutted, and the price low, some of them were brought to Massachusetts. The statistics of the trade are somewhat scattered, and it is difficult to bring them together, but enough is known to bring the subject home to us. In 1795, one informant of Dr. Belknap could remember two or three entire cargoes, and the Doctor himself remembered one somewhere between 1755 and 1765 which consisted almost wholly of children. Sometimes the vessels of the neighboring colony of Rhode Island, after having sold their prime slaves in the West Indies, brought the remnants of their cargoes to Boston for sale. *Coll. M. H. S.*, i., iv., 197.

The records of the slave-trade and slavery everywhere are the same—the same disregard of human rights, the same indifference to suffering, the same contempt for the oppressed races, the same hate for those who are injured. It has been asserted that in Massachusetts, not only were the miseries of slavery mitigated, but some of its worst features were wholly unknown. But the record does not bear out the suggestion; and the traditions of one town at least preserve the memory of the most brutal and barbarous[1] of all, "raising slaves for the market." *Barry's Hanover*, 175.

The first newspapers published in America illustrate among their advertisements the peculiar features of the institution to which we refer, and in their scanty columns of intelligence may be found thrilling accounts of the barbarous murders of masters and crews by the hands of their slave-cargoes.[2] The case of the Amistad negroes had its occasional parallel in the colonial history of the traffic—excepting that the men of New England had a sympathy at home in the 17th and 18th centuries, which was justly withheld from their Spanish and Portuguese imitators in the 19th. Nor was that region wholly exempt from the terror by day and by night of slave insurrections. In *Coffin's Newbury*, 153, is a notice of a conspiracy of Indian and negro slaves "to obtain their inalienable rights,"— apparently a scheme of some magnitude.

---

[1] "The slave-trade can be supported only by barbarians; for civilized nations purchase slaves, but do not produce them." Gibbon, *Extraits de mon Journal*, Oct. 19, 1763. What would the historian of the Decline and Fall of the Roman Empire have said of the Virginia of the nineteenth century!

[2] *Boston News Letter*, No. 1399, *New England Weekly Journal*, No. 214, *Boston News Letter*, No. 1422, No. 1423.

As the advantages of advertising came to be understood, the descriptions of slave property became more frequent and explicit. Negro men, women, and children were mixed up in the sales with wearing apparel, Gold Watches, and other Goods[1]—" very good Barbados Rum" is offered with "a young negro that has had the Small Pox"[2]—and competitors offer "Likely negro men and women juft arrived"[3]— "negro men *new* and negro boys who have been in the country fome time,"[4] and alfo "juft arrived, a choice parcel of negro boys and girls."[5] " A likely negro man *born in the country*, and bred a Farmer, fit for any fervice,"[6] "a negro woman about 22 years old, with a boy about 5 months,"[7] &c., a " likely negro woman about 19 years and a child of about fix months of age *to be fold together or apart*,"[8] and "a likely negro man, *taken by execution*, and to be fold by publick auction at the Royal Exchange Tavern in King Street, at fix o'clock this afternoon,"[9] muft conclude thefe extracts.

At this point it may be neceffary to interpofe a caution with reference to the judgment which muft be pronounced againft the policy which has been illuftrated

[1] Bofton News Letter, No. 1402.   [2] N. E. Journal, No. 200.
[3] N. E. Journal, No. 217.   [4] N. E. Journal, No. 230.
[5] Bofton News Letter, No. 1438, Auguft 12th to 19th, 1731.
[6] This man was offered for fale by the Widow and Adminiftratrix to the Eftate of Thomas Amory in 1731. Bofton News Letter, No. 1413.
[7] Bofton News Letter, No. 1487, July 20th to July 27th, 1732.
[8] N. E. Weekly Journal, No. 267, May 1ft, 1732.
[9] The Bofton Gazette and Country Journal, No. 594, Auguft 18, 1766. This advertifement is a concluſive anſwer to the claim that " no evidence is found of fuch taking in execution in Maffachufetts." *Dane's Abridgment*, II., 314.

in thefe notes ; and a recent writer of Englifh hiftory has fo clearly ftated our own views, that his language requires very little change here.

It would be to mifread hiftory and to forget the change of times, to fee in the Fathers of New England mere commonplace flavemongers ; to themfelves they appeared as the elect to whom God had given the heathen for an inheritance; they were men of ftern intellect and fanatical faith, who, believing themfelves the favorites of Providence, imitated the example and affumed the privileges of the chofen people, and for their wildeft and worft acts they could claim the fanction of religious conviction. In feizing and enflaving Indians, and trading for negroes, they were but entering into poffeffion of the heritage of the faints; and New England had to outgrow the theology of the Elizabethan Calvinifts before it could underftand that the Father of Heaven refpected neither perfon nor color, and that his arbitrary favor—if more than a dream of divines—was confined to fpiritual privileges. *Compare Froude's Hiftory of England, Vol.* VIII., 480.

It was not until the ftruggle on the part of the colonifts themfelves to throw off the faft-clofing fhackles of Britifh oppreffion culminated in open refiftance to the mother-country, that the inconfiftency of maintaining flavery with one hand while pleading or ftriking for freedom with the other, compelled a reluctant and gradual change in public opinion on this fubject.

If it be true that at no period of her colonial and provincial hiftory was Maffachufetts without her "proteſtants" againſt the whole ſyſtem; their example was powerleſs in that day and generation. The words and thoughts of a Williams, an Eliot, and a Sewall, fell unheeded and unnoticed on the ears and hearts of the magiſtrates and people of their time, as the acorn fell two centuries ago in the foreſts by which they were ſurrounded.[1]

V.

But the humane efforts of Roger Williams and John Eliot to abate the ſeverity of judgment againſt captives, and mitigate the horrors of ſlavery in Maſſachuſetts, hardly amounted to a poſitive proteſt againſt the inſtitution itſelf. In their time there was no public opinion againſt ſlavery, and probably very little exerciſe of private judgment againſt it. Even among the Quakers the inner light had not yet diſcloſed its enormity, or awakened tender conſciences to its utter wickedneſs.

There were two ſignal exceptions to the general

---

[1] In this ſentence, as originally printed in the Hiſtorical Magazine, a "Dudley" was included among thoſe indicated as having been in advance of their contemporaries on this ſubjeƈt. The reference was to Paul Dudley, who was the author of a traƈt, publiſhed in 1731, entitled, "An Eſſay on the Merchandiſe of Slaves and Souls of Men. With an Application to the Church of Rome." This title, and references to the traƈt by others, gave us the impreſſion that it was againſt Slavery; but an opportunity recently enjoyed of examining the traƈt itſelf, showed the miſtake. It is altogether ‹an Application to the Church of Rome,"—in faƈt, "an oration againſt Popery," of which Maſſachuſetts had a much greater horror than of ſlavery.

theory and practice of that period on this subject, both of which deserve to be had in everlasting remembrance. We shall make no apology for noticing them in this place, although their connection with the history of slavery in Massachusetts is very remote.

Among the "Acts and Orders made at the Generall Court of Election held at Warwicke this 18th day of May, anno 1652," "The Commissioners of Providence and Warwicke being lawfully mett and sett," on the second day of their session (19th May, 1652), enacted and ordered as follows, viz.:

"WHEREAS, there is a common course practised among Englishmen to buy negers, to that end they may have them for service or slaves for ever; for the preventinge of such practices among us, let it be ordered, that no blacke mankind or white being forced by covenant bond, or otherwise, to serve any man or his assighnes longer than ten yeares, or untill they come to bee twentiefour yeares of age, if they bee taken in under fourteen, from the time of their cominge within the liberties of this Collonie. And at the end or terme of ten yeares to sett them free, as is the manner with the English servants. And that man that will not let them goe free, or shall sell them away elsewhere, to that end that they may be enslaved to others for a long time, hee or they shall forfeit to the Collonie forty pounds." *R. I. Records*, i., 248.

This noble act stands out in solitary grandeur in the middle of the seventeenth century, the first legislative enactment in the history of this continent, if not of the world, for the suppression of involuntary servitude. But, unhappily, it was not enforced, even in the towns over which the authority of the Commiſſioners extended.¹

The other exception to which we have referred is to be found in the following declaration againſt ſlavery by the Quakers of Germantown, Pennſylvania, in 1688. Theſe were a "little handful" of German Friends from Cresheim, a town not far from Worms, in the Palatinate.

We are indebted to the curious and zealous reſearch of Mr. Nathan Kite, of Philadelphia, for the publication of this intereſting memorial. It appeared in *The Friend*, *Vol.* xvii., *No.* 16, *January* 13, 1844. The paper from which Mr. Kite copied was the original. At the foot of the addreſs, John Hart, the clerk of the Monthly Meeting, made his minute, and that paper having been then forwarded to the Quarterly Meeting, received a few lines from Anthony Morris, the clerk of that body, to introduce it to the Yearly Meeting, to which it was then directed.

"This is to the monthly meeting held at Richard Worrell's:

"Theſe are the reaſons why we are againſt the traffic of men-body, as followeth: Is there any that would be done or handled at this manner? viz., to be ſold or made a ſlave for all the time of his life? How fearful and faint-hearted are many at ſea, when they ſee a ſtrange veſſel, being afraid it ſhould be a Turk,

---

¹ Compare *Arnold*, i., 240. We omit his miſtaken deference to Maſſachuſetts in regard to the Act of 1646—ſo long miſunderſtood or miſrepreſented as a proteſt againſt ſlavery. See *ante*, pp. 28-30. Alſo *Bancroft*, i., 174, and *Hildreth*, i., 373.

and they should be taken, and sold for slaves into
Turkey. Now, what is *this* better done, than Turks
do? Yea, rather it is worse for them, which say they
are Christians; for we hear that the most part of such
negers are brought hither against their will and consent, and that many of them are stolen. Now, though
they are black, we cannot conceive there is more
liberty to have them slaves, as [than] it is to have
other white ones. There is a saying, that we should
do to all men like as we will be done ourselves;
making no difference of what generation, descent, or
colour they are. And those who steal or rob men,
and those who buy or purchase them, are they not all
alike? Here is liberty of conscience, which is right
and reasonable; here ought to be likewise liberty of
the body, except of evil-doers, which is another case.
But to bring men hither, or to rob and sell them
against their will, we stand against. In Europe, there
are many oppressed for conscience-sake; and here
there are those oppressed which are of a black colour.
And we who know that men must not commit adultery
—some do commit adultery *in* others, separating
wives from their husbands, and giving them to others:
and some sell the children of these poor creatures to
other men. Ah! do consider well this thing, you
who do it, if you would be done at this manner—and
if it is done according to Christianity! You surpass
Holland and Germany in this thing. This makes an
ill report in all those countries of Europe, where they
hear of [it,] that the Quakers do here handel men as
they handel there the cattle. And for that reason
some have no mind or inclination to come hither.

And who shall maintain this your cause, or plead for it? Truly, we cannot do so, except you shall inform us better hereof, viz.: that Christians have liberty to practise these things. Pray, what thing in the world can be done worse towards us, than if men should rob or steal us away, and sell us for slaves to strange countries; separating husbands from their wives and children. Being now this is not done in the manner we would be done at, [by]; therefore, we contradict, and are against this traffic of men-body. And we who profess that it is not lawful to steal, must, likewise, avoid to purchase such things as are stolen, but rather help to stop this robbing and stealing, if possible. And such men ought to be delivered out of the hands of the robbers, and set free as in Europe. Then is Pennsylvania to have a good report, instead, it hath now a bad one, for this sake, in other countries: Especially whereas the Europeans are desirous to know in what manner *the Quakers* do rule in *their* province; and most of them do look upon us with an envious eye. But if this is done well, what shall we say is done evil?

" If once these slaves (which they say are so wicked and stubborn men,) should join themselves—fight for their freedom, and handel their masters and mistresses, as they did handel them before; will these masters and mistresses take the sword at hand and war against these poor slaves, like, as we are able to believe, some will not refuse to do? Or, have these poor negers not as much right to fight for their freedom, as you have to keep them slaves?

" Now consider well this thing, if it is good or

bad. And in cafe you find it to be good to handel thefe blacks in that manner, we defire and require you hereby lovingly, that you may inform us herein, which at this time never was done, viz., that Christians have fuch a liberty to do fo. To the end we fhall be fatisfied on this point, and fatisfy likewife our good friends and acquaintances in our native country, to whom it is a terror, or fearful thing, that men fhould be handelled fo in Pennfylvania.

"This is from our meeting at Germantown, held ye 18th of the 2d month, 1688, to be delivered to the monthly meeting at Richard Worrell's.

    "GARRET HENDERICH,
    DERICK OP DE GRAEFF,
    FRANCIS DANIEL PASTORIUS,
    ABRAM OP DE GRAEFF.

"At our monthly meeting, at Dublin, ye 30th 2d mo., 1688, we having infpected ye matter, above mentioned, and confidered of it, we find it fo weighty that we think it not expedient for us to meddle with it *here*, but do rather commit it to ye confideration of ye quarterly meeting; ye tenor of it being related to ye truth.

 "On behalf of ye monthly meeting,
      "JO. HART.

"This abovementioned, was read in our quarterly meeting, at Philadelphia, the 4th of ye 4th mo., '88, and was from thence recommended to the yearly meeting, and the above faid Derrick, and the other two mentioned therein, to prefent the fame to ye above said meeting, it being a thing of too great weight for this meeting to determine.

"Signed by order of ye meeting.

"ANTHONY MORRIS."

The minutes of the Yearly Meeting, held at Burlington in the same year, record the result of this first effort among the Quakers.

"At a Yearly Meeting, held at Burlington the 5th day of the 7th Month, 1688.

"A paper being here presented by some German Friends Concerning the Lawfulness & Unlawfulness of Buying & Keeping of Negroes It was adjudged not to be so proper for this Meeting to give a Positive Judgment in the Case It having so general a Relation to many other Parts & therefore at present they Forbear It." *Extract from the Original Minutes, copied by Nathan Kite. Compare Bettle, in Penn. Hist. Soc. Coll.*, I., 365.

Richard Baxter has been represented as having "echoed the opinions of Puritan Massachusetts." *Bancroft*, III., 412. We have already shown that the Puritans of Massachusetts were not hostile to slavery. Neither was Baxter; for he expressly recognized the lawfulness of the purchase and use of men as slaves, although he denounced man-stealing as piracy. The principal point of his Christian Directory (published in 1673) in this matter, was concerning the religious obligations growing out of the relation of master and slave. *Works*, IV., 212–20., XVII., 330., XIX., 210.

Morgan Godwyn, a clergyman of the Church of England, who wrote and publifhed in 1680 "The Negro's and Indian's Advocate, fuing for their Admiffion into the Church," etc., hardly intimates a doubt of the lawfulnefs of their flavery, while he pleads for their humanity and right to religion againft a very general opinion of that day, which denied them both.

Dean Berkeley, in his famous fermon before the Venerable Society in 1731, fpeaks of "the irrational contempt of the Blacks, as Creatures of another Species, who had no right to be inftructed or admitted to the Sacraments." *Sermon, p.* 19.

And George Keith (then Quaker), whose paper againft the practice was faid to be given forth by the appointment of the meeting held by him in the city of Philadelphia, about the year 1693, gave a ftrict charge to Friends "that they fhould fet their negroes at liberty, *after fome reafonable time of fervice.*" *Gabriel Thomas's Hiftory of Pennfylvania, etc.,* 1698, *pp.* 53, 54. This was probably the pamphlet quoted by Dr. Franklin in his letter to John Wright, 4th November, 1789. *Works,* x., 403.

Keith appears fimply to have repeated the words of George Fox in Barbadoes in 1671, when he urged the religious training of the negroes, as well as kind treatment, in place of "cruelty towards them, as the manner of fome hath been and is; and that after certain years of fervitude they fhould make them free." *Journal,* II., 140. For a more particular account of this teftimony of Fox, see *The Friend, Vol.* XVII., *pp.* 28, 29. 4to. Phil. 1843. The explicit answer of Fox to the charge that the Quakers "taught the negroes to rebel," shows very clearly that anti-slavery doctrines were no part of the Quaker creed at that time. *Ibid., pp.* 147–9. Compare 454. See also *Ralph Sandiford's Brief Examination, etc.,* Preface.

And for half a century afterwards "that people were as greedy as any Body in keeping Negroes for their Gain," so as to induce the belief that they "approved of it as a People with one consent unanimously." *Lay,* 84. Ralph Sandiford, in 1729, in his "Brief Examination," etc., thus bemoaned the fact, "that it hath defaced the present Dispensation."

"Had the Friends stood clear of this Practice, that it might have been answered to the Traders in Slaves that there is a People called *Quakers* in *Pennsylvania* that will not own this practice in Word or Deed, then would they have been a burning and a shining Light to these poor Heathen, and a Precedent to the Nations throughout the Universe which might have brought them to have seen the Evil of it in themselves, and glorifyed the Lord on our Behalf, and like the Queen of the *East,* to have admired the Glory and Beauty of the Church of God. But instead thereof, the tender seed in the Honest-hearted is under Suffering, to see both Elders and Ministers as it were cloathed with it, and their offspring after them filling up the Measure of their Parents' Iniquity; which may be suffered till such Time that Recompence from Him that is just to all his Creatures opens that Eye the god of this World has blinded. Though I would not be understood to pervert the Order of the Body, which consists of Servants and Masters, and the

Head cannot say to the Foot, *I have no need of thee;* but it is the Converting Men's Liberty to our Wills, who have not, like the Gibeonites, offered themselves willingly, or by Consent given their Ear to the Doorpost, but are made such by Force, in that Nature that desires to Lord it over their Fellow Creatures, is what is to be abhorred by all Christians." *pp.* 9, 10.

Again, he says in another place: " But in Time this dark Trade creeping in amongst us to the very Ministry, because of the profit by it, hath spread over others like a Leprosy, to the Grief of the Honesthearted." *Preface.*

Public sentiment and opinion against slavery were first aroused and stimulated in America in the latter part of the seventeenth century by sympathy for the Christian captives, Dutch and English, who were enslaved by the Turks and the pirates of Northern Africa. *Lay's " All Slave-keepers Apostates."* The efforts to ransom and release these unfortunate persons, excited by the terrible sorrow of relatives and friends, kinsmen and countrymen, brought home to some minds (though few) the injustice of their own dealings with the negroes. The earliest writers against slavery urged that argument with peculiar force and unction, but with little effect. They seem to have made no impression on the legislation of the colonies, and curious and zealous research only can recover the memorials of their righteous testimonies.

The earliest positive public challenge to slavery in Massachusetts of which we have any knowledge, was in the year 1700, when a learned, pious, and honored magistrate entered the lists alone, and founded his folitary blaft in the ears of his brother magiftrates and the people, who liftened in amazement and wonder, not unmingled with forrow and contempt. His performance is all the more remarkable from the fact that it ftands out in the hiftory of the time feparate and diftinct as "the voice of one crying in the wildernefs."

SAMUEL SEWALL, at that time a Judge of the Superior Court, and afterwards Chief-Juftice, publifhed a brief tract in 1700, entitled: "*The Selling of Jofeph a Memorial.*" It filled three pages of a folio fheet, ending with the imprint: "*Bofton of the Maffachufetts; Printed by Bartholomew Green and John Allen. June 24th, 1700.*"

The author prefented a copy of this tract "not only to each member of the General Court at the time of its publication, but alfo to numerous clergymen and literary gentlemen with whom he was intimate." *MS. Letter.* Compare *Briffot*, I., 224. Although thus extenfively circulated at that day, it has for many years been known apparently only by tradition, as nearly all the notices of it which we have feen are confined to the fact of its publication early in the eighteenth century, the date being nowhere correctly ftated.

Beyond this, it appears to have been unknown to our hiftorians, and is now reproduced probably for the firft time in the prefent century. Indeed, we have met with no quotation even from it later than 1738, when it was reprinted in Pennfylvania, where antiflavery took an earlier and deeper root, and bore earlier fruit, than in any other part of America.[1]

---

[1] It was reprinted as a part of Benjamin Lay's tract, "*All Slave-Keepers that keep the Innocent in Bondage, Apoftates* . . . ," in which it occupies

Its rarity and peculiar intereſt will juſtify us in placing the reprint before our readers in this connection. It is ſomewhat remarkable that ſo ſignal a teſtimony againſt ſlavery ſhould have eſcaped the reſearch of thoſe who have in their cuſtody "the hiſtoric fame" of Maſſachuſetts. It is a moſt honorable memorial of its venerated author.

"*THE SELLING OF JOSEPH A MEMORIAL.*
By the Hon'ble JUDGE SEWALL in New England.

"*FORASMUCH as* LIBERTY *is in real value next unto* Life; *None ought to part with it themſelves, or deprive others of it, but upon moſt mature conſideration.*

"The Numerouſneſs of Slaves at this Day in the Province, and the Uneaſineſs of them under their Slavery, hath put many upon thinking whether the Foundation of it be firmly and well laid; ſo as to ſuſtain the Vaſt Weight that is built upon it. It is moſt certain that all Men, as they are the Sons of *Adam,* are Co-heirs, and have equal Right unto Liberty, and all other outward Comforts of Life. GOD *hath given the Earth [with all its commodities] unto the Sons of Adam, Pſal.,* 115, 16. *And hath made of one Blood all Nations of Men, for to dwell on all the face of the Earth, and hath determined the Times before appointed, and the bounds of their Habitation: That they ſhould ſeek the Lord. Foraſmuch then as we are the Offspring of* GOD, &c. *Acts* 17. 26, 27, 29. Now, although the Title given by the laſt ADAM doth infinitely better Men's Eſtates, reſpecting GOD and themſelves; and grants them a moſt beneficial and inviolable Leaſe under the Broad Seal of Heaven, who were before only Tenants at Will; yet through the Indulgence of GOD to our Firſt Parents after the Fall, the outward Eſtate of all and every of their Children, remains the

---

pp. 199–207 incluſive. The title of Lay's tract gives the imprint, "*Philadelphia, Printed for the Author,* 1737 ;" but it was not publiſhed until the following year. *See The American Weekly Mercury,* No. 973, Aug. 17–24, 1738, and following numbers ; eſpecially No. 982, Oct. 19–26, 1738, in which is printed the repudiation of Lay and his book, by the Yearly Meeting.

same as to one another. So that Originally, and Naturally, there is no such thing as Slavery. *Joseph* was rightfully no more a Slave to his Brethren, than they were to him; and they had no more Authority to *Sell* him, than they had to *Slay* him. And if *they* had nothing to do to sell him; the *Ishmaelites* bargaining with them, and paying down Twenty pieces of Silver, could not make a Title. Neither could *Potiphar* have any better Interest in him than the *Ishmaelites* had. Gen. 37, 20, 27, 28. For he that shall in this case plead *Alteration of Property*, seems to have forfeited a great part of his own claim to Humanity. There is no proportion between Twenty Pieces of Silver and LIBERTY. The Commodity itself is the Claimer. If *Arabian* Gold be imported in any quantities, most are afraid to meddle with it, though they might have it at easy rates; lest it should have been wrongfully taken from the Owners, it should kindle a fire to the Consumption of their whole Estate. 'Tis pity there should be more Caution used in buying a Horse, or a little lifeless dust, than there is in purchasing Men and Women: Whereas they are the Offspring of GOD, and their Liberty is,

. . . *Auro pretiosior Omni.*

" And seeing GOD hath said, *He that Stealeth a Man, and Selleth him, or if he be found in his Hand, he shall surely be put to Death.* Exod. 21, 16. This Law being of Everlasting Equity, wherein Man-Stealing is ranked among the most atrocious of Capital Crimes: What louder Cry can there be made of that Celebrated Warning.

Caveat Emptor!

" And all things considered, it would conduce more to the Welfare of the Province, to have White Servants for a Term of Years, than to have Slaves for Life. Few can endure to hear of a Negro's being made free; and indeed they can seldom use their Freedom well; yet their continual aspiring after their forbidden Liberty, renders them Unwilling Servants. And there is such a disparity in their Conditions, Colour, and Hair, that they can never embody with us, & grow up in orderly Families, to the Peopling of the Land; but still remain in our Body Politick as a kind of extravasat Blood. As many Negro Men as there are among us, so many empty Places are there in our Train Bands, and the places taken up of Men that might make Husbands for our Daughters. And the Sons and Daughters of *New England* would become more like *Jacob* and *Rachel*, if this Slavery were thrust quite out of Doors. Moreover it is too well known what Temptations Masters are under, to connive at the Fornication of their Slaves; lest they should be obliged to find them Wives, or pay their Fines. It seems to be practically pleaded that they might be lawless; 'tis thought much of, that the Law should have satisfaction for their Thefts, and other Immoralities; by which means, *Holiness to the Lord* is more rarely engraven upon this sort of Servitude. It is likewise most lamentable to think, how in taking Negroes out of *Africa*, and selling of them here, That which GOD has joined together, Men do boldly rend asunder; Men from their Country, Husbands from their Wives, Parents from their Children. How horrible is the Uncleanness, Mortality, if not Murder, that the Ships are guilty of that bring great Crouds of these miserable Men and Women. Methinks when we are bemoaning the barbarous Usage of our Friends and Kinsfolk in *Africa*, it might not be unreasonable to enquire whether we are not culpable in forcing the *Africans* to become Slaves amongst ourselves. And it may be a question whether all the Benefit received by *Negro* Slaves will balance the Accompt of Cash laid out upon them; and for the Redemption of our own enslaved Friends out of *Africa*. Besides all the Persons and Estates that have perished there.

" Obj. 1. *These Blackamores are of the Posterity of Cham, and therefore are under the Curse of Slavery.* Gen. 9, 25, 26, 27.

" *Ans.* Of all Offices, one would not beg this; viz. Uncall'd for, to be an Executioner of the Vindictive Wrath of God; the extent and duration of which is to us uncertain. If this ever was a Commission; How do we know but that it is long since out of Date ? Many have found it to their Cost, that a Prophetical Denunciation of Judgment against a Person or People, would not warrant them to inflict that evil. If it would, *Hazael* might justify himself in all he did against his master, and the *Israelites* from 2 *Kings* 8, 10, 12.

" But it is possible that by cursory reading, this Text may have been mistaken. For *Canaan* is the Person Cursed three times over, without the mentioning of *Cham*. Good Expositors suppose the Curse entailed on him, and that this Prophesie was accomplished in the Extirpation of the *Canaanites*, and in the Servitude of the *Gibeonites*.

Vide Pareum. Whereas the Blackmores are not descended of *Canaan*, but of *Cush*. Psal. 68, 31. *Princes shall come out of Egypt* [Mizraim]. *Ethiopia* [Cush] *shall soon stretch out her hands unto God.* Under which Names, all *Africa* may be comprehended; and their Promised Conversion ought to be prayed for. *Jer.* 13, 23. *Can the Ethiopian change his Skin?* This shows that Black Men are the Posterity of *Cush*. Who time out of mind have been distinguished by their Colour. And for want of the true, *Ovid* assigns a fabulous cause of it.

> *Sanguine tum credunt in corpora summa vocato*
> *Æthiopum populos nigrum traxisse colorem.*
> Metamorph. lib. 2.

"Obj. 2. *The* Nigers *are brought out of a Pagan Country, into places where the Gospel is preached.*

"*Ans.* Evil must not be done, that good may come of it. The extraordinary and comprehensive Benefit accruing to the Church of God, and to *Joseph* personally, did not rectify his Brethren's Sale of him.

"Obj. 3. *The* Africans *have Wars one with another: Our Ships bring lawful Captives taken in those wars.*

"*Answ.* For aught is known, their Wars are much such as were between *Jacob's* Sons and their Brother *Joseph*. If they be between Town and Town; Provincial or National: Every War is upon one side Unjust. An Unlawful War can't make lawful Captives. And by receiving, we are in danger to promote, and partake in their Barbarous Cruelties. I am sure, if some Gentlemen should go down to the *Brewsters* to take the Air, and Fish: And a stronger Party from *Hull* should surprise them, and sell them for Slaves to a Ship outward bound; they would think themselves unjustly dealt with; both by Sellers and Buyers. And yet 'tis to be feared, we have no other Kind of Title to our *Nigers*. Therefore all things whatsoever ye would that men should do to you, do you even so to them: for this is the Law and the Prophets. Matt. 7, 12.

'Obj. 4. Abraham *had Servants bought with his Money and born in his House.*

Slavery in Massachusetts. 87

"*Anf.* Until the Circumstances of *Abraham's* purchase be recorded, no Argument can be drawn from it. In the mean time, Charity obliges us to conclude, that He knew it was lawful and good.

"It is Observable that the *Israelites* were strictly forbidden the buying or selling one another for Slaves. *Levit.* 25. 39. 46. *Jer.* 34. 8-22. And GOD gaged His Blessing in lieu of any loss they might conceit they suffered thereby, *Deut.* 15. 18. And since the partition Wall is broken down, inordinate Self-love should likewise be demolished. GOD expects that Christians should be of a more Ingenuous and benign frame of Spirit. Christians should carry it to all the World, as the *Israelites* were to carry it one towards another. And for Men obstinately to persist in holding their Neighbours and Brethren under the Rigor of perpetual Bondage, seems to be no proper way of gaining Assurance that God has given them Spiritual Freedom. Our Blessed Saviour has altered the Measures of the ancient Love Song, and set it to a most Excellent New Tune, which all ought to be ambitious of Learning. *Matt.* 5. 43. 44. *John* 13. 34. These *Ethiopians*, as black as they are, seeing they are the Sons and Daughters of the First *Adam*, the Brethren and Sisters of the Last ADAM, and the Offspring of GOD; They ought to be treated with a Respect agreeable.

" *Servitus perfecta voluntaria, inter Christianum & Christianum, ex parte servi patientis sæpe est licita, quia est necessaria; sed ex parte domini agentis, & procurando & exercendo, vix potest esse licita; quia non convenit regulæ illi generali: Quæcunque volueritis ut faciant vobis homines, ita & vos facite eis.* Matt. 7. 12.

" *Perfecta servitus pœnæ, non potest jure locum habere, nisi ex delicto gravi quod ultimum supplicium aliquo modo meretur: quia Libertas ex naturali æstimatione proxime accedit ad vitam ipsam, & eidem a multis præferri solet.*

" Ames. Cas. Confc. Lib. 5. Cap. 23. Thes. 2. 3."

Thus signally and clearly did Judge Sewall expose the miserable pretences on which slavery and the slave-trade were then justified in Massachusetts, as they continued to be long years after he " slept with his fathers." And he exhibited in his correspondence his desire that " the wicked practice of slavery" might be taken away, as well as his ſtrong conviction that there would be "no great progreſs in Goſpellizing till then." *Letter to Henry Newman, Dec.—Jan.*, 1714-15. It is manifeſt that he was far in advance of his day and generation in theſe views, and he has himſelf left the record that he met more "frowns and hard words" than ſympathy! His teſtimony did not go unchallenged, nor was its publication allowed to paſs without reply. JOHN SAFFIN, a judge of the ſame court with Judge Sewall, and a ſlaveholder, printed an anſwer the next year, of which we regret to ſay we have been able to find no copy. Could it be found, it would undoubtedly be an intereſting document and very important in illuſtration of the hiſtory of ſlavery in Maſſachuſetts. We might naturally expect to find in it ſome references to the laws, the principles, and the practices of the Puritan Fathers of that colony.[1]

---

[1] Since this portion of our work was firſt printed, in the Hiſtorical Magazine for June, 1864, Sewall's tract has been reprinted by the Maſſachuſetts Hiſtorical Society, from an original preſented to its Library by the Hon. Robert C. Winthrop. *Proc. M. H. S.*, 1863-64, *pp.* 161-5. And, what is of much more importance in this connection, a copy of Saffin's anſwer has been diſcovered. It is a ſmall quarto, entitled " A | Brief and Candid Anſwer to a late | Printed Sheet entituled | THE SELLING OF JOSEPH | whereunto is annexed, | a True and Particular Narrative by way of Vindication of the | Author's Dealing with and Proſecution of his Negro Man Servant | for his vile and exhorbitant Behaviour towards his Maſter and his | Tenant, Thomas Shepard ; which hath been wrongfully repreſented | to their Prejudice and Defamation. | By JOHN SAFFIN, Eſqr. : | Boſton : Printed in the Year 1701." The original is now in the poſſeſſion of GEORGE BRINLEY, Eſq., of Hartford, Conn. We are indebted to the reſearch and ſagacity of Mr. J. HAMMOND TRUMBULL, Preſident of the Connecticut Hiſtorical Society, for the diſcovery of Saffin's tract and permiſſion to make the preſent uſe of it. Saffin's original petitions to the General Court in regard to this affair, one referring to his pamphlet as in print, etc., etc., are preſerved in the *Maſſ. Archives*, IX., 152, 153.

Slavery in Massachusetts. 89

The following letter from Judge Sewall, which illustrates the subject further, was addressed

"*To the Rev^d. & aged Mr. John Higginson.*"

Apr. 13, 1706.

"Sir,

"I account it a great Favour of God, that I have been priviledged with the Acquaintance and Friendship of many of the First Planters in New England: and the Friendship of your self, as such, has particularly oblig'd me. *It is now near Six years agoe since I printed a Sheet in defence of Liberty. The next year after, Mr. Saffin set forth a printed Answer. I forbore troubling the Province with any Reply, untill I saw a very Severe Act passing against Indians and Negros, and then I Reprinted that Question, as I found it stated and answered in the Athenian Oracle; which I knew nothing of before last Autumn was twelve moneths, when I accidentally cast my Eye upon it. Amidst the Frowns and hard Words I have met with for this Undertaking, it is no small refreshment to me, that I have the Learned, Reverend & Aged Mr. Higginson for my Abetter. By the interposition of this Brest-Work, I hope to carry on and manage this Enterprise with Safety and Success.* I have inclosed the Prints. I could be glad of your Answer to one Case much in agitation among us at this day: viz., Whether it be not for the Honor of G. and of N. E. to reserve entire and untouch'd the Indian Plantation of Natick, and other Lands under the same Circumstances? that the lying of those Lands unoccupied and undesired by the English, may be a valid and Lasting Evidence, that we desire the Con-

verfioh and Wellfare of the Natives, and would by no means Extirpat them, as the Spaniards did? There is one thing more I would mention, and that is, I am verily perswaded that the Set time for the Drying up of the Apocalyptical Euphrates, is very nigh, if not come: and I earneftly befpeak the Affiftance of your Prayers in that momentous Concern: wch I do with the more Confidence, becaufe you were Lifted in that Service above fifty years ago. Pray, Sir! Come afrefh into the Confederation. Let me alfo entreat your Prayers for me, and my family, that the Bleffing of G. may reft upon the head of every one in it by reafon of the good will of Him who dwell'd in the Bufh. My fervice to Madam Higginfon. I am, Sir,
"Your humble Servt.
"S. S."

We are unable to give any account of the Act againft Indians and Negroes, whofe feverity induced Sewall to renew his efforts in their behalf. Thefe efforts were probably fuccefsful, as none appears to have been paffed into a law at all anfwering to his defcription in its provifions, and in point of time; or if paffed, it muft have been fpeedily repealed. If the Act referred to fhould be found, it might furnifh a ftriking illuftration of the views of the time concerning the ftatus of thefe unhappy races of men.

We fhall therefore re-produce here "that Queftion" as "ftated and anfwered in the Athenian Oracle," which Sewall ufed to fo good purpofe in defending the rights of Indians and Negroes againft the hoftile legiflation of Maffachufetts, in the early years of the eighteenth century.

From the *Athenian Oracle*, Vol. II., pp. 460–63.

"Q. *We read in* Gen. 17. 12: And he that is eight days old shall be Circumcised among you, every Man-child in their Generation. He that is born in the House, or bought with Money of any Stranger that is not of thy Seed. *This was God's Covenant with* Abraham, *and in him with all the Jews; which Covenant by Chrift's coming into the World, being abolifhed, and the Covenant of Baptifm inftituted in its ftead;* The Queftion is, *Whether thofe Merchants and Planters in the* Weft Indies, *as well all other parts of the World, that buy Negroes, or other Heathen Servants or Slaves, are not indifpenfably bound to bring fuch Servants to be Baptized, as well as* Abraham *was to Circumcife his Stranger Servants? Confequently, what's to be thought of thofe Chriftian Mafters, who refufe to let fuch Servants be baptized; becaufe if they were, they wou'd have their freedom at a certain term of Years allow'd by the Laws of the feveral Plantations?*

"A. We have met with this Queftion before, though to comply with the Gentleman's defire, we'll here give it a larger Anfwer; tho' in the firft Place, we muft obferve a falfe fuppofition in the wording of it. That God's Covenant with *Abraham* was abolifhed by the Covenant he made with us by our Saviour, and confequently they are two *different Covenants;* whereas they were rather the *fame Covenant*, with two different *Seals;* we fay the Covenant God made with *Abraham*, was not a *Covenant of Works*, but of *Faith*, as well as that he makes by Chrift with all Believers; nay, was the very fame with it, Chrift being promifed in God's Covenant with *Abraham*, when 'twas faid, *That in his feed fhould all the Nations of the Earth be blefsed;* which is interpreted of Chrift by the infpired Writers; and this is further evident from the Apoftles way of Arguing, *Rom.* 4. 11. 13. *He received the Sign of Circumcifion, a Seal of the Righteoufnefs of the Faith, which he had yet being uncircumcifed, that he might be Father of all them that believe, though they be not Circumcifed;* for the Promife that he fhould be the Heir of the World, was not to Abraham, or to his feed through the Law; but through Faith, etc.

"Now to the Queftion. If *Abraham* was oblig'd to Circumcife all that were born of his Houfe, and that were bought with money of

the *Stranger* (the Samaritan Verſion has it בָּרְבָרָה *Barbarah*, whence
Βάρβαρος a Barbarian, names that all Nations have ever ſince flung at
one another, and the *Hebrews* as often call'd by it among the Greeks
as any. If he was to do this, ought not all Chriſtians by *Parity* of
Reaſon to do the like by their *Slaves* and *Servants ?* We anſwer,
Yes, and much more, as the *Goſpel* is now more clearly revealed than
'twas to *Abraham*, who indeed ſaw Chriſt, and rejoic'd, but 'twas in
darker *Types* and *Prophecies*. But in order to a more full ſatisfac-
tion of this Difficulty, it may be further convenient to enquire; whether Negro's Children are to be *Baptized*, and for grown Perſons what
Preparation is required of 'em? To the firſt, a great Man of our
Church was of an opinion, That a Negro's Child ought to be baptiz'd,
as well as any others; the Promiſe reaching *To all that were afar off,
as well as to Believers and their Children*, and in this caſe, the right
of the child is in the Maſter,[1] not the Slave; and if Chriſt dy'd for
all, why ſhould not the Vertues of his Death be apply'd to all; who do
nothing to refiſt it, for the waſhing away their Original Pravity?
Again, as we argue in the caſe of Infant Baptiſm. If Infants were in
the Covenant before Chriſt, how come they ſince to be excluded? So
we may here, and perhaps more generally; If all Infants, born in
Abraham's houſe, or bought with Money of the Stranger or *Barbarian*
(who often ſold their own Children then, as they do now) if they were
then to have the Seal of the Covenant, how have they ſince forfeited
it? Why mayn't they be capable of a nobler Seal, 'tis true, but yet of
the ſame Covenant made with all Mankind by Chriſt, that *promiſ'd
Seed*, in whom, as before, all Nations ſhould be bleſſed, and the breach
repaired that was made in *Adam;* as was, we are ſure, the expreſs
opinion of St. *Jerom*, who in his diſputation with the *Pelagian*,
Ep. 17, has remarkable Expreſſions. *Why are Infants Baptized,
ſays the Pelagian?* The Orthodox anſwers, *That in Baptiſm their*

[¹ At a meeting of the General Aſſociation of the Colony of Connecticut, 1738, "It was inquired—whether the infant ſlaves of Chriſtian maſters
may be baptized in the right of their maſters—they ſolemnly promiſing to
train them in the nurture and admonition of the Lord: and whether it is the
duty of ſuch maſters to offer ſuch children and thus religiouſly to promiſe.
Both queſtions were affirmatively anſwered. *Records as reported by Rev.
C. Chapin, D. D., quoted in Jones's Religious Inſtruction of the Negroes, etc.,
p. 34.*]

Sins may be remitted. The *Pelagian* replies, Where did they ever sin? The *Orthodox* rejoyns, that S. *Paul* shall answer for him, who says in the fifth of the *Rom.*, *Death reign'd from* Adam *to* Moses, *even over those who had not sinn'd, according to the similitude of* Adam's *Transgression.* And he quotes St. *Cyprian* in the same place, both to his and our Purpose, *That if Remission of Sins is given even to greater and more notorious Sinners, and none is Excepted from Grace, none prohibited from Baptism, much less ought an Infant to be deny'd' Baptism, who has no Sin of his own, but only that of his Father* Adam *to answer for.* This for Children, and there's yet less doubt of those who are of Age to answer for themselves, and would soon learn the Principles of our Faith, and might be taught the Obligation of the Vow they made in Baptism, as there's little doubt but *Abraham* instructed his *Heathen Servants*, who were of Age to learn, in the Nature of *Circumcision*, before he *Circumcis'd* them; nor can we conclude much less from God's own noble Testimony of him, *Gen.* 18. 19. *I know him, that he will command his Children and his Household, and they shall keep the way of the Lord.*

"What then should hinder but these be *Baptized?* If only the Covetousness of their Masters, who for fear of losing their Bodies, will venture their Souls; which of the two are we to esteem the greater Heathens? Now that this is notorious Matter of Fact, that they are so far from persuading those poor Creatures to Come to *Baptism*, that they discourage them from it, and rather hinder them as much as possible, though many of the wretches, as we have been informed, earnestly desire it; this we believe, none that are concern'd in the Plantations, if they are ingenuous, will deny, but own they don't at all care to have them Baptized. Talk to a *Planter* of the *Soul* of a *Negro*, and he'll be apt to tell ye (or at least his Actions speak it loudly) that the Body of one of them may be worth twenty Pounds; but the Souls of an hundred of them would not yield him one Farthing; and therefore he's not at all solicitous about them, though the true Reason is indeed, because of that Custom of giving them their Freedom after turning Christians, which we know not if it be Reasonable; we are sure the Father of the *Faithful* did not so by those Servants whom he had Circumcised. 'Tis no where required in Scripture. St. *Paul* indeed bids Masters not be *cruel* and *unreasonable* to their Slaves, especially if Brethren or Christians; but he no where bids them give 'em their Liberty, nor do's Chriſtianity alter any *Civil Right;* nor do's the ſame Apoſtle, in all his excellent Plea for *Oneſimus,* once tell his *Maſter* 'tis his Duty to ſet him *Free;* all he deſires is, he'd again *receive* and *forgive* him; nay, he tells Servants, 'tis their Duty, in whatever ſtate they are call'd therein to abide; beſides, ſome Perſons, nay, Nations ſeem to be born for Slaves; particularly many of the *Barbarians* in *Africa,* who have been ſuch almoſt from the beginning of the World, and who are in a much better Condition of Life, when Slaves among us, then when at Liberty at Home, to cut Throats and Eat one another, eſpecially when by the Slavery of their Bodies, they are brought to a Capacity of Freeing their Souls from a much more unſupportable Bondage. Though in the mean time, if there be ſuch a Law or Cuſtom for their *Freedom,* to encourage 'em to Chriſtianity, be it reaſonable or otherwiſe, this is certain, that none can excuſe thoſe who for that Reaſon ſhould any way hinder or diſcourage 'em from being Chriſtians; ſome of whoſe excuſes are almoſt too ſhameful to repeat, ſince they ſeem to reflect on the Chriſtian Religion, as if that made Men more untractable and ungovernable, than when bred in Ignorance and Heatheniſm, which muſt proceed from the Perverſeneſs of ſome Tempers, as before, fitter for *Slaves* than *Freedom;* or for want of good Inſtruction, when they have nothing but the name of Chriſtianity, without underſtanding any thing of the Obligation thereof; or Laſtly, From the bad Examples of their Maſter's themſelves, who live ſuch lives as often ſcandalize theſe honeſter Heathens."

We ſhall force no inferences from this document as to the character of the legiſlation againſt which it was directed. It is an argument for the "right to Religion," in that day ſo univerſally denied, in practice at leaſt, to enſlaved Indians and Negroes, and their offspring, that it would be ſtrange, if true, that Maſſachuſetts furniſhed any but occaſional exceptions to the prevailing rule.[1]

---

[1] " Slaves were admitted to be church members at a period when church members had peculiar political privileges." *Quincy's Reports,* 30, *note.* This is Mr. Justice Gray's ſtatement on the following authorities :

Slavery in Maſſachuſetts. 95

We have previouſly noticed Sewall's "eſſay" to prevent Indians and Negroes being rated with brutes in the tax-laws, in the year 1716. Three years later, a new occaſion preſented itſelf for the renewal of his efforts in behalf of the oppreſſed. A maſter had killed his negro ſlave, and was about to anſwer for the offence before the Court. One of the judges ſeems to have deſired the aid and counſel of the Chief Juſtice in his

---

1. *Winthrop's Journal*, II., 26, and Savage's note. "Mo. 2. 13. [1641]. A negro maid, ſervant to Mr. Stoughton of Dorcheſter, being well approved by divers years' experience, for ſound knowledge and true godlineſs, was received into the church and baptized." Mr. Savage's note is, "Similar inſtances have been common enough ever ſince."

2. *Ancient Charters*, 117. "To the end the body of the freemen may be preſerved of honeſt and good men: It is ordered, that henceforth no man ſhall be admitted to the freedom of this Commonwealth, but ſuch as are members of ſome of the churches within the limits of this juriſdiction."

3. *Bancroft's Hiſtory U. S.*, I., 360. "The ſervant, the bondman, might be a member of the church, and therefore a freeman of the Company."

Notwithſtanding this array of authority, we muſt ſuggeſt our doubts, 1ſt. Whether the notice itſelf by Winthrop is not a palpable evidence of the extraordinary and exceptional character of the incident that a negro maid-ſervant ſhould be baptized and received into the church? Mr. Savage's remark cannot be regarded as authority, not being ſuſtained by references to any ſimilar inſtances. 2d. Whether a ſingle inſtance has ever been found or is known in the hiſtory of Maſſachuſetts, during the period referred to, in which a ſervant or bondman, black or white, actually became a freeman of the Company?

Mr. Palfrey indulges in ſome pleaſing ſpeculations on this topic. "A negro ſlave might be a member of the church, and this fact preſents a curious queſtion. As a church-member, he was eligible to the political franchiſe; and if he ſhould be actually inveſted with it, he would have a part in making laws to govern his maſter,—laws with which his maſter, if a non-communicant, would have had no concern, except to obey them." Touchſtone wiſely ſaid there was "much virtue in If," and Dr. South has a maxim that "we are not to build certain rules on the contingency of human actions." Whether the hiſtorian recalled either "inſtance," we cannot ſay; but here he evidently recognized the impropriety of conſtructing hiſtory on a frame of conjectural contingencies, and frankly admitted at the end of his

preparations for the case, and Sewall's Letter-Book preserves the following memoranda of what he communicated.

"The poorest Boys and Girls in this Province, such as are of the lowest Condition; whether they be English, or Indians, or Ethiopians : They have the same Right to Religion and Life, that the Richest Heirs have.

"And they who go about to deprive them of this Right, they attempt the bombarding of HEAVEN, and the Shells they throw, will fall down upon their own heads.

"Mr. Justice Davenport, Sir, upon your desire, I have sent you these *Quotations*, and my *own Senti-*

---

note, "it is improbable that the Court would have made a slave—while a slave—a member of the Company, though he were a communicant." *History of New England*, II., 30, *note.* As to baptism of slaves in Massachusetts, see *ante, pp.* 58–59. Compare *Hurd's Law of Freedom and Bondage, Vol.*I., *pp.* 165, 210, 358. The famous French *Code Noir* of 1685 obliged every planter to have his Negroes baptized, and properly instructed in the doctrines and duties of Christianity. Nor was this the only important and humane provision of that celebrated statute, to which we may seek in vain for any parallel in British Colonial legislation. Its influence was felt in England, and may have given rise to those humane instructions, one of which we have already quoted (*p.* 52). Another required his Majesty's Governors "with the assistance of our Council to find out the best means to facilitate and encourage the Conversion of Negros and Indians to the Christian Religion." *N. Y. Col. Doc.*, III., 374. Evelyn, in his Diary, gives an interesting account of the determination of the King, James II., on this point. At Winchester, 16 September, 1685, he says, "I may not forget a resolution which his Majesty made, and had a little before entered upon it at the Council Board at Windsor or Whitehall, that the negroes in the Plantations should all be baptized, exceedingly declaiming against the impiety of their masters prohibiting it, out of a mistaken opinion that they would be *ipso facto* free; but his Majesty persists in his resolution to have them christened, which piety the Bishop blessed him for." *Works*, II., 245. This was good Bishop Ken, the Christian Psalmist.

ments. I pray GOD, the Giver and Guardian of Life, to give his gracious Direction to you, and the other Justices; and take leave, who am your brother and most humble servant,

"Samuel Sewall.

"Boston, July 20, 1719.

"I inclosed also the *Selling of Joseph*, and my Extract out of the *Athenian Oracle*.

"To Addington Davenport, Esqr., etc., going to Judge Sam¹. Smith of Sandwich, for killing his Negro."

That such arguments were necessary, or even regarded as appropriate on such an occasion, is a fact full of meaning. We have previously intimated a doubt whether the slave could claim any right or privilege of protection under the laws which were known as the "*Liberties of Servants;*" and in connection with the instructions to Andros in 1688, we have called the attention of the reader to the distinction between the *Christian* servants or slaves and the *Indians and Negroes*. The former were to be protected against the inhuman severity of ill-masters or overseers, while the latter were to be so far advanced in the scale of humanity, that the "*wilful* killing" of them should "be punished with *death*, and a fitt penalty imposed for the maiming of them."

We cannot, however, at present attempt to determine what were the actual legal restraints upon the power of a master over his slave, in Massachusetts. We do not know that the materials for such a determination exist anywhere save in such records as remain of those ancient tribunals of the Colony and Province by which alone the rights of persons and of property were then, as now, judicially ascertained and regulated. There are abundant modern statements of opinion on these points, but we cannot recall a single instance in which these statements are fortified by good and sufficient testimony from the ancient and contemporary records or authorities; and we cannot doubt that the reader of these notes will sympathize in our desire to rest on facts rather than opinions. For example, in the particular case above referred to, the awful solemnity with which the Chief Justice communicates his charge to his brother magistrate when about to "judge" a master for "killing his Negro," gives peculiar interest to the result; and it is greatly to be regretted that the record of the trial, conviction, and punishment of such an offender should be concealed among the neglected rubbish of any Massachusetts Court-House. If Samuel Smith of Sandwich was hung for the murder of his slave in Massachusetts in the year 1719, it is due to the historic fame of the Province that the world should know it!

We are perfectly aware that the opinion has prevailed that the negro or mulatto or Indian slave in Massachusetts, "always had many rights which raised him far above the *absolute* slave." These are nowhere more favorably stated than by Nathan Dane, in his great work on American Law. *Abridgment*, II., 313. He considers the subject in eight points of view:

"1. The master has no control over the religion

of such slave, any more than over the religion of any other member of his family;

"2. None over his life; if he killed him, he was punishable as for killing a freeman;

"3. The master was liable to his slave's action, for beating, wounding or immoderately chastising him, as much as for immoderately correcting an apprentice, or a child;

"4. The slave was capable of holding property, as a devisee or legatee, and as recovered for wounds, etc., so much so, if the master took away such property, his slave could sue him by *prochein ame*;

"5. If one took him from his master without his consent, he could not have trover, but only sue, as for taking away his other servant; on the whole the slave had the right of property and of life, as apprentices had, and the only difference was 'an apprentice is a servant for time, and the slave is a servant for life.' In Connecticut, the slave was, by statute, specially forbidden to contract; no such statute is recollected in Massachusetts;

"6. If a slave married a free woman, with the consent of his master, he was emancipated, for his master had suffered him to contract a relation inconsistent with a state of slavery; 'hereby the master abandoned his right to him as a slave, as a minor child is emancipated from his father when he is married.' *Ld. Raymond*, 356;

"7. A slave however could be sold, and in some states be taken in execution for his master's debts; but no evidence is found of such taking in execution in Massachusetts;

"8. On the principles of the Englifh Common Law, men may be made *flaves for life* for *crimes*, and fo clearly, by our prefent law. Property in a negro [was] acquired without deed. 1 *Dal.*, 169."

Now, if all thefe points had been well taken and could be fortified by the neceffary amount of hiftorical teftimony, they would unqueftionably make a very good cafe. But unhappily they are mainly theoretical ftatements derived from abftract reafoning on general principles, of which no fuch applications were thought of in the period to which they are affigned. Yet the formality with which they are ftated, and the dignified place they hold in a book of great authority, give them an importance beyond the conjectures which are generally ventured as to how far the lot of the flave was mitigated in Maffachufetts.

Mr. Dane copied them with but flight alterations, chiefly in favor of Maffachufetts, from the treatife of Judge Reeve on "*Domeftic Relations,*" *pp.* 340-41, publifhed in 1816. There is no reference to the ftatutes, nor to any judicial decifions on any point, excepting as here quoted, either in original or copy.

Shall we be accounted prefumptuous, if we add a few comments as well as a reference to the facts already prefented, which muft throw great doubts over the whole array of rights thus claimed as having been accorded to flaves in Maffachufetts?

The right to religion and life was not clearly recognized as belonging equally to bond-flave and freeman. Mr. Dane altered Judge Reeve's ftatement of the latter point. Judge Reeve faid, " if he killed him, he was *liable to the same punishment* as for killing a freeman." The alteration indicates the nature of the doubt which may have arisen in the mind of Mr. Dane when he wrote it, "he was *punishable* as for killing a freeman." No doubt he was punishable. The incident which we have presented of the master called to answer before the Court for the fact of killing his negro shows this. So too, in the first Massachusetts Code, even "the Bruite Creature" is protected against "Tirrany and Crueltie" by the very next statute after that which establishes slavery—a significant sequence!

Here let it be remembered that the original law of slavery in Massachusetts gave to slaves "all the liberties and Christian usages which the law of God, established in Israel concerning such persons, doth morally require." Now the Mosaic Law here recognized and reënacted did not protect the life of a heathen slave against his master's violence, by the penalty of "life for life," and although such violence might be punished, the kind and degree of punishment is not now to be ascertained. *Exodus*, xxi., 20, 21. And there is a marked distinction to be observed in regard to the Hebrew, though a slave, who is favorably compared with the hired servant and sojourner in contrast with the bondman. *Leviticus*, xxv., 39, 40. To what extent the "rigor" of heathen bondage among the Jews was softened into "liberties and Christian usages" among the Puritans is a question of fact and not of opinion. What was morally required by the law of God established in Israel, in this as in all similar business, was a matter reserved for their own decision, in their own General Court and other tribunals. And this general provision in the original law seems to have been the only one to which the slave could appeal, or more properly by which the conduct of the master could be regulated, in the government and disposition of his chattel. It is certain that most of the special provisions of the law respecting masters and servants had no application to slaves, and we have already expressed the doubt whether slaves enjoyed any of the privileges of servants under that law.

Where is the evidence that Indians and Negroes in bondage were entitled to protection as other servants? and that the master was liable to his slave's action for beating, wounding, or immoderately chastising, etc.? It is far more probable that the condition of the servant was practically assimilated to that of the slave, than that the slave shared any of the privileges accorded by statute to the servant. It would add much to our knowledge on this subject, if the examples should be adduced to show at what period in the history of Massachusetts the Indian and negro slave *first* acquired a status in Court as a prosecutor, or in any other capacity than as a criminal at the bar, before which he was often enough called to answer under the unjust and unequal legislation of that period. If it was at any time before the American Revolution—how came it to pass that, in 1783, a fine of forty shillings against a master for "beating, bruising, and otherwise evilly intreating" his negro-slave, gave "a mortal wound to slavery in Massachusetts?" And further, if a slave could recover against his master damages for cruelty, why was it necessary to resort to the suit "by *prochein ame*" to enable him to keep his recovery?

Again, where is the evidence that flaves were capable of holding property, etc., beyond the occafional and exceptional permiffion to enjoy fome privileges as a *peculium*, with the profits of which they might in fome cafes be enabled even to purchafe their manumiffion? Could flaves take and hold real eftate in Maffachufetts? "No fervant, either man or maid," was permitted "to give, fell or truck any commodity whatfoever without licenfe from their Mafters, during the time of their fervice, under pain of fine, or corporal punifhment, at the difcretion of the Court, as the offence fhall deferve." *Mafs. Laws, Ed.* 1672, *p.* 104. Is it probable that a flave was on any better footing in this refpect than a white fervant?

As to the form of action by which a mafter fhould fue for the unlawful taking of his flave without his confent—the only examples of fuch fuits in Maffachufetts to which we are able to refer, contradict the opinion that he could not have trover, but muft fue in trefpafs *per quod fervitium amifit*. *Goodfpeed* v. *Gay, Mafs. Sup. Court Records,* 1763, *fol.* 47, 101. *Allifon* v. *Cockran, Ibid.* 1764, *fol.* 103. The right to maintain trover for a negro was a matter of courfe in Maffachufetts, for there can be no queftion as to the fact that he might be held and fold as a chattel under the laws of that Colony and Province, and trover lies by any one who has any fpecial property in a chattel, with the right to immediate poffeffion. *Compare Gray, in Quincy's Reports,* 93, *note,* where all the authorities are cited.

The marriage of flaves in Maffachufetts has already

been noticed, and it is obvious that the legiflators of Maffachufetts never intended that fuch marriages fhould confer any rights or impofe any duties which were incompatible with the ftate of flavery; and it may fafely be alleged that no inftance can be produced of the emancipation of a flave as a legal confequence of marriage with a free woman.[1]

The candor of the admiffion "that a flave however could be fold, and in fome ftates be taken in execution for his mafter's debts," is unhappily qualified by the affertion that "no evidence is found of fuch taking in execution in Maffachufetts." The only reafon it was not found was, that it was not hunted; for the failure to find it muft have been either from want of difpofition or lack of diligence.

But we have faid enough on thefe topics to put thofe who are moft interefted upon inquiry. Thofe who are familiar with fuch refearches and have opportunities of eafy reference to the records and files of the Courts in Maffachufetts during the period of which we are writing, can probably collate a fufficient number of examples to fettle all thefe queftions by authority. They will undoubtedly illuftrate the gradual amelioration of all the various forms of oppreffion, but thefe changes muft be held to mark the era of their hiftorical development. If they prove that the doubts we have

---

[1] We have been unable to verify the reference to "Lord Raymond, 356," as to the analogous emancipation of a minor child "from his father when he is married"—but we have high authority for the ftatement that the laws of Maffachufetts know of no fuch emancipation. 15 *Mafs. Reports*, 203.

suggested are not well founded, we shall be most gratified with the result.

The ultimate theory of slavery in all ages and nations has been reduced to a very brief and comprehensive statement. Dr. Maine, in his admirable treatise on Ancient Law, says that "the simple wish to use the bodily powers of another person as a means of ministering to one's own ease or pleasure is doubtless the foundation of slavery and as old as human nature." And again, "there seems to be something in the institution of slavery which has at all times either shocked or perplexed mankind, however little habituated to reflection, and however slightly advanced in the cultivation of its moral instincts." To satisfy the conscience of the master, the Greeks established the idea of intellectual inferiority of certain races and consequent natural aptitude for the servile condition. The Romans declared the doctrine of a supposed agreement between victor and vanquished, in which the first stipulated for the perpetual services of his foe, and the other gained in consideration the life which he had legitimately forfeited. *Compare Maine*, 162–66.

The Puritans of New England appear to have been neither shocked nor perplexed with the institution, for which they made ample provision in their earliest code. They were familiar with the Greek and Roman ideas on the subject, and added the conviction that slavery was established by the law of God, and that Christianity always recognized it as the antecedent Mosaic practice. On these foundations, is it strange that it held its place so long in the history of Massachusetts?

It has been said that the firſt ſtep towards the deſtruction of ſlavery was the reſtraint or prohibition of the importation of ſlaves. But it would be abſurd to regard laws for this purpoſe as an expreſſion of humane conſideration for the negroes. Graham, in his hiſtory, characterizes ſuch a view of the moſt ſtringent one ever made in any of the Colonies, as an "impudent abſurdity." *Hiſt. U. S.*, IV., 78. We have already noticed the Maſſachuſetts acts of 1705, with the additional acts of 1728 and 1739, impoſing and enforcing the collection of an import duty of four pounds per head upon all negroes brought into the Province.

There is no indication in the acts themſelves, nor have we been able to find any evidence, that they were intended other than as revenue acts, beyond that which we have preſented in theſe notes.

We have heretofore quoted the inſtruction of the town of Boſton in 1701. It is not improbable that it was the reſult of Judge Sewall's efforts in 1700. Fruitleſs as it was, it ſhows that even then ſome were wiſe enough to ſee that the importation of negroes was not ſo beneficial to the Crown or Country as that of white ſervants would be. In 1706, an eſſay or "*Computation that the Importation of Negroes is not ſo profitable as that of White Servants*," was publiſhed in Boſton, which may properly be reproduced here. It was the firſt newſpaper article againſt the importation of negroes publiſhed in America, and appeared in the *Boſton News-Letter*, No. 112, June 10, 1706. We are inclined to attribute this article alſo to Judge Sewall.

Slavery in Maſſachuſetts.

" By laſt Year's Bill of Mortality for the Town of *Boſton*, in *Number* 100 *News-Letter*, we are furniſhed with a Liſt of 44 Negroes dead laſt year, which being computed one with another at 30*l.* per Head, amounts to the Sum of One Thouſand three hundred and Twenty Pounds, of which we would make this Remark : That the Importing of Negroes into this or the Neighboring Provinces is not ſo beneficial either to the Crown or Country, as White Servants would be.

" For Negroes do not carry Arms to defend the Country as Whites do.

" Negroes are generally Eye-Servants, great Thieves, much addicted to Stealing, Lying and Purloining.

" They do not People our Country as Whites would do whereby we ſhould be ſtrengthened againſt an Enemy.

" By Encouraging the Importing of White Men Servants, allowing ſomewhat to the Importer, moſt Huſbandmen in the Country might be furniſhed with Servants for 8, 9, or 10*l.* a Head, who are not able to launch out 40 or 50*l.* for a Negro the now common Price.

" A Man then might buy a White Man Servant we ſuppoſe for 10*l.* to ſerve 4 years, and Boys for the ſame price to Serve 6, 8, or 10 years ; If a White Servant die, the Loſs exceeds not 10*l.* but if a Negro dies, 'tis a very great loſs to the Huſbandman ; Three years Intereſt of the price of the Negro, will near upon if not altogether purchaſe a White Man Servant.

" If Neceſſity call for it, that the Huſbandman muſt fit out a Man againſt the Enemy ; if he has a Negro he cannot ſend him, but if he has a White Servant, 'twill anſwer the end, and perhaps save his Son at home.

" Were Merchants and Maſters Encouraged as already ſaid to bring in Men Servants, there needed not be ſuch Complaint againſt Superiors Impreſſing our Children to the War, there would then be Men enough to be had without Impreſſing.

" The bringing in of ſuch Servants would much enrich this Province becauſe Huſbandmen would not only be able far better to manure what Lands are already under Improvement, but would alſo improve a great deal more that now lyes waſte under Woods, and enable this Province to ſet about raiſing of Naval Stores, which would be greatly advantageous to the Crown of England, and this Province.

" For the raiſing of Hemp here, ſo as to make Sail-cloth and

Cordage to furnish but our own shipping, would hinder the Importing it, and save a considerable sum in a year to make Returns for which we now do, and in time might be capacitated to furnish England not only with Sail-cloth and Cordage, but likewise with Pitch, Tar, Hemp, and other Stores which they are now obliged to purchase in Foreign Nations.

"Suppose the Government here should allow Forty Shillings per-head for five years, to such as should Import every of these years 100 White Men Servants, and each to serve 4 years, the cost would be but 200*l.* a year, and a 1000*l.* for the 5 years. The first 100 Servants, being free the 4th year they serve the 5th for Wages, and the 6th there is 100 that goes out into the Woods, and settles a 100 Families to Strengthen and Baracado us from the Indians, and also a 100 Families more every year successively.

"And here you see that in one year the Town of Boston has lost 1320*l.* by 44 Negroes, which is also a loss to the Country in general, and for a less loss (if it may be improperly be so called) for a 1000*l.* the Country may have 500 Men in 5 years time for the 44 Negroes dead in one year.

"A certain person within these 6 years had two Negroes dead computed both at 60*l.* which would have procured him six white Servants at 10*l.* per head to have Served 24 years, at 4 years apiece, without running such a great risque, and the Whites would have strengthened the Country, that Negroes do not.

"'Twould do well that none of those Servants be liable to be Impressed during their Service of Agreement at their first Landing.

"That such Servants being Sold or Transported out of this Province during the time of their Service, the Person that buys them be liable to pay 3*l.* into the Treasury."

A third of a century after the publication of Judge Sewall's tract, another made its appearance, entitled "A Testimony against that Anti-Christian Practice of making Slaves of Men Wherein it is shewed to be contrary to the Dispensation of the Law, and Time of the Gospel, and very opposite both to Grace and Nature. By Elihu Coleman. Matthew 7. 12.

Therefore all things whatfoever ye would that men fhould do unto you, do ye even fo to them, for this is the Law and the Prophets. Printed in the year 1733." *MS. Copy in the Library of the American Antiquarian Society.* This writer was a minifter of the Society of Friends, and of Nantucket. His work was written in 1729-30. *Coffin's Newbury, p. 338. Macy's Nantucket, p. 279.*

At the Nantucket Monthly Meeting, in 1716, it was determined as "yᵉ fenfe and judgment of this meeting, that it is not agreeable to truth for Friends to purchafe flaves and hold them term of life." *Macy's Nantucket, p. 281.*

In 1755, March 10, the town of Salem authorized a petition to the General Court againft the importation of negroes. *Felt's Salem,* II., 416. There may have been other occafional efforts of this fort, but they muft have been comparatively few and fruitlefs.

We have thus noticed the moft important, if not the only anti-flavery demonftrations which appear in the hiftory of Maffachufetts down to the period immediately preceding the Revolution. Excepting thofe already mentioned, we know of no public advocates for the flave in that Colony and Province until the cry of refiftance to Britifh tyranny began to refound through the Colonies.

James Otis's great fpeech in the famous Caufe of the Writs of Affiftance in 1761—the firft fcene of the firft act of oppofition to the arbitrary claims of Great Britain—declared the rights of man, inherent and inalienable. In that fpeech the poor negroes were not forgotten. None ever afferted their rights in ftronger terms. *Adams's Works,* x., 315. Mr. Bancroft poftpones Otis's "proteft againft negro flavery" to a later year (1764), when he tranflated the "fcathing fatire" of Montefquieu in his affertion and proof of the rights of the Britifh Colonies. This difference in time is not material for our prefent purpofe. Many years were to pafs away before his views on this fubject were accepted by the children's children of thofe to whom his words then founded like a rhapfody and an extravagance.

It was a ftrong arm, and it ftruck a fturdy blow, but the wedge recoiled and flew out from the tough black knot of flavery, which was deftined to outlaft the ﬁerceft fires of the Revolution in Maffachufetts, thus kindled with live coals from the altar of univerfal liberty.

John Adams heard the words of Otis, and "fhuddered at the doctrine he taught," and to the end of his long life continued "to fhudder at the confequences that may be drawn from fuch premifes." Yet John Adams "adored the idea of gradual abolitions." *Works,* x., 315. For his later views on emancipation, see *Works,* vi., 511., x., 379.

The views expreffed by Otis muft have founded ftrangely in the ears of men who "lived (as John Adams himfelf fays he did) for many years in times when the practice [of flavery] was not difgraceful, when the beft men in my vicinity thought it not inconfiftent with their character." *Works,* x., 380. If there was a prevailing public fentiment againft flavery in Maffachufetts—as has been conftantly claimed of late—the people of that day, far lefs demonftrative than their defcendants, had an extraordinary way of not fhowing it. Hutchinfon, who was undoubtedly the man of his time moft familiar with the hiftory of his native province, fays in his firft volume, publifhed in 1764, *p*. 444, "Some judicious perfons are of opinion that the permiffion of flavery has been a publick mifchief." This is certainly the indication of a very mild type of oppofition—by no means of a pervading public fentiment.

John Adams was not alone in his aftonifhment at the ideas expreffed by Otis. Thefe ideas were new as they were ftartling to the people of Maffachufetts in that day. And to the calm judgment of the hiftorian there is nothing ftrange in the fact that the foremoft man of his time in that province fhould have fhuddered at the doctrines which Otis taught. More than a century paffed away before all the ancient badges of fervitude could be removed from the colored races in Maffachufetts, if indeed it be even now true that none of thofe difabilities which fo ftrongly mark the focial ftatus of the negro ftill linger in the legiflation of that State.

VI.

Among the ftrongeft indications of the coming change in opinion on this fubject, the "fuits for liberty," as they are called, challenge attention. They are alfo known as "fuits for freedom," and "fuits for fervice," in which flaves "fued their mafters for freedom and for recompence for their service, after they had attained the age of twenty-one years."[1] *M. H. S. Coll.*, i., iv. 202.

There had been a case in Connecticut as early as 1703, in which a master was summoned to answer, before a County Court, "to Abda, a mulatto, in an action of the case, for his unjust holding and detaining the said Abda in his service as his bondsman, for the space of one year last past." The damages were laid at 20*l*. The result was a verdict against the master for 12*l*. damages—"thereby virtually establishing Abda's right to freedom." *J. H. Trumbull's Notes from the Original Papers, etc. Conn. Courant, Nov.* 9, 1850. In this case, the ground on which the slave rested his claim appears to have been his white blood.

The earliest of these cases in Massachusetts, of which we have any knowledge, is noticed in the Diary of John Adams. It was in the Superior Court at Salem, in 1766. Under date of Wednesday, November 5th, he says: "Attended Court; heard the trial of an action of trespass, brought by a mulatto woman, for damages, for restraining her of her liberty. This is called suing for liberty; the first action that ever I knew of the sort, though I have heard there have been many." *Works*, ii., 200.

[1] If any of these decisions in Massachusetts sustained the claims for wages, they are in strong contrast with the highest English authority of the period. Many actions were brought in the English Courts, by negro slaves against their masters for wages; but Lord Mansfield, the great oracle of the Common Law, was accustomed to deal very summarily with them. He has left a very emphatic record on this point:

"When slaves have been brought here, and have commenced actions for their wages, I have always nonsuited the plaintiff." *The King* v. *the Inhabitants of Thames Ditton.* 4 *Doug.*, 300.

We suppose this to have been the case of *Jenny Slew* vs. *John Whipple, jr.,* the record of which we copy here.

"JENNY SLEW of Ipswich in the County of Essex, spinster, Pltff., agst. JOHN WHIPPLE, Jun., of said Ipswich Gentleman, Deft., in a Plea of Trespass for that the said John on the 29th day of January, A. D. 1762, at Ipswich aforesaid with force and arms took her the said Jenny, held and kept her in servitude as a slave in his service, and has restrained her of her liberty from that time to the fifth of March last without any lawfull right & authority so to do and did her other injuries against the peace & to the damage of said Jenny Slew as she faith the sum of twenty-five pounds. This action was first brought at last March Court at Ipswich when & where the parties appeared & the case was continued by order of Court to the then next term when & where the Pltff appeared & the said John Whipple Jun, came by Edmund Trowbridge, Esq. his attorney & defended when he said that there is no such person in nature as Jenny Slew of Ipswich aforesaid, Spinster, & this the said John was ready to verify wherefore the writ should be abated & he prayed judgment accordingly which plea was overruled by the Court and afterwards the said John by the said Edmund made a motion to the Court & praying that another person might endorse the writ & be subject to cost if any should finally be for the Court but the Court rejected the motion and then the Deft. saving his plea in abatement aforesaid said that he is not guilty as the plaintiff contends, & thereof put himself on the Country, & then the cause was continued to this term, and now the Pltff. reserving to herself the liberty of joining issue on the Deft's plea aforesaid in the appeal says that the defendant's plea aforesaid is an insufficient answer to the Plaintiff's declaration aforesaid and by law she is not held to reply thereto & she is ready to verify wherefore for want of a sufficient answer to the Plaintiff's declaration aforesaid she prays judgment for her damages & costs & the defendant consenting to the waving of the demurrer on the appeal said his plea aforesaid is good & because the Pltff refuses to reply thereto He prays judgment for his cost. It is considered by the Court that the defendant's plea in chief aforesaid is good & that the said John Whipple recover of the said Jenny Slew costs tax at
the Pltff appealed to the next Superior Court of Judicature to be holden

for this County & entered into recognizance with sureties as the law directs for prosecuting her appeal to effect." *Records of the Inferior Court of C. C. P., Vol. —, (Sep. 1760 to July 1766), page 502.*

"JENNY SLEW of Ipswich, in the County of Essex, Spinster, Appellant, versus JOHN WHIPPLE, Jr. of said Ipswich, Gentleman Appellee from the judgment of an Inferior Court of Common Pleas held at Newburyport within and for the County of Essex on the last Tuesday of September 1765 when and where the appellant was plaint., and the appellee was defendant in a plea of trespass, for that the said John upon the 29th day of January, A. D. 1762, at Ipswich aforesaid with force and arms took her the said Jenny held & kept her in servitude as a slave in his service & has restrained her of her liberty from that time to the fifth of March 1765 without any lawful right or authority so to do & did other injuries against the Peace & to the damage of the said Jenny Slew, as she saith, the sum of twenty-five pounds, at which Inferior Court, judgment was rendered upon the demurrer then that the said John Whipple recover against the said Jenny Slew costs. This appeal was brought forward at the Superior Court of Judicature &c., holden at Salem, within & for the County of Essex on the first Tuesday of last November, from whence it was continued to the last term of this Court for this County by consent & so from thence unto this Court, and now both parties appeared & the demurrer aforesaid being waived by consent & issue joined upon the plea tendered at said Inferior Court & on file. The case after full hearing was committed to a jury sworn according to law to try the same who returned their verdict therein upon oath, that is to say, they find for appellant reversion of the former judgment four pounds money damage & costs. It's therefore considered by the Court, that the former judgment be reversed & that the said Slew recover against the said Whipple the sum of four pounds lawful money of this Province damage & costs taxed 9*l*. 9*s*. 6*d*.

"Exon. issued 4 Dec. 1766." *Records of the Superior Court of Judicature (Vol. 1766-7), page 175.*

The case of *Newport* vs. *Billing* has been previously noticed, *p.* 22, *note*. It is not improbable that this was the case in which John Adams was engaged, in the latter part of September, 1768, when he "attended the Superior Court at Worcefter and the next week proceeded to Springfield, where I was accidentally engaged in a caufe between a negro and his mafter." *Works*, II., 213.

The next cafe was that which has been for more than half a century the grand *cheval de bataille* of the champions of the hiftoric fame of Maffachufetts—the cafe of *James* v. *Lechmere*, in Middlefex, in 1769. This is the cafe referred to in a recent paper read before the Maffachufetts Hiftorical Society, in which the writer felt at liberty to "indulge a pride equally juft and generous, that here, in the Courts of the Province, the ruling of Lord Mansfield [in the cafe of Somerfet] was anticipated by two years, in favor of perfonal freedom and human rights." *M. H. S. Proc.*, 1863-4, *p.* 322. That is to fay, as the fame writer expreffes it elfewhere, in the cafe of *James* v. *Lechmere*, "the right of a mafter to hold a flave had been denied, by the Superior Court of Maffachufetts, and upon the fame grounds, fubftantially, as thofe upon which Lord Mansfield difcharged Somerfet,[1] when his cafe came before him." *Wafhburn's Judicial Hift. of Mafs.*, 202. Compare alfo *M. H. S.*

---

[1] The abfurdity of the claim fet up for Maffachufetts is not diminifhed by the faft that no cafe in the hiftory of Englifh Law has been more mifunderftood and mifreprefented than the Somerfet cafe itfelf.

Thirteen years later (27 April, 1785), Lord Mansfield himfelf ftated expresfly "that his decifion went no farther than that the mafter cannot by force compel the flave to go out of the Kingdom." At the fame time he alfo faid, with reference to the alleged extinftion of villenage, "villains in grofs may in point of law fubfift at this day. But the change of cuftoms and manners has effeftually abolifhed them in point of faft." *The King* v. *The Inhabitants of Thames Ditton*, 4 *Doug.*, 300. In the fame year, the

Proc., 1855–58, *pp.* 190–91, and *Coll.*, IV., iv., *pp.* 334–5.

It is a pity to difturb thefe cherifhed fancies, but the truth is that this cafe, fo often quoted "as having determined the unlawfulnefs of flavery in Maffachufetts, is *fhown by the records and files of Court to have been brought up from the Inferior Court by fham demurrer, and, after one or two continuances, fettled by the parties. Rec.*, 1769, *fol.* 196." *Gray in Quincy's Reports*, 30, *note.*

We muft not omit to note in paffing another interefting fact recently developed. James Somerfet, the fubject of the great Englifh "fuit for liberty," was not a Virginia or Weft India flave, as has been

fame great exponent of Englifh Law expresfly recognized property in flaves on board a flave-trader, in an action on a policy of affurance. The demand on the policy was for the lofs of a great many flaves by mutiny. *Jones vs. Schmoll.* 1 *Term Reports*, 130, *note.* Add to all this the notorious facts that flaves were bought and fold in England long after the time when it has been alleged that "Lord Mansfield *firft* eftablifhed the grand doctrine that the air of England is too pure to be breathed by a flave;" that it was not until 1807 that fhe abolifhed her flave-trade, and twenty-feven weary years more elapfed before fhe fet her flaves free in her colonies; and we can, without referring to the earlier hiftory of her royal and parliamentary, national and individual patronage of flavery and the flave-trade, or her cowardly fympathy with the flaveholders' rebellion, eftimate the value of Earl Ruffell's recent declaration, that Great Britain has always been hoftile to flavery. "The Britifh nation have always entertained, and ftill entertain, the deepeft abhorrence of laws by which men of one color were made flaves of men of another color. The efforts by which the United States Government and Congrefs have fhaken off flavery have, therefore, the warmeft fympathies of the people of thefe Kingdoms." *Earl Ruffell to Mr. Adams, Auguft* 20, 1865. No language or hiftory within our knowledge furnifhes fit epithet or parallel for fuch confummate hypocrify and recklefs difregard of the truth of hiftory. It would be an infult to the "hiftoric fame" of that unhappy Jewifh fect to refer to the Pharifees. Perhaps it is enough to fay it is the empty "palaver" of a Britifh Prime Minifter!

generally stated, but a negro-slave from Massachusetts! where he lived with his owner, Mr. Charles Stewart, who held an office in the customs and resided in Boston. *Proc. M. H. S.*, 1863–64, *p.* 323.

Mr. Stewart left Boston on the first of October, 1769, and arrived in London on the tenth of November following. He was accompanied by this slave, who continued in his service until the first of October, 1771, when he ran away. His owner found means to seize and secure him, and had placed him on board a vessel bound for Jamaica, in the custody of the captain, who was to carry him there to be sold. This was on the 26th November, 1771. He was rescued by a writ of habeas corpus, and the proceedings in the case terminated in his release on the 22d June, 1772.

There was a case in Nantucket, about the years 1769–1770, in which Mr. Rotch, a member of the Society of Friends, received on board a vessel called the Friendship, at that time engaged in the whale-fishery, and commanded by Elisha Folger, a young slave by the name of " Boston," belonging to the heirs of William Swain. At the termination of the voyage, he paid to " Boston " his proportion of the proceeds. The master, John Swain, brought an action against the captain of the vessel, in the Court of Common Pleas of Nantucket, for the recovery of his slave; but the jury returned a verdict in favor of the defendant, and the slave is said to have been "manumitted by the magistrates." Swain took an appeal from this judgment to the Supreme Court at Boston, but never prosecuted it. *Lyman's Report*, 1822.

Another cafe is mentioned in a letter of Thomas Pemberton, dated at Bofton, March 12, 1795, in reply to the Circular of Dr. Jeremy Belknap, dated Bofton, February 17, 1795, as follows:

"The firft inftance I have heard of a negro requefting his freedom *as his right* belonged, I am informed, to Dr. Stockbridge, of Hanover, in Plymouth County. His mafter refufed to grant it, but by affiftance of lawyers he obtained it, this about the year 1770."

Mr. Gray mentions the cafe of *Cæfar* vs. *Taylor*, in Effex, 1772, in which " the wife of a flave was not allowed to teftify againft him," and " the defendant in an action of falfe imprifonment was not permitted under the general iffue to prove that the plaintiff was his flave." *Quincy's Reports*, 30, *note*.

In September or October, 1773, an action was brought in the Inferior Court, in Effex, againft Richard Greenleaf, of Newburyport, by Cæfar [Hendrick], a colored man, whom he claimed as his flave, for holding him in bondage. He laid the damages at fifty pounds. A letter from Newburyport, October 10th, fays, "We have lately had our Court week when the novel cafe of Cæfar againft his mafter in an action of fifty pounds lawful money damages for detaining him in flavery was litigated before a jury of the County, who found for the *plaintiff eighteen pounds damages and cofts.*" John Lowell, Efq., afterward Judge Lowell, was counfel for the plaintiff. *Coffin's Newbury*, 241, 339.

Nathan Dane notices this cafe in his Abridgment and Digeft of American Law. He fays:

"As early as 1773, many negroes claimed their freedom, and brought actions of trespass against their masters for restraining them. A. D. 1773, one Cæsar brought trespass against his master, and declared that he, with force and arms, assaulted the plaintiff and imprisoned him, and so with force and arms against the plaintiff's will, hath there held, kept, and restrained him in servitude, as the said G.'s slave, for so long á time, etc.

"In this case the master protested the plaintiff was his *mulatto slave*, and that he, the master, was not held by law to answer him; but for plea the master said he was not guilty. The parties agreed any special matter might be given in evidence, etc. Counsel, Farnham and Lowell." *Dane's Abridgment*, II., 426.

Another case is mentioned as " brought on at the Inferior Court of Common Pleas for the County of Essex for July term [1774], between Mr. Caleb Dodge of Beverly, and his negro servant, in which the referees gave a verdict in favor of the negro, by which he obtained his freedom, there being no law of the province to hold a man to serve for life." *The Watchman's Alarm*, etc., *p.* 28, *note*. Yet the writer of this pamphlet suggested the "abolishing of this vile custom of slave-making, either by a law of the province, Common Law, (which I am told has happily succeeded in many instances of late) or by a voluntary releasement." *Ibid., p.* 27.

Mr. Dane also refers to the case of *Cæsar* vs. *Taylor*, and gives the following view of the subject generally:

"In these cases there seem to have been doubts

if flavery exifted in Maffachufetts; the caufes were generally argued on general principles; the mafters urged, in fupport of flavery, the practice of ancient and fome modern nations; alfo the Provincial Statutes of 10 W. 3., ch. 6.; 1 & 2 Anne, ch. 2.; and 4 & 5 Anne, ch. 6.

"The plaintiffs argued that by Englifh Law, *flavery* could not exift, and that we had nothing to do with any other, except the Provincial Statutes; that if thefe eftablifhed flavery, it was merely by *implication*, and that natural liberty was never to be taken away by implication; that at common law *partus non fequitur ventrem*, though it might be otherwife by the civil law, which England, in this cafe, had never adopted; that marriage and providing for children was a right and a duty which only free perfons could perform; that the Gofpel forbid men to fell their brethren; and that the plaintiffs were *Chriftians*, and, if held in flavery, could not perform their Chriftian duties; that even villainage is abolifhed by Englifh law, and that the common law abhorred flavery. But it was admitted by the plaintiff's counfel, that flavery might be eftablifhed by exprefs law; and the defendants urged, and it feems long to have been underftood, that the Provincial Statutes did expreffly recognize and eftablifh flavery, as in the cafes above ftated, and in many others.

"In 1773, etc., fome flaves did recover againft their mafters; but thefe cafes are no evidence that there could not be flaves in the Province, for fometimes mafters permitted their flaves to recover to get clear of maintaining them as *paupers* when old and infirm;

the effect, as then generally underſtood, of a judgment againſt the maſter on this point of ſlavery; hence, a very feeble defence was often made by the maſters, eſpecially when ſued by the old or infirm ſlaves, as the maſters could not even manumit their ſlaves, without indemnifying their towns againſt their maintenance, as town paupers." *Dane's Abridgment,* ii., 426–7.

Chief-Juſtice Parſons alſo, in the caſe of *Winchendon* vs. *Hatfield in error,* confirms this view.

"Several negroes, born in this country of imported ſlaves demanded their freedom of their maſters by ſuit at law, and obtained it by a judgment of court. The defence of the maſter was feebly made, for ſuch was the temper of the times, that a reſtleſs diſcontented ſlave was worth little; and when his freedom was obtained in a courſe of legal proceedings, the maſter was not holden for his future ſupport, if he became poor." iv *Maſs. Reports,* 128.

The reference by the Chief-Juſtice to the circumſtance that theſe negroes litigant were " born in this country," points to the queſtion, whether hereditary ſlavery was legal in Maſſachuſetts? which is alſo touched in the previous reference by the counſel for the ſlaves, as ſtated by Mr. Dane, to the difference between the rules of the Common Law and the Civil Law.

The Rev. Dr. Belknap, in his account of theſe ſuits, ſays, "On the part of the blacks it was pleaded, that the royal charter expreſſly declared all perſons born or reſiding in the province, to be as free as the King's ſubjects in Great Britain; that by the laws of England, no man could be deprived of his liberty but by the judgment of his peers; that the laws of the province refpecting an evil exifting, and attempting to mitigate or regulate it, did not authorize it; and, on fome occafions, the plea was, that though the flavery of the parents be admitted, yet no difability of that kind could defcend to children." *M. H. S. Coll.*, I., iv., 203.

How far the arguments here noticed were urged in thefe various fuits, and whether in any of them thefe points were judicially ftated and determined, we are unable to fay. We have previoufly examined the legal hiftory of hereditary flavery in Maffachufetts; and it may be proper in this connection to add fomething with refpect to the other pleas mentioned by Belknap. And firft, the alleged rights of the Indians and Negroes under the royal charter, and laws of England. The provifion referred to is fubftantially the fame in both Colony and Province charters, and is in the words following, viz:

"That all and every of the fubjects of us, our heirs and fucceffors, which go to and inhabit within our faid province and territory, and every of their children which fhall happen to be born there, or on the feas in going thither, or returning from thence, fhall have and enjoy all liberties and immunities of free and natural fubjects within the dominions of us, our heirs and fucceffors, to all intents, conftructions, and purpofes whatfoever, as if they and every of them were born within our realm of England."

The preamble to the Body of Liberties in 1641, which declares the civil privileges of the inhabitants of the Colony, might alfo have been referred to in this line of argument. Still, it is a hiftorical fact that the guaranties of the royal charters, and the Common Law of England as a perfonal law of privilege, did not extend to Aliens, Negroes, or Indians.[1]

The other plea, "that the laws of the province refpecting an evil exifting, and attempting to mitigate or regulate it did not authorize it," could avail nothing againft the other ftern hiftorical fact that flavery exifted in Maffachufetts "by virtue and equity of an exprefs Law of the Country warranting the fame, eftablifhed by a General Court, and fufficiently publifhed; or in cafe of the defect of a Law in any particular cafe, by the word of God, . . . to be judged by the General Court." Was it faid that the colony-law was annulled with the Charter, by the authority of which it was made? Still the ufage had prevailed and acquired force as the common law of the Province. The validity of the judgment againft the Charter in 1684, which was denied by the Houfe of Commons, and "queftioned by very great authority in England," was never admitted in Maffachufetts. 9 *Gray*, 517. There was nothing in the repeal of the Colony charter to affect the private rights of the colonifts. *Ibid.*, 518. And generally the rights of the inhabitants, as well as the penalties to which they might be fubjected, continued to be determined by the effect and according to the form of the colonial and provincial legiflation, i. e. the common law of Maffachufetts, rather than by

---

[1] See Hurd's *Law of Freedom and Bondage in the United States, Vol.* I., *pp.* 196, 197, 201 ; a perfect treafure-houfe of law and hiftory on its fubject, for which every ftudent of American Hiftory owes him a large debt of gratitude.

the ancient common law of England. 5 *Pickering*, 203. 7 *Cuſhing*, 76, 77. 13 *Pickering*, 258. 13 *Metcalf*, 68–72.

But whatever may have been the pleas or arguments in theſe ſuits, or the opinions which influenced their various reſults; the faƈt remains that, although "the bonds of ſlavery" may have been "looſened" by theſe proceedings, and "the verdiƈts of juries in favor of liberty," the legal effeƈt of ſuch verdiƈts reached none but the parties immediately concerned; and the inſtitution of ſlavery continued to be recognized by law in Maſſachuſetts, defying all direƈt attempts to deſtroy it.

The queſtion however had been raiſed, and ſlavery was challenged. Dr. Belknap ſays, that "the controverſy began about the year 1766." *M. H. S. Coll.* i., iv., 201. We ſhall endeavor to indicate the principal features of its progreſs in their juſt relations, without diſparagement and without exaggeration.

The town of Worceſter, by inſtruƈtions in 1765, required their repreſentative to "uſe his influence to obtain a law to put an end to that unchriſtian and impolitic praƈtice of making ſlaves of the human ſpecies, and that he give his vote for none to ſerve in His Majeſty's Council, who will uſe their influence againſt ſuch a law." *Boſton News-Letter*, June 4, 1765, quoted by *Buckingham, Newſpaper Literature*, i., 31.

The town of Boſton, in May, 1766, inſtruƈted their Repreſentatives as follows, viz.: "And for the total aboliſhing of ſlavery among us, that you move for a law to prohibit the importation and the purchasing of flaves for the future." *Lyman's Report*, 1822.

This action was confirmed by a new vote in the following year. At the Town-Meeting on the 16th of March, 1767, the queftion came up, as to whether the Town would adhere to that part of its Inftructions, and it paffed in the affirmative.[1] *Drake's Bofton*, 728–9. It is alfo faid, though probably true of a later period only, that " In fome of the country towns they voted to have no flaves among them, and that their mafters be indemnified from any expence, [after they had granted them freedom] that might arife by reafon of their age, infirmities, or inability to fupport themfelves." *Letter of Mr. Thomas Pemberton to Dr. Jeremy Belknap, Bofton, Mch.* 12, 1795.

In 1767, an anonymous tract of twenty octavo pages againft flavery made its appearance. It was entitled " *Confiderations on Slavery, in a Letter to a Friend.*" It was written by Nathaniel Appleton, a merchant of Bofton, afterwards a member of the firft Committee of Correfpondence and a zealous patriot during the Revolutionary ftruggle. *Appleton Memorial*, 36.

On March 2d, 1769, the reverend Samuel Webfter of Salifbury, Maffachufetts, publifhed " an earneft addrefs to my country on flavery." An extract is given by Mr. Coffin in his *Hiftory of Newbury, p.* 338.

---

[1] The reader will note the coincidence of this proceeding with that in the Legiflature on the fame day, when it was " *Ordered, that the Matter fubfide.*" See *poft, p.* 127.

James Swan, "a Scotfman," and merchant in Bofton, publifhed "A Diffuafion to Great Britain and the Colonies, from the Slave-Trade to Africa— fhewing the Injuftice thereof, etc." It feems to have been in "the form of a fermon," and the writer was apparently better fatisfied with a fecond edition revifed and abridged, which he put forth in 1773, at the earneft defire of the Negroes in Bofton, in order to anfwer the purpofe of fending a copy to each town.

In 1767, the firft movement was made in the Legiflature to procure the paffage of an act againft flavery and the flave-trade.

On the 13th March, a bill was brought into the Houfe of Reprefentatives "to prevent the *unwarrantable and unufual* Practice or Cuftom of inflaving Mankind in this Province, and the importation of flaves into the fame." It was read a firft time, and the queftion was moved, whether a fecond reading be referred to the next feffion of the General Court? which was paffed in the negative. Then it was moved, that a claufe be brought into the bill, for a limitation to a certain time, and the queftion being put, it paffed in the affirmative; and it was further ordered, that the bill be read again on the following day, at ten o'clock. *Journal*, 387.

On the 14th, the bill "to prevent the *unwarrantable and unnatural* Practice," etc., was read a fecond time, and the queftion was put whether the third reading be referred to the next May feffion? This paffed in the negative, and it was ordered that the Bill be read a third time on Monday next at three o'clock. *Ibid.*, 390.

On the 16th, "The Bill for preventing the *unnatural and unwarrantable* Cuſtom of enſlaving Mankind in this Province, and the Importation of Slaves into the Same, was Read according to order, and, after a Debate,

"*Ordered that the Matter ſubſide*, and that Capt. Sheaffe, Col. Richmond, and Col. Bourne, be a Committee to bring in a Bill for laying a Duty of Impoſt on Slaves importing into this Province." *Ibid.*, 393.

On the 17th, a Bill for laying a Duty of Impoſt upon the Importation of Slaves into this Province was read a firſt and ſecond time, and ordered for a third reading on the next day at eleven o'clock. *Ibid.*, 408.

On the 18th, "the bill for laying an Impoſt on the Importation of Negro and other Slaves, was read a third time, and the queſtion was put, whether the enacting this bill ſhould be referred to the next May ſeſſion, that the Minds of the Country may be known thereupon? Paſſed in the Negative. Then the Question was put, Whether a clauſe ſhall be bro't in to limit the Continuance of the Act to the Term of one year? Paſſed in the Affirmative, and Ordered, that the Bill be recommitted." *Ibid.*, 411. In the afternoon of the ſame day, the bill was read with the amendment, and having paſſed to be engroſſed, was "ſent up by Col. Bowers, Col. Gerriſh, Col. Leonard, Capt. Thayer, and Col. Richmond." *Ibid.*, 411.

The bill was read a firſt time in the Council on the 19th of March, and on the 20th was read a ſecond time and paſſed to be engroſſed "as taken into a new draft." On being ſent down to the Houſe of Reprefentatives for concurrence, in the afternoon of the fame day, it was "Read and unanimoufly non-concurred, and the Houfe adhere to their own Vote. Sent up for concurrence." *Ibid. Compare Gen. Court Records, May* 1763 *to May* 1767, *p.* 485.

And thus the bill difappeared and was loft. It was the neareft approach to an attempt to abolifh flavery, within our knowledge, in all the Colonial and Provincial legiflation of Maffachufetts. The bills againft the importation of flaves cannot juftly be regarded as direct attempts to abolifh the inftitution of flavery, whatever may have been the motives which influenced the action concerning them. The bill itfelf of 1767 has not been found, and it is not unlikely that its provifions may have been lefs pofitive and ftringent than its title, which is the chief authority for what little anti-flavery reputation it enjoys. Could it be recovered, it might illuminate the record we have given, and throw much light on the fubject generally. It is apparent from the record that whatever may have been the height to which the zeal of anti-flavery had carried the agitation of the fubject on this occafion, it was duly " ordered, that the Matter fubfide;"[1] so that it was only an Impoft Act which finally tried to ftruggle forth into exiftence, and perifhed in the effort. If indeed it was an attempt at abolition, the failure was fo fignal and decifive that it was not renewed until ten years afterward, when, as we fhall fee, it failed again.

[1] The reader will fee hereafter, in the frequent ufe of this parliamentary phrafe by the Legiflature of Maffachufetts, that an order to "*fubfide*" continued to be their favorite method of reducing anti-flavery inflammation.

That terror of infurrection, fo often and aptly illuftrated in the common phrafe of "fleeping over a volcano," that continuous and awful dread which confcious tyranny feels, but hates to acknowledge, we have already faid, was not unknown even in Maffachufetts, where the fervile clafs was always a comparatively fmall element of the population. In times of civil commotion and popular excitement, the danger was more imminent, and the fear was more freely expreffed.

During the difficulties between the people of the town of Bofton and the Britifh foldiers in 1768, John Wilfon, a captain in the 59th Regiment, was accufed of exciting the flaves againft their mafters, affuring them that the foldiers had come to procure their freedom; and that, "with their affiftance, they fhould be able to drive the Liberty Boys to the devil." He was arrefted on the complaint of the felectmen, and was bound over for trial; "but, owing to the manœuvres of the Attorney-General, the indictment was quafhed, and Wilfon left the Province about the fame time." *Drake's Bofton*, 754.

There was a fimilar alarm in September, 1774. It is noticed in one of the letters of Mrs. John Adams to her hufband, dated at Bofton Garrifon, 22d September, 1774.

"There has been in town a confpiracy of the negroes. At prefent it is kept pretty private, and was difcovered by one who endeavored to diffuade them from it. He being threatened with his life, applied to Juftice Quincy for protection. They conducted in this way, got an Irifhman to draw up a petition to the Governor [Gage], telling him they would fight for him provided he would arm them, and engage to liberate them if he conquered. And it is said that he attended so much to it, as to consult Percy[1] upon it, and one Lieutenant Small has been very busy and active. There is but little said, and what steps they will take in consequence of it I know not. I wish most sincerely there was not a slave in the province; it always appeared a most iniquitous scheme to me to fight ourselves for what we are daily robbing and plundering from those who have as good a right to freedom as we have. . You know my mind upon this subject." *Adams Letters*, 1., 24.

In 1771, the subject of the Slave-Trade was again introduced into the Legislature. On the 12th April, in that year, a bill "to prevent the Importation of Slaves from Africa" was read the first time and ordered to a second reading on the following day at ten o'clock. *Journal*, 211. On the 13th, the bill was read the second time, and the further consideration was postponed till the following Tuesday morning. *Ibid.*, 215. On the 16th the bill was re-committed. *Ibid.*, 219.

On the 19th, a "Bill to prevent the Importation of Negro Slaves into this Province" was read the first time and ordered a second reading "to-morrow at eleven o'clock." *Ibid.*, 234. On the 20th, it was "read a second time and ordered to be read again on Monday next, at Three o'clock." On the 22d, it

---

[1] Brigadier-General the Right Honorable Hugh, Earl Percy, afterwards Duke of Northumberland, was Colonel of the 5th Regiment, or Northumberland Fusileers, at that time stationed in Boston.

was read the third time, and paſſed to be engroſſed. *Ibid.*, 236. On the 24th, it was read and paſſed to be enacted. *Ibid.*, 240.

It was duly ſent to the Council for concurrence, and on the ſame day, " James Otis, Eſq., came down from the honorable Board, to propoſe an Amendment on the engroſſed bill for preventing the Importation of Slaves from *Africa*, and laid the Bill on the Table;" whereupon " The Houſe took the propoſed Amendment into conſideration, and concur'd with the honorable Board therein, then the Bill was ſent up to the honorable Board." *Ibid.*, 242–3.

We have been unable to procure any record of the doings of the Council on the ſubject, excepting the following entry in the Records of the General Court:

" Wedneſday, April 24, 1771, etc. etc. An Engroſſed Bill intituled ' An Act to prevent the Importation of Negro Slaves into this Province ' having paſſed the Houſe of Repreſentatives to be Enacted. In Council, Read a third time and paſſed a concurrence to be enacted."

This act failed to obtain the approval of Governor Hutchinſon, and we are fortunately able to preſent his views on the ſubject, as communicated to Lord Hillſborough, Secretary of State for the Colonies, in a letter dated May, 1771.

" The Bill which prohibited the importation of Negro Slaves appeared to me to come within his Majeſty's Inſtruction to Sir Francis Bernard, which reſtrains the Governor from Aſſenting to any Laws of a new and unuſual nature. I doubted beſides whether the chief motive to this Bill which, it is said, was a scruple upon the minds of the People in many parts of the Province of the lawfulness, in a meerly moral respect, of so great a restraint of Liberty, was well founded, slavery by the Provincial Laws giving no right to the life of the servant and a slave here considered as a Servant would be who had bound himself for a term of years exceeding the ordinary term of human life, and I do not know that it has been determined he may not have a Property in Goods, notwithstanding he is called a Slave.

"I have reason to think that these three [1] bills will be again offered to me in another Session, I having intimated that I would transmit them to England that I might know his Majesty's pleasure concerning them." 27 *Mass. Archives*, 159–60.

These are interesting and important suggestions. It is apparent that at this time there was no special instruction to the royal governor of Massachusetts, forbidding his approval of acts against the slave-trade. Hutchinson evidently doubted the genuineness of the "chief motive" which was alleged to be the inspiration of the bill, the "meerly moral" scruple against slavery; but his reasonings furnish a striking illustration of the changes which were going on in public opinion, and the gradual softening of the harsher features of slavery under their influence. The non-importation agreements throughout the Colonies, by which America was trying to thwart the commercial selfishness of her rapacious Mother, had rendered the

[1] The other two bills were a *Marine Corporation Bill* and a *Salem Militia Bill*.

provincial viceroys peculiarly senfitive to the flighteft manifeftation of a difpofition to approach the facred precincts of thofe prerogatives by which King and Parliament affumed to bind their diftant dependencies: and the "fpirit of non-importation" which Maffachufetts had imperfectly learned from New York was equally offenfive to them, whether it interfered with their cherifhed "trade with Africa," or their favorite monopolies elfewhere.

In 1773, the attempt to difcourage the flave-trade was renewed. The reprefentatives from Salem had been inftructed, May 18, 1773, to ufe their exertions to prevent the importation of negroes into Maffachufetts "as repugnant to the natural rights of mankind, and highly prejudicial to the Province." *Felt, Annals*, II., 416. The town of Medford alfo directed their member to "ufe his utmoft influence to have a final period put to that moft cruel, inhuman and unchriftian practice, the flave-trade." *Swan's Diffuafion, etc., Revifed Ed.*, 1773, p. x. The town of Leicefter, May 19, 1773, inftructed their reprefentative on this fubject, as follows:

" And, as we have the higheft regard for (fo as even to revere the name of) liberty, we cannot behold but with the greateft abhorrence any of our fellow creatures in a ftate of flavery.

" Therefore we ftrictly enjoin you to ufe your utmoft influence that a ftop may be put to the flavetrade by the inhabitants of this Province; which, we apprehend, may be effected by one of thefe two ways: either by laying a heavy duty on every negro imported or brought from Africa or elfewhere into this

Province; or, by making a law, that every negro brought or imported as aforesaid should be a free man or woman as soon as they come within the jurisdiction of it; and that every negro child that shall be born in said government after the enacting such law should be free at the same age that the children of white people are; and, from the time of their birth till they are capable of earning their living, to be maintained by the town in which they are born, or at the expense of the Province, as shall appear most reasonable.

"Thus, by enacting such a law, in process of time will the blacks become free; or, if the Honorable House of Representatives shall think of a more eligible method, we shall be heartily glad of it. But whether you can justly take away or free a negro from his master, who fairly purchased him, and (although illegally; for such is the purchase of any person against their consent, unless it be for a capital offence) which the custom of this country has justified him in, we shall not determine; but hope that unerring Wisdom will direct you in this and in all your other important undertakings." *Washburn's Leicester*, 442.

The town of Sandwich, in Barnstable County, voted, May 18, 1773, "that our representative is instructed to endeavor to have an Act passed by the Court, to prevent the importation of *slaves* into this country, and that all children that shall be born of such Africans as are now slaves among us, shall, after such Act, be free at 21 years of age." *Freeman's History of Cape Cod*, II., 114.

There may have been other towns in which similar

measures were taken to influence the action of the Legiflature, but we have no knowledge of any beyond thofe already noticed. The negroes themfelves alfo began to move in the matter, encouraged by the "fpirit of liberty which was rife in the land."

On the 25th June, 1773, in the afternoon feffion of the Houfe of Reprefentatives, a petition was read "of Felix Holbrook, and others, Negroes, praying that they may be liberated from a State of Bondage, and made Freemen of this Community; and that this Court would give and grant to them fome part of the unimproved Lands belonging to the Province, for a Settlement, or relieve them in fuch other Way as fhall feem good and wife upon the Whole." Upon this it was "ordered, that Mr. Hancock, Mr. Greenleaf, Mr. Adams, Capt. Dix, Mr. Paine, Capt. Heath, and Mr. Pickering confider this Petition, and report what may be proper to be done." *Journal, p.* 85.

This "Committee on the Petition of Felix Holbrook, and others, in behalf of themfelves and others; praying to be liberated from a State of Slavery, reported" on the 28th June, 1773, P. M., "that the further Confideration of the Petition be referred till next Seffion," and it was fo referred accordingly. *Ibid.*, 94.

Among other indications of the growing intereft in the fubject, is the fact that at the annual commencement of Harvard College, Cambridge, July 21, 1773, a forenfic difputation on the legality of enflaving the Africans was held by two candidates for the bachelor's degree; namely, Theodore Parfons and Eliphalet Pearfon, both of whom were natives of Newbury.

The queftion was "whether the flavery, to which Africans are in this province, by the permiffion of law, fubjected, be agreeable to the law of nature?" The work was publifhed at Bofton, the fame year, in an octavo pamphlet of forty-eight pages. *Coffin's Newbury*, 339.

The following letter alfo fhows that the bufinefs before the Legiflature was not wholly neglected or forgotten during the interval between the feffions.

SAMUEL ADAMS TO JOHN PICKERING, JR.

"Bofton, Jan'. 8, 1774.

"Sir,

"As the General Affembly will undoubtedly meet on the 26th of this month, the Negroes whofe petition lies on file, and is referred for confideration, are very folicitous for the Event of it, and having been informed that you intended to confider it at your leifure Hours in the Recefs of the Court, they earneftly wifh you would compleat a Plan for their Relief. And in the meantime, if it be not too much Trouble, they afk it as a favor that you would by a Letter enable me to communicate to them the general outlines of your Defign. I am, with fincere regard," etc.

On the 26th January, 1774, P.M., "a Petition of a number of Negro Men, which was entered on the Journal of the 25th of June laft, and referred for Confideration to this Seffion," was "read again, together with a Memorial of the fame Petitioners and *Ordered*, that Mr. Speaker, Mr. Pickering, Mr. Hancock, Mr.

Adams, Mr. Phillips, Mr. Paine, and Mr. Greenleaf confider the fame and report." *Journal,* 104.

All this preliminary preparation refulted at length in "a Bill to prevent the Importation of Negroes and others as Slaves into this Province," which was read the firft time on the 2d March, 1774, and ordered to be read again the next day. *Ibid.,* 221. On the 3d, it was read the fecond time in the morning, and in the afternoon the third time, and paffed to be engroffed, when it was fent up to the Council Board for concurrence, by Col. Gerrifh, Col. Thayer, Col. Bowers, Mr. Pickering, and Col. Bacon. *Ibid.,* 224. On the 4th March, the bill was returned as "paffed in Council with Amendments." *Ibid.,* 226. On the 5th, the Houfe voted to concur with the Council, *ibid.,* 228; and on the 7th, paffed the bill to be enacted. *ibid.,* 237. On the 8th, it received the final fanction of the Council, and only required the approval of the Governor to become a law. That approval, however, it failed to obtain; the only reafon given in the record being "the Secretary faid [on returning the approved bills] that his Excellency had not had time to confider the other Bills that had been laid before him."[1] *Ibid.,* 243. Compare alfo for Council proceedings, *General Court Records,* xxx., 248, 264.

To this hiftory, derived from the records, we are fortunately able to add a copy of the Bill itfelf, which is preferved in the *Mafs. Archives, Domeftic Relations,* 1643-1774, *Vol.* 9, 457.

[1] The General Court was prorogued March 9th, and diffolved March 30th, 1774. *General Court Records,* xxx., 280-81.

ANNO REGNI REGIS GEORGII TERTII &c DECIMO QUARTO

AN ACT to prevent the importation of Negroes or other Perſons as Slaves into this Province; and the purchaſing them within the ſame; and for making proviſion for relief of the children of ſuch as are already ſubjected to ſlavery Negroes Mulattoes & Indians born within this Province.

WHEREAS the Importation of Perſons as Slaves into this Province has been found detrimental to the intereſt of his Majeſty's ſubjects therein; And it being apprehended that the abolition thereof will be beneficial to the Province—

Be it therefore Enacted by the Governor Council and Houſe of Repreſentatives that whoſoever ſhall after the Tenth Day of April next import or bring into this Province by Land or Water any Negro or other Perſon or Perſons whether Male or Female as a Slave or Slaves ſhall for each and every ſuch Perſon ſo imported or brought into this Province forfeit and pay the ſum of one hundred Pounds to be recovered by preſentment or indictment of a Grand Jury and when ſo recovered to be to his Majeſty for the uſe of this Government: or by action of debt in any of his Majeſty's Courts of Record and in caſe of ſuch recovery the one moiety thereof to be to his majeſty for the uſe of this Government the other moiety to the Perſon or Perſons who ſhall ſue for the ſame.

And be it further Enacted that from and after the Tenth Day of April next any Perſon or Perſons that ſhall purchaſe any Negro or other Perſon or Perſons as a Slave or Slaves imported or brought into this Province as aforeſaid ſhall forfeit and pay for every Negro or other Perſon ſo purchaſed Fifty Pounds to be recovered and diſpoſed of in the ſame way and manner as before directed.

And be it further Enacted that every Perſon, concerned in importing or bringing into this Province, or purchaſing any ſuch Negro or other Perſon or Perſons as aforeſaid within the ſame; who ſhall be unable, or refuſe, to pay the Penalties or forfeitures ordered by this Act; ſhall for every ſuch offence ſuffer Twelve months impriſonment without Bail or mainpriſe.

Provided allways that nothing in this act contained ſhall extend to ſubject to the Penalties aforeſaid the Maſters, Mariners, Owners or

Slavery in Massachusetts. 139

Freighters of any such Vessel or Vessels, as before the said Tenth Day of April next shall have sailed from any Port or Ports in this Province, for any Port or Ports not within this Government, for importing or bringing into this Province any Negro or other Person or Persons as Slaves who in the prosecution of the same voyage may be imported or brought into the same. *Provided* he shall not offer them or any of them for sale.

Provided also that this act shall not be construed to extend to any such Person or Persons, occasionally hereafter coming to reside within this Province, or passing thro' the same, who may bring such Negro or other Person or Persons as necessary servants into this Province provided that the stay or residence of such Person or Persons shall not exceed Twelve months or that such Person or Persons within said time send such Negro or other Person or Persons out of this Province there to be and remain, and also that during said Residence such Negro or other Person or Persons shall not be sold or alienated within the same.

∀ *And be it further Enacted and declared that nothing in this act contained shall extend or be construed to extend for retaining or holding in perpetual servitude any Negro or other Person or Persons now inslaved within this Province but that every such Negro or other Person or Persons shall be intituled to all the Benefits such Negro or other Person or Persons might by Law have been intituled to, in case this act had not been made.*

In the House of Representatives March 2, 1774. Read a first & second Time. March 3, 1774. Read a third Time & passed to be engrossed. Sent up for Concurrence.

          T. CUSHING, *Spkr.*

In Council March 3, 1774. Read a first Time. 4. Read a second Time and passed a Concurrence to be Engrossed with the Amendment at ∀ dele the whole Clause. Sent down for Concurrence.

          THOS. FLUCKER, *Secry.*

In the House of Representatives March 4, 1774. Read and concurred.

          T. CUSHING, *Spkr.*

That portion of the title to the bill which we have

italicized is ſtricken out in the original. We have alſo retained and italicized the clauſe which was ſtricken out by the amendment of the Council. They form a part of the hiſtory of the bill, though not of the bill itſelf as " paſſed to be enacted."

Such was the reſponſe of the Great and General Court of Maſſachuſetts to the petition of her negro-ſlaves in 1773-4. They prayed that they might be "liberated from a State of Bondage, and made Freemen of the Community; and that this Court would give and grant to them ſome part of the unimproved Lands belonging to the Province for a Settlement, or relieve them in ſuch other Way as ſhall ſeem good and wiſe upon the Whole." Not one of their prayers was anſwered. It would ſeem that an attempt was made to include in the bill, an indirect legiſlative approval of ſome of the doctrines maintained by Counſel for the negroes in the "freedom ſuits;" but even this failed; and a prohibitory act againſt the importation of ſlaves was offered to the Governor for his approval, which it was known beforehand could not be obtained.

Whether Hutchinſon had actually received an inſtruction from the Crown on the ſubject at this time or not, there is no room for doubt as to the general policy of Great Britain. She had aided her colonial offspring to become ſlaveholders; ſhe had encouraged her merchants in tempting them to acquire ſlaves; ſhe herſelf excelled all her competitors in ſlave-ſtealing; and from the reign of Queen Anne, the ſlave-trade was among her moſt envied and cheriſhed monopolies, its protection and increaſe being a principal feature in her commercial policy. The great "diſtinction" of the Treaty of Utrecht, as the Queen expreſſly called it, was that the Aſſiento or Contract for furniſhing the Spaniſh Weſt Indies with Negroes, ſhould be made with England, for the term of thirty years, in the ſame manner as it had been enjoyed by the French for ten years before. *Queen's Speech*, 6 *June*, 1712.

This was what her great ſtatesmen and divines of the Church of England were ſo eager and proud to ſecure for their country! For all her ſacrifices in the war, the millions of treaſure she had ſpent, the blood of her children ſo prodigally ſhed, with the glories of Blenheim, of Ramillies, of Oudenarde, and Malplaquet, England found her conſolation and reward in seizing and enjoying, as the lion's ſhare[1] of reſults of the Grand Alliance againſt the Bourbons, the excluſive right for thirty years of ſelling African ſlaves to the Spaniſh Weſt Indies and the Coaſt of America! *Compare Macknight's Bolingbroke*, 346–8. Who will wonder that men who had thus been taught to believe "that the Negro-Trade on the Coaſt of Africa was the chief and fundamental ſupport of the Britiſh Colonies and Plantations" in America, ſhould frown upon legiſlation in the colonies ſo utterly inconſiſtent with the intereſts of Britiſh Commerce, or that the

---

[1] By the articles of the Grand Alliance, England and all the other states ſubſcribing them were pledged neither to enter into any ſeparate treaty with the enemy, nor ſeek to negotiate for themſelves any exceptional privilege to the excluſion of the other members of the Confederacy. Of courſe this obligation was totally diſregarded by England, who inſiſted on the conceſſion of the Aſſiento Contract by France and Spain before the propoſals for peace were even communicated to the reſt of the Allies!

modeſt efforts of Maſſachuſetts in 1774, ſhould be met by Hutchinſon and Gage with the ſame ſpirit which, in 1775, dictated the reply of the Earl of Dartmouth to the earneſt remonſtrance of the Agent of Jamaica againſt the policy of the government: "We cannot allow the colonies to check or discourage, in any manner, a traffic ſo beneficial to the nation." *Bridges' Jamaica,* II., 475. *Notes.*

We cannot be accuſed of belittling the reſiſtance thus preſented to any colonial interference with the ſlave-trade, when we expreſs our regret that the legislative annals of Maſſachuſetts record no attempt to repeal the local laws by which ſlavery had been eſtabliſhed, regulated, and maintained. Such a meaſure, which ſhould alſo have granted the relief prayed for by the negroes in their petition, and embodied the wiſe ſuggeſtions of the town of Leiceſter (*ante, p.* 133), might well have encountered leſs ſerious oppoſition from the ſervants of the Crown than this twice-rejected non-importation act of 1774.[1]

In the brief ſeſſion of the General Court at Salem, in June, 1774, after Hutchinſon's ſucceſſor, Gage, the laſt Royal Governor, had commenced his adminiſtration, the ſame bill ſubſtantially, for the variations are unimportant, was hurried through the forms of legislation. It was introduced, read a firſt, ſecond, and third time, and paſſed to be engroſſed on the ſame day,

---

[1] The rhetorical flouriſhes with which Lord Mansfield ornamented his deciſion in the famous caſe of Somerſet would have furniſhed an excellent preamble to ſuch an act. The caſe was well known in Maſſachuſetts, having been reprinted more than once. But the General Court of Maſſachuſetts had no more intention than Lord Mansfield had power to aboliſh ſlavery at that period.

10th June. *Journal,* 27. On the 16th, the engroffed bill was read and paffed to be enacted. *Ibid.,* 41. In the Council, on the fame day, it was read a third time and paffed a concurrence to be enacted. *Gen. Court Records,* xxx., 322. On the following day, June 17th, the General Court was diffolved. Like that of which it was a copy, the bill appears " not to have been confented to by the Governor."

The fact is not to be difguifed that thefe efforts were political movements againft the government as much as anything elfe. Sympathy for the flave, and moral fcruples againft flavery, became lefs urgent and troublefome after the royal negative had become powerlefs againft the legiflation of the people of Maffachufetts. The fact that moft of the States were flow or relaxed their efforts, after the power came into their hands, and they were "uncontrolled by the action of the Mother Country," would not diminifh the credit due to Maffachufetts, if fhe had taken the lead and maintained it. But that honor is not hers! Nor did the feparate action of any of the States effectually limit, much lefs deftroy, this infamous traffic.

The Continental Affociation, adopted and figned by all the members of the Congrefs on the 20th of October, 1774, for carrying into effect the non-importation, non-confumption, and non-exportation refolve of the 27th of September, provided for the difcontinuance of the Slave-Trade. The Continental Congrefs, on the 6th of April, 1776, formally "*Refolved,* That no flave be imported into any of the thirteen United Colonies." There is reafon to believe that this refolution received the unanimous affent of the Congrefs. *Force's Dec. of Independence, p.* 42. But no provifion was made in the Articles of Confederation to hinder the importation of flaves, and this pernicious commerce was never absolutely crushed until the power of the nation was exercifed againft it under the authority of the Conftitution.

Slavery, however, was not forgotten or neglected for want of notice. In the firft Provincial Congrefs of Maffachufetts, October 25, 1774,

"Mr. Wheeler brought into Congrefs a letter directed to Doct. Appleton, purporting the propriety, that while we are attempting to free ourfelves from our prefent embarraffments, and preferve ourfelves from flavery, that we alfo take into confideration the ftate and circumftances of the negro flaves in this province. The fame was read, and it was moved that a Committee be appointed to take the fame into confideration. After fome debate thereon, the queftion was put, whether the matter now fubfide, and it paffed in the affirmative." *Journals,* 29.

In May, 1775, the Committee of Safety (Hancock and Warren's Committee) came to a formal refolution, which is certainly one of the moft fignificant documents of the period.

"*Refolved,* That it is the opinion of this Committee, as the conteft now between Great Britain and the Colonies refpects the liberties and privileges of the latter, which the Colonies are determined to maintain, that the admiffion of any perfons, as foldiers, into the army now raifing, but only fuch as are freemen, will be inconfiftent with the principles that are to be fupported, and reflect dishonor on this Colony, and that no flaves be admitted into this army upon any confideration whatever."

This refolution being communicated to the Provincial Congrefs (June 6, 1775), was read, and ordered to lie on the table for further confideration. It was probably allowed to "fubfide," like the former propofition. The prohibition againft the admiffion of flaves into the Maffachufetts Army clearly recognizes flavery as an exifting inftitution.

The negroes of Briftol and Worcefter having petitioned the Committee of Correfpondence of the latter county to affift them in obtaining their freedom, it was refolved, in a Convention held at Worcefter, June 14, 1775, "That we abhor the enflaving of any of the human race, and particularly of the negroes in this country, and that whenever there fhall be a door opened, or opportunity prefent for anything to be done towards the emancipation of the negroes, we will ufe our influence and endeavor that fuch a thing may be brought about." *Lincoln's Hift. of Worcefter*, 110.

The high tory writers of 1775 were not flow to avail themfelves of the argument of inconfiftency againft the whigs of the day. One writer faid:

"Negroe flaves in Bofton! It cannot be! It is neverthelefs very true. For though the Boftonians have grounded their rebellions on the 'immutable laws of nature,' and have refolved in their Town Meetings, that 'It is the firft principle in civil fociety, founded in nature and reafon, that no law of fociety can be binding on any individual, without his confent given by himfelf in person, or by his representative of his own free election; yet, notwithstanding the immutable laws of nature, and this public resolution of their own in Town Meetings, they actually have in town two thousand Negroe slaves, who neither by themselves in person, nor by representatives of their own free election ever gave consent to their present state of bondage." *Mein's Sagittarius's Letters, pp.* 38, 39.

On June 5th, 1774, two discourses on liberty were delivered at the North Church in Newburyport, by Nathaniel Niles, M. A.,—which were printed in a pamphlet of sixty pages. A brief passage near the close of the first discourse presents a strong argument against the institution. *pp.* 37, 38.

In 1774, Deacon Benjamin Colman, of Byfield Church, Newbury, Massachusetts, made himself conspicuous in his neighborhood by his exertions against slavery. In the Essex Journal, of Newburyport, July 20, 1774, an essay of his was published, in which he says:

"And this iniquity *is established by law in this province*, and although there have been some feeble attempts made to break the yoke and set them at liberty, yet the thing is not effected, but they are still kept under the civil yoke of bondage.' *Coffin's Newbury*, 340.

In the following year, Sept. 16, 1775, the same zealous deacon addressed a letter to a member of the General Court, " by whom (he thought) this idolatry should be thrown down, and a reformation take place by the authority of that legislative power." His appeals to the love of freedom, which was then the cry of the whole land, are moſt forcible, and his ſtrong fears of the further judgments of God as a conſequence of this "capital ſin of theſe States," ſlavery, are full of warning. He concludes with the following paragraph, which is not leſs intereſting in this connection from the ſpecial reference to Boſton—in his pious improvement of an important fact already ſet forth in theſe Notes:

"But, Sir, you may be ready too haſtily to conclude from this writing that my mind is ſo faſtened upon the ſlave-trade, as if it were the only crime that we were chargeable with, or that God was chaſtening us for. As I have ſaid before, ſo ſay I again, our tranſgreſſions are multiplied, but yet this crime is more particularly pointed at than any other. WAS BOSTON THE FIRST PORT ON THIS CONTINENT THAT BEGAN THE SLAVE-TRADE, *and are they not the firſt ſhut up by an oppreſſive act, and brought almoſt to deſolation, wherefore, Sir, though we may not be peremptory in applying the judgments of God, yet I cannot paſs over ſuch providences without a remark.* But to conclude. I entreat and beſeech you by all the love you have for this town, by all the regard you have for this diſtreſſed, bleeding province, as for the American Colonies in general, that you exert yourſelf, and improve your utmoſt endeavors at the Court to obtain a diſcharge for the ſlaves from their bondage. If this was done, I ſhould expect ſpeedy deliverance to ariſe to us, but if *this oppreſſion is ſtill continued and maintained by authority*, I can only ſay, my ſoul ſhall weep in ſecret places for that crime." *Ibid.*, 342.

VII.

In the autumn of 1776, sympathy for the slave in Massachusetts received a fresh impulse. Two negro men, captured on the high seas, were advertised for sale at auction, as a part of the cargo and appurtenances of a prize duly condemned in the Maritime Court.[1] This advertisement roused the spirit of hostility to slavery to a remarkable degree, and the Legislature were excited to begin the work of reform apparently with great earnestness and vigor.

On Friday, Sept. 13, 1776, at the afternoon session, the Massachusetts House of Representatives

"*Resolved*, That Wednesday next, at three o'clock in the afternoon, be assigned for choosing a committee to be joined with a Committee of the Honorable Board, to take under consideration the condition of the African Slaves, now in this State, or that hereafter may be brought into it, and to report." *Jour. H. of R.*, 105.

We find no record of proceedings in accordance with this resolution until a little more than a month later, when, on the 19th of October, 1776, it was "Ordered, that Mr. Sergeant, Mr. Murrey, Mr. Appleton, and Capt. Stone, with such as the honorable

---

[1] This was the Hannibal, a sloop of sixty tons, commanded by William Fitzpatrick, and taken while on a voyage from Jamaica to Turk's Island. *Am. Archives*, v., iii., 258. An advertisement in the *New England Chronicle*, August 15, 1776, announces the Maritime Court for y͡e Middle District to be held at Boston, 5th September, 1776, to try the Justice of the Capture of the Sloop called the Hannibal, etc., and her Cargo and Appurtenances.

House may join be a Committee to take under confideration the condition of the African flaves now in this State [or that may be hereafter brought into this State] or may be hereafter brought into it and report." *Journal H. of R., p.* 127. This refolution was concurred in by the Council, and William Sever, Benjamin Greenleaf, and Daniel Hopkins, Efqrs., were joined on the part of the Board. *Gen. Court Records, Vol.* xxxiii., *p.* 55. We have made diligent fearch for further action under this refolution and appointment of the Committee, but have failed to difcover any trace of it. The matter was probably "allowed to fubfide" again.

On the fame day, however, in which the Houfe firft determined to give attention to the condition of the African flaves, on the 13th of September, 1776, their refolution to that effect was immediately followed by another "to prevent the fale of two negro men lately brought into this State, as prifoners taken on the high feas, and advertifed to be fold at Salem, the 17th inft., by public auction." *Journal, p.* 105. The refolve does not appear on the Journal, but from the files preferved among the Archives of the State, we are enabled to prefent it as thus originally paffed, viz.:

"IN THE HOUSE OF REPRESENTATIVES, SEPT. 13, 1776:

"WHEREAS this Houfe is credibly informed that two negro men lately brought into this State as prifoners taken on the High Seas are advertifed to be fold at Salem, the 17th inftant, by public auction,

"*Refolved,* That the felling and enflaving the human fpecies is a direct violation of the natural rights alike vested in all men by their Creator, and utterly inconsistent with the avowed principles on which this and the other United States have carried their struggle for liberty even to the last appeal, and therefore, that all persons connected with the said negroes be and they hereby are forbidden to sell them or in any manner to treat them otherways than is already ordered for the treatment of prisoners of war taken in the same vessell or others in the like employ and if any sale of the said negroes shall be made, it is hereby declared null and void.

"Sent up for concurrence,

"SAM^L. FREEMAN, *Speaker*, *P. T.*

"In Council, Sept. 14, 1776. Read and concurred as taken into a new draught. Sent down for concurrence.

JOHN AVERY, *Dpy. Secy.*

"In the House of Representatives, Sept. 14, 1776. Read and non-concurred, and the House adhere to their own vote. Sent up for concurrence.

J. WARREN, *Speaker.*

"In Council, Sept. 16, 1776. Read and concurred as now taken into a new draft. Sent down for concurrence.

JOHN AVERY, *Dpy. Secy.*

"In the House of Representatives, Sept. 16, 1779. Read and concurred.

J. WARREN, *Speaker.*

"Consented to.

JER. POWELL,
W. SEVER,
B. GREENLEAF,
CALEB CUSHING,
B. CHADBOURN,
JOHN WHETCOMB,
ELDAD TAYLOR,
S. HOLTEN,

JABEZ FISHER,
B. WHITE,
MOSES GILL,
DAN'L. HOPKINS,
BENJ. AUSTIN,
WM. PHILLIPS,
D. SEWALL,
DAN'L HOPKINS."

We give a more particular account of the legislative history and progress of this resolve, derived from the journals.

The fubject reappears on the Journal of the Houfe of the 14th September, as follows :

"David Sewall, Efq., brought down the refolve which paffed the Houfe yefterday, forbidding the fale of two negroes, with the following vote of Council thereon, viz.: *In Council,* Sept. 14, 1776. Read and concurred, as taken into a new draught. Sent down for concurrence. Read and non-concurred, and the Houfe adhere to their own vote. Sent up for concurrence." *Ibid.,* 106.

The members of the Council prefent on the 14th September, 1776, were

JAMES BOWDOIN,	MOSES GILL,
BENJAMIN GREENLEAF,	BENJAMIN AUSTIN,
RICHARD DERBY,	SAMUEL HOLTEN,
JER. POWELL,	BENJAMIN WHITE,
CALEB CUSHING,	HENRY GARDNER,
BENJAMIN CHADBURN,	JABEZ FISHER,
WILLIAM SEAVER,	WILLIAM PHILLIPS,
JOHN WINTHROP,	DAVID SEWALL,
THOMAS CUSHING,	JOSEPH CUSHING,
ELDAD TAYLOR,	DANIEL HOPKINS.

General Court Records, etc., p. 581.

The Council Minutes, as contained in the *General Court Records,* March 13, 1776—*Sept.* 18, 1776, *pp.* 581–2, under the date of September 14th, 1776, give the refolve as finally paffed, with the addition, "In Council. Read and concurred. Confented to by the major part of the Council." This, however, is an error, as appears not only from the entry on the

Journal of the Houſe and the original document from the files as given above, but alſo from the following minute of the Council in the ſame volume of Records. Under date of 16th September—the following members of Council being preſent,

JER. POWELL,	BENJAMIN GREENLEAF,
JOHN WINTHROP,	ELDAD TAYLOR,
JNO. WHETCOMB,	WILLIAM PHILLIPS,
WILLIAM SEAVER,	CALEB CUSHING,
BENJAMIN CHADBURN,	SAMUEL HOLTEN,
JABEZ FISHER,	DAVID SEWALL,—

Rev. Mr. [John] Murray came up with a Meſſage from the Houſe to acquaint the Board that it was their deſire to know whether the reſolve reſpecting the ſale of Negroes at Salem had paſſed.

David Sewall, Eſq., went down with a meſſage to acquaint the Hon. Houſe that it was under conſideration of the Board. *Ibid.*, *pp.* 585, 589.

On the ſame day, 16th September, 1776, the final diſpoſition of the matter in the Houſe is thus recorded in their journal.

"John Whitcomb, Eſq., brought down the reſolve forbidding the ſale of two negroes, with the following vote of Council thereon, viz.: *In Council*, Sept. 16, 1776. Read and concurred, as now taken into a new draught. Sent down for concurrence. Read and concurred." *Ibid.*, 109. The reſolve, as finally paſſed by the General Court, appears in the printed volume of reſolves for that period.

"LXXXIII. Resolve forbidding the sale of two Negroes brought in as Prisoners; Passed September 14, [16th,] 1776.

" Whereas this Court is credibly informed that two Negro Men lately taken on the High Seas, on board the sloop *Hannibal,* and brought into this State as Prisoners, are advertized to be sold at *Salem,* the 17th instant, by public Auction :
" *Resolved,* That all Persons concerned with the said Negroes be, and they are hereby forbidden to sell them, or in any manner to treat them otherwise than is already ordered for the Treatment of Prisoners taken in like manner; and if any Sale of the said Negroes shall be made it is hereby declared null and void; and that whenever it shall appear that any Negroes are taken on the High Seas and brought as Prisoners into this State, they shall not be allowed to be Sold, nor treated any otherwise than as Prisoners are ordered to be treated who are taken in like Manner." *Resolves, p.* 14.

The high-toned, bold, and unequivocal declaration of anti-slavery principles, with which it originally set out, is gone; but it is still the most honorable document of Massachusetts legislation concerning the negro. To appreciate its importance and properly to understand this subject of negro captures and recaptures, it is necessary to extend our inquiry beyond the limits of the legislation of a single Colony; and we shall therefore make no apology for presenting to the reader in this place the results of our examination of the national legislation and action with reference thereto.

Its practical importance was obvious, and the necessity of an uniform rule was too apparent to admit of a doubt. Accordingly the Continental Congress, on the 14th of October, 1776—just one month after the proceedings in the Legislature of Massachusetts concerning the two negroes captured in the Hannibal—appointed a special Committee of three members (Mr. Rich. Henry Lee, Mr. Wilson, and Mr. Hall) "to consider what is to be done with Negroes taken by vessels of war, in the service of the United States." We have found no report of this Committee, nor are we able to say what action, if any, was taken until a later period of the war.

The Continental Congress, by resolutions of 25th November, 1775, had recommended it to the several Legislatures to erect Courts, or give jurisdiction to the Courts in being, for the purpose of determining concerning captures. Still, from the beginning, Congress exercised the power of controlling, by appeal, the several admiralty jurisdictions of the States. *Journal, 6th March, 22d May,* 1779, *21st March, 24th May,* 1780. *Journal H. of R. Pa., Jan.* 31, 1780.

Congress had prescribed a rule of the distribution of prizes, and an early act of Massachusetts is curiously illustrative of the doctrine of a divided sovereignty. By Chapter XVI. of the laws of 1776, it was provided that distribution should take place according to the Laws of this Colony, when prizes were taken by the Forces or the Inhabitants thereof; and when they shall be taken by the fleet and army of the United Colonies, then to distribute and dispose of them according to the Resolves and Orders of the Congress. *Compare Chapter* x., 1776, *and Chapter* i., 1775, *p.* 9.

Massachusetts ratified the Articles of Confederation in 1778, and the confederation was completed March 1st, 1781. The ninth article gave to the United States in Congress assembled the sole and exclusive right of establishing rules for deciding, in all cases, what captures on land or water shall be legal, and in what manner prizes taken by land or naval forces in the service of the United States shall be divided or appropriated, as well as establishing courts for receiving and determining finally appeals in all cases of captures.

Accordingly, Congress proceeded to legislate on the subject, and, during the year 1781, completed an ordinance, ascertaining what captures on water shall be lawful, in pursuance of the powers delegated by the confederation in such cases. On the 4th of June, 1781, an ordinance was reported for establishing a court of appeals, etc. On the 25th of the same month the subject was discussed, and, on the 17th of July, 1781, the ordinance having been further debated, was recommitted, and the committee were instructed to prepare and bring an ordinance for regulating the proceedings of the admiralty courts of the several States in cases of capture, to revise and collect into one body the resolutions of Congress and other convenient rules of decision, and to call upon the several Legislatures to aid by necessary provisions the powers reserved to Congress by the Articles of Confederation on the subject of captures from the enemy. On the 21st of September, 1781, Congress resumed the second reading of the ordinance respecting captures, and on the question to agree to the following paragraph, the yeas and nays were required by Mr. Matthews, of South Carolina: "On the recapture by a citizen of any negro, mulatto, Indian, or other person from whom labor or service is lawfully claimed by *another citizen*, specific restitution shall be adjudged to the claimant, whether the original capture shall have been made on land or water, a reasonable salvage being paid by the claimant to the recaptor, not exceeding one-fourth part of the value of such labor or service, to be estimated according to the laws of the State *of which the claimant shall be a citizen :* but if the service of such negro, mulatto, Indian or other person, captured below high water mark, shall not be legally claimed *by a citizen of these United States,* he shall be set at liberty."

It was adopted by a vote of twenty ayes to two noes. Both noes were from the South Carolina delegates. By the method of voting in that Congress, the vote was seven States in the affirmative, and one in the negative—four States not voting. The affirmative States were Georgia, Virginia, Maryland, Pennsylvania, New York, Rhode Island, and Massachusetts. States not voting, North Carolina, Delaware, New Jersey, and Connecticut, although all their delegates present voted in the affirmative. On the 27th September, when the ordinance came up for a third reading, an attempt was made to obtain a second vote on this paragraph, but it was ruled to be out of order. The ordinance was farther debated November 8, 13, 30, and some important changes were made, which will appear on comparison of the passages in italics. It was finally passed, apparently without opposition, on the 4th of December, 1781, as follows:

"On the recapture by a citizen of any negro, mulatto, Indian, or other person, from whom labor or service is lawfully claimed by *a State or a citizen of a State*, specific restitution shall be adjudged to the claimant, whether the original capture shall have been made on land or water, *and without regard to the time of possession by the enemy*, a reasonable salvage being paid by the claimant to the recaptor, not exceeding 1-4th of the value of such labor or service, to be estimated according to the laws of the State *under which the claim shall be made*.

"But if the service of such negro, mulatto, Indian, or other person, captured below high water mark, shall not be legally claimed *within a year and a day from the sentence of the Court*, he shall be set at liberty." Thus the action of the legislative authorities—colonial or state and continental or national—was virtually an affirmation of the received law on the subject, which was founded on the doctrine of *post liminium* derived from the civil law.

This, however, applied only to recaptures. There is no special provision for cases of capture of slaves belonging to the enemy—to whom probably the old doctrine was held to apply, that they were lawful prize, and as such liable to sale for the benefit of the captors. This had been the general, if not universal, rule.

Sir Leoline Jenkins, in a letter written in 1674, respecting negroes in a Dutch prize-vessel, says that it will not be controverted that on the statute of Prize "negroes are to be reputed Goods and merchandizes in this ship, as they are, generally speaking, a part of the commerce of those parts." *Wynne's Life of Sir L. Jenkins, p.* 707, *quoted by John C. Hurd.*

Negroes, captured in Canada, during the wars

between the Englifh and French, were fent to the Weft India Iflands for fale. *Col. Doc.*, x., 131.; *bis*, 138, 140. In 1747, the Englifh having captured a negro fervant, the French took pains to reclaim him, but the Englifh refufed to furrender him on the ground that *every negro is a flave, wherever he happens to be, and in whatever Country he may refide.* *N. Y. Col. Doc.*, x., 210. This precedent was referred to in a fimilar cafe in 1750, with a fimilar decifion, which was *acquiefced in by both Englifh and French.* *Ib.*, 213. See alfo the 47th article of Capitulation for the Surrender of Canada in 1760. *N. Y. Col. Doc.*, x., 1118.

In 1761, upon the reduction of Martinico, Maj.-Gen. Monckton ordered the negroes which were taken to be fold, and the money to be divided amongft the fubalterns attached to his army. *Ibid.*, VIII., 250.

During the American War, the flaves of the rebel colonifts were regarded by the Englifh as proper fubjects of prize and booty. The *N. E. Chronicle*, July 4, 1776, ftates that the "negroes carried off when the [Britifh] Army and Fleet were obliged to evacuate the Town and Harbor [of Bofton] were fent to Louifburgh, to dig Coal for their Tyrannical Mafters. Thefe Blacks, were commanded by a certain Captain Lindfey." It was eftimated that not lefs than 30,000 were carried off from Virginia. *Hildreth*, III., 355. And thoufands were carried off from South Carolina, Georgia, and other States. Mr. Jefferfon, in his letter to Gordon, refers to thofe who were fent to the Weft Indies, and exchanged for rum, fugar, coffee, and fruit. *Works*, II., 427.

In 1779, Sir Henry Clinton iffued the following proclamation:

"*By his Excellency, Sir* HENRY CLINTON, *K.B., General, and Commander-in-Chief of all His Majefty's Forces within the Colonies lying on the Atlantic Ocean, from Nova Scotia to Weft Florida, inclufive, &c., &c., &c. :*

" PROCLAMATION.

" WHEREAS, The Enemy have adopted a practice of enrolling NEGROES among their troops: I do hereby give Notice, that all NEGROES taken in Arms, or upon any military Duty, fhall be purchafed for [*the public fervice at*] a ftated price; the Money to be paid to the Captors.

"But I do moft ftrictly forbid any Perfon to fell or claim Right over any NEGROE, the Property of a Rebel, who may take refuge with any part of this Army : And I do promife to every NEGROE who fhall defert the Rebel Standard full Security to follow within thefe Lines any occupation which he fhall think proper.

"Given under my Hand, at Head-Quarters, PHILIPSBURGH, the 30th day of June 1779.

"H. CLINTON.

"By his Excellency's Command,
"JOHN SMITH, Secretary."

When this proclamation was firft iffued, the words enclofed within brackets were not in it. They were added in the publication two months later—with a ftatement that the omiffion was a miftake of the printers.

This method of dealing with captive negroes was not confined to the Britifh Army at that time.

At the capture of Stony Point by General Wayne, three negroes were taken among the fpoils, and although we have not been able to determine what dif-

position was finally made of them, the following letter of General Wayne on the subject is not without interest here. Writing from New Windsor on the 25th July, 1779, to Lieut.-Col. Meigs, he says:

"The wish of the officers to free the three Negroes after a few Years Service meets my most hearty approbation, but as the Chance of War or other Incidents may prevent the officer [owner] from Complying with the Intention of the Officers, it will be proper for the purchaser or purchasers to sign a Condition in the Orderly Book.

" . . . I would chearfully join them in their Immediate Manumission—if a few days makes no material difference, I could wish the sale put off until a Consultation may be had, and the opinion of the Officers taken on this Business." *Dawson's Stony Point, pp.* 111, 118.

The discussions which arose out of the breaches of the Treaty of Peace in 1783, which put negroes on the same footing with any other article of property, and the settlement made by Mr. Jay's Treaty in 1794, furnish an authoritative statement of the prevailing views of public law concerning the status of negroes. Hamilton, in his Camillus, No. III., says:

"Negroes, by the law of the States, in which slavery is allowed, are personal property. They, therefore, on the principle of those laws, like horses, cattle, and other moveables, were liable to become booty—and belonged to the enemy [captor] as soon as they came into his hands." *American Remembrancer,* I., 57.

Gen. Washington, the Continental Congress, and

the Commiffioners appointed by Congrefs in 1783 to fuperintend the embarkation of the Britifh from New York, all concurred in this view. Indeed the Commiffioners, Egbert Benfon, William S. Smith, and Daniel Parker, fhowed concluſively that they had no hefitation in confidering negroes, horfes, and other property, as being precifely on the fame footing; and felected a claim for a negro as one of the ftrongeft that could be found to enforce a compliance with the ftipulation in the Seventh Article of the Treaty. Nor did the Britifh Miniftry at any period of the negotiations raife any queftion as to this doctrine.

The differences of opinion, and the arguments of both parties in the National Congrefs, only confirm the fact, which indeed is obvious enough from the language of the Article. This was in 1795, during the firft feffion of the fourth Congrefs, when the Houfe of Reprefentatives embraced many of the ableft men in the country. *Debates on the Britifh Treaty*, Part II., pp. 129, 147, 253, 291-2, 301. *Papers relative to Great Britain*, pp. 5-9.

After the laft war with England fimilar difficulties and difcuffions arofe with reference to the firft article of the Treaty of Ghent, which protected the rights of our citizens in their "flaves or other private property." After a long ftruggle of the characteriftic diplomacy of Great Britain to evade it, a large fum was paid as indemnity for the flaves carried off in violation of the treaty ftipulation.

The doctrine of prize in negroes fell only with the Slave-Trade, and the Courts of England were very flow to recognife its fall. As late as 1813, Sir William

Scott condemned one hundred and ninety-nine flaves, as "good and lawful prize to the captors," declaring at the fame time that "flaves are deemed *perfonal property*, and pafs to the captors under the words of the Prize Act, 'Goods or Merchandizes.'"   1 *Dodfon's Reports*, 263.

The earlieft judicial recognition, within our knowledge, of the fact that negroes were no longer to be held and taken as "good and lawful prize to the captors," was in the United States Diftrict Court, in South Carolina, in July, 1814. It appears that the queftion was regarded as new. The Court previoufly had not proceeded to condemnation of flaves brought in as prize of war; but ordered their confinement as prifoners.[1] And in fome cafes, they had been received as fuch by the Britifh authority refident at Charlefton. The intereft of parties requiring a formal decifion on the point of prize, the libel was filed, in this cafe, *Jofeph Almeida, Captain of the American Privateer Caroline*, v. *Certain Slaves*. Mr. Juftice Drayton faid he had never had any doubt on the fubject, and declared that "Slaves captured in time of war cannot be libelled as prize: nor will the Diftrict Court of the United States confider them as prifoners of war. The Court confiders the difpofition of them as a matter of State, in which the judiciary fhould not interfere." *Hall's Law Journal*, v., 459.

In view of all thefe facts, the Maffachufetts Refolve of September 16th, 1776, juftly challenges our admiration. It lights up the dreary record with a

[1] They were informally confidered as prifoners, not fo decreed by Court.

sudden and brilliant glare, as of a light shining in great darkness. Although shorn of its magnanimous declaration of principles, in its progress through the legislature, its terms would still introduce a new theory and practice into the law of nations, annihilating the doctrine of prize in negroes, which had been everywhere maintained before, and which continued without question elsewhere. If it was really adhered to, it deserves all the honor that has been claimed for it as a long stride in advance of all the world in civilization and humanity. But the Legislature of Massachusetts could only regulate the action of their own prize Courts and their own citizens, and did not at that time attempt to give law to the whole continent. They then recognized the fact that they could not divest the title of slave-owners in the other Colonies in captured slaves, and their obligation to restore them in cases of recapture. Called upon to deal with a larger number of negroes, under circumstances more embarrassing than in the case already detailed, they appear to have been satisfied with their own declared position, and did not attempt to extend the principle of their new rule to all negro slaves who came or were brought within their jurisdiction.

In the month of June, 1779, the prize-ship, Victoria, was brought into the port of Boston. The Victoria was a Spanish ship which had cleared from South Carolina for Cadiz. On her passage she was attacked by an English privateer, made a successful resistance, and captured her assailant, who had on board thirty-four negroes which had been taken from the plantations of several gentlemen in South Carolina.

The Spaniard, after taking the negroes on board and injuring the veffel, difmiffed her. A few days afterward the fhip fell in with and was taken by two Britifh letters of marque and ordered into New York. On her paffage there fhe was recaptured by the Hazard and Tyrannicide, two veffels in the fervice of Maffachufetts, and brought fafely into port. On the 21ft of June, by order of the Board of War, fhe was placed in charge of Capt. Johnfon, to direct the unloading, etc., in behalf of the State. The Board of War immediately reprefented to the Legiflature the facts relating to the negroes thus "taken on the high feas and brought into the State;" being evidently unable to apply the refolution of 1776 to this cafe.

On the 23d of June, 1779, it was ordered in the Houfe of Reprefentatives, "that Gen. Lovell, Capt. Adams, and Mr. Cranch be a committee to confider what is proper to be done with a number of negroes brought into port in the prize fhip called the Lady Gage."[1] *Journal*, p. 60. The next day, "the committee appointed to take into confideration the ftate and circumftances of a number of negroes lately brought into the port of Bofton, reported a refolve directing the Board of War to inform our delegates in Congrefs of the ftate of facts relative to them, to put them into the barracks on Caftle Ifland, and caufe them to be fupplied and employed." *Ibid.*, pp. 63, 64. The refolution was immediately paffed and concurred in by the Council. It appears in the printed volume, among the Refolves of June, 1779.

[1] This name of "Lady Gage" is probably a miftake, for this proceeding evidently led to the refolution of the following day.

Slavery in Massachusetts.   165

"CLXXX. Resolve on the Representation of the Board of War respecting a number of negroes captured and brought into this State. Passed June 24, 1779.

"On the representation made to this Court by the Board of War, respecting a number of negroes brought into the Port of Boston, on board the Prize Ship Victoria:

"*Resolved*, that the Board of War be and they are hereby directed forthwith to write to our Delegates in Congress, informing them of the State of Facts relating to said Negroes, requesting them to give information thereof to the Delegates from the State of *South Carolina*, that so proper measures may be taken for the return of said Negroes, agreeable to their desire.

"And it is further *Resolved*, that the Board of War be and they hereby are directed to put the said Negroes, in the mean time, into the barracks on Castle Island in the Harbor of Boston, and cause them to be supplied with such Provision and Clothing as shall be necessary for their comfortable support, putting them under the care and direction of some Prudent person or Persons, whose business it shall be to see that the able-bodied men may be usefully employed during their stay in carrying on the Fortifications on said Island, or elsewhere within the said Harbor; and that the Women be employed according to their ability in Cooking, Washing, etc. And that the said Board of War keep an exact Account of their Expenditures in supporting said Negroes." *Resolves, p.* 51.

This resolve was immediately carried into execution. On the 28th of June, Edward Revely, the prize-master, was ordered to "deliver Thos. Knox from ship Victoria the Negroes that are on board for the purpose of their being sent to Castle Island pr. Order of Court," and accordingly there were "34 Negroes delivered." At the same time, the Board of War ordered the "issue to the Negroes at Castle Island—1 lb. of Beef, 1 lb. of Rice pr. day," upon the orders of Lt.-Col. Revere, the commandant of Castle

Island. *Minutes Board of War.* His letter of instructions from the Board is as follows:

"War Office, 28 June, 1779.

"Lt.-Col. Revere,

"Agreeable to a Resolve of Court we send to Castle Island and place under your care the following Negroes, viz.:

[19] Men,
[10] Women,
[5] Children,

lately brought into this Port in the Spanish retaken Ship Victoria. The Men are to be employed on the Fortifications there or elsewhere in the Harbor, in the most useful manner, and the Women and Children, according to their ability, in Cooking, Washing, etc. They are to be allowed for their subsistence One lb. of Beef, and one lb. of Rice per day each, which Commissary Salisbury will furnish upon your order, and this to continue until our further orders.

"By Order of the Board."

In accordance with the resolve of Court, the Board of War, by their President, Samuel P. Savage, addressed a letter to Messrs. Gerry, Lovell, Holten, etc., etc., delegates from Massachusetts in the Continental Congress, dated War Office, 29th June, 1779, in which are set forth the principal facts in the case, and the instructions of the Legislature. In conclusion, the President says, "Every necessary for the speedy discharge of these people, we have no doubt you will take, that as much expense as possible may be saved to those who call themselves their owners." This letter also gives the number of the negroes, and the names of the several gentlemen from whose plantations they were taken, viz.:

"5 Men 4 Women 4 Boys 1 Girl belonging to Mr. Wm. Vryne.

"9 Men 1 Woman belonging to Mr. Anthony Pawley.

"1 Man belonging to Mr. Thomas Todd.

"2 Men 3 Women belonging to Mr. Henry Lewis.

"2 Men 2 Women belonging to Mr. William Pawley.

"One of the negroes is an elderly sensible man, calls himself James, and says he is free, which we have no reason to doubt the truth of. He also says that he with the rest of the Negroes were taken from a place called Georgetown." *Mass. Archives, Vol.* 151, 292–94.

These negroes were not all detained at Castle Island, until their owners were heard from. One method of providing for them is noticed in the following extract:

"In 1779, Col. Paul Revere, who commanded there [Castle Island] had several orders from the Council to let part of them [negroes quartered on the Island] live as servants, with persons in different towns. An express condition of such license was, they should be returned whenever the public authorities required." *Felt: Coll. Am. Stat. Assoc.*, 1., 206–7.

These orders of the Council began as soon as the negroes were sent to the Island, the first one we have found bearing date June 30th, 1779, by which Mr. Joſhua Brackett was to have a Negro Boy "ſuch as he may chooſe," etc. *Maſs. Archives, Vol.* 175, 374. See alſo ſimilar order for three Negro Boys to be delivered to Hon. Henry Gardner, July 5, 1779. *Ibid.*, 385.

Moſt of them, however, muſt have remained at Caſtle Iſland, as appears from a return of the negroes there, October 12th, 1779. It is a ſingular circumſtance that ſuch a return ſhould be made, apparently to the Legiſlature, with a brief and touching report, from John Hancock—one of the moſt intereſting documents connected with this ſubject. The original, from which we copy, is in the *Maſs. Archives, Vol.* 142, 170. The portions which are in *italics* are in the autograph of Hancock.

BOSTON, Octr. 12, 1779. A Return of ye Negroes at Caſtle Iſland, Viz. :

Negro Men.

1. ANTHONY.
2. PARTRICK.
3. PADDE.
4. ISAAC.
5. QUASH.
6. BOBB.
7. ANTHONEY
8. ADAM.

9. JACK.
10. GYE.
11. JUNE.
12. RHODICK.
13. JACK.
14. FULLER.
15. LEWIS.

The above men are ſtout fellows.

Negro Boys.

No. 1. SMART.
2. RICHARD.

Boys very ſmall.

Negro Woomen.
No. 1. KITTEY.
2. LUCY.
3. MILLEY.
4. LANDER.
Pretty large.

Negro Girls.
No. 1. LYSETT.
2. SALLY.
3. MERCY.

Rather stout.

Gentlemen,
The Scituation of thefe Negroes is pitiable with refpect to Cloathing.
I am, Gen^t.
Your very hum. Servt.
John Hancock.¹

Oct. 12, 1779.

On the 15th of November, 1779, a petition was read in the Council, from Ifaac Smith, John Codman, and William Smith, in behalf of William Vereen and others, of the State of South Carolina, then in Bofton, praying that a number of Negroes which were taken from them by a Britifh privateer, and retaken by two armed veffels belonging to Maffachufetts, might be delivered to them. The Council, upon hearing the petition, ordered "that Mofes Gill, Efq., with fuch as the Honorable Houfe fhall join, be a Committee to take into confideration this petition, and report what may be proper to be done thereon." The refolution was immediately fent to the Houfe, who concurred, and joined Capt. Williams of Salem, and Mr. Davis of Bofton, for the Committee.

On the 17th of November, another petition was prefented in Council, from John Winthrop, "pray-

¹ John Hancock had been appointed "Captain of the Caftle and Fort on Governor's Ifland," on the 6th of October, 1779. *Refolves*, CLXXVIII, *p.* 111. Compare *Journal, pp.* 54, 60.

ing that certain negroes, who were brought into this State by the *Hazard* and *Tyrannicide,* may be delivered to him." This petition was alfo committed to the "committee appointed on the petition of Ifaac Smith and others," by a concurrent vote of both Houfes.

On the 18th of November, "Jabez Fifher, Efq., brought down a report of the Committee of both Houfes on the petition of Ifaac Smith, being by way of refolve, directing the Board of War to deliver fo many of the negroes therein mentioned, as are now alive. Paffed in Council, and fent down for concurrence." The order of the Houfe is, "Read and concurred, as taken into a new draught." Sent up for concurrence."

It is printed among the refolves of November, 1779.

"XXXI. Refolve relinquifhing this State's claim to a number of Negroes, paffed November 18, 1779.

"Whereas a number of negroes were re-captured and brought into this State by the armed veffels Hazard and Tyrannicide, and have fince been fupported at the expenfe of this State, and as the original owners of faid Negroes now apply for them:

"Therefore *Refolved,* That this Court hereby relinquifh and give up any claim they may have upon the faid owners for re-capturing faid negroes: Provided they pay to the Board of War of this State the expence that has arifen for the fupport and cloathing of the Negroes aforefaid." *Refolves, p.* 131.[1]

The Maffachufetts act of April 12, 1780, more effectually providing for the fecurity, fupport, and exchange of prifoners of war brought into the State,

---

[1] The original refolve is in *Mafs. Archives, Vol.* 142, 29, and is endorfed "Negroes captured in the fhip Victoria," and "Entered page 454."

was paſſed in accordance with the Reſolutions of Congreſs, adopted January 13th, 1780. *Laws,* 1780, *Chap.* v., *pp.* 283, 4. It declares with reference to "all Priſoners of War, whether captured by the Army or Navy of the United States, or armed Ships or Veſſels of any of the United States, or by the Subjects, Troops, Ships, or Veſſels of War of this State, and brought into the ſame, or caſt on ſhore by ſhipwreck on the coaſt thereof . . . . . , all ſuch priſoners, ſo brought in or caſt on ſhore (including Indians, Negroes, and Molatoes) be treated in all reſpects as priſoners of war to the United States, any law or reſolve of this Court to the contrary notwithſtanding." A previous law of 1777, repealed by this act, contained no ſpecial proviſion concerning this claſs of captures. *Laws,* 1777, *Chap.* xxxv., *p.* 114.

On Friday, the 23d of January, 1784, Governor Hancock ſent a meſſage to the Legiſlature, tranſmitting papers received during the receſs from October 28th, 1783, to January 21ſt, 1784, "among which (he ſays) is one from his Excellency the Governor of South Carolina, reſpecting the detention of ſome Negroes here, belonging to the ſubjects of that State. I have communicated it to the Judges of the Supreme Judicial Court—their obſervations upon it are with the Papers. I have made no reply to the letter, judging it beſt to have your deciſion upon it." *Journal H. of R., Vol.* IV., *pp.* 308, 9. The Secretary, in communicating the meſſage to the Houſe, ſaid he had laid the papers before the Senate, with his Excellency's requeſt to ſend them to the Houſe. *Ibid., p.* 310.

On the fame day, in the Senate, the meffage was read with accompanying papers, and referred to a joint committee of both Houfes. *Senate Journal*, iv., 277. *Houfe Journal*, iv., 311.

On the 23d of March following, a report of the committee, "by way of order," was read and accepted in the Senate, and concurred in by the Houfe. *Senate Journal*, iv., 441. In the Houfe, "The Hon. Mr. Warner brought down the report of the Committee on Governor Gerrard's[1] letter, being an Order requefting his Excellency the Governor to tranfmit a copy of the opinions of the Judges of the Supreme Judicial Court on the cafe complained of, for the information of the faid Governor Gerrard." *Houfe Journal*, iv., 496. The order is printed among the Refolves, March, 1784.

"CLXXI. Order requefting the Governor to write to Governor *Guerard* of *South Carolina*, inclofing the letter of the Judges of the Supreme Judicial Court, March 23d, 1784.

"*Ordered*, that his Excellency the Governor be requefted to write to Excellency *Benjamin Guerard*, Governor of *South Carolina*, inclofing for the information of Governor Guerard, the letter of the Judges of the Supreme Judicial Court of this Commonwealth, with the copy in the faid letter referred to, upon the fubject of Governor *Guerard's* letter, dated the fixth October, 1783." *p.* 141.

[1] Benjamin Guerard was Governor of the State of South Carolina from 1783 to 1785.

We have made diligent efforts to find the papers referred to among the files preferved in the State-Houfe at Bofton, but without fuccefs. We have alfo endeavored to procure them from the Archives of the State of South Carolina, with no more fatisfactory refult. Fortunately, however, we have been favored with the following extracts and memorandum, which were made by Mr. Bancroft at Columbia, S. C., feveral years ago.

From Mr. Bancroft's MSS., America, 1783, Vol. II.

GOVERNOR GUERARD TO GOVERNOR HANCOCK, 6th October, 1783.

EXTRACT. "That fuch adoption is favoring rather of the Tyranny of Great Britain which occafioned her the lofs of thefe States—that no act of Britifh Tyranny could exceed the encouraging the negroes from the State owning them to defert their owners to be emancipated—that it feems arbitrary and domination —affuming for the Judicial Department of any one State, to prevent a reftoration voted by the Legiflature and ordained by Congrefs. That the liberation of our negroes difclofed a fpecimen of Puritanifm I fhould not have expected from gentlemen of my Profeffion."

MEMORANDUM. "He had demanded fugitives, carried off by the Britifh, captured by the North, and not given up by the interference of the Judiciary." "Governor Hancock referred the fubject to the Judges."

JUDGES CUSHING AND SARGENT TO GOVERNOR HANCOCK, Boston, Dec. 20, 1783.

EXTRACT. "How this determination is an attack upon the spirit, freedom, dignity, independence, and sovereignty of South Carolina, we are unable to conceive. That this has any connection with, or relation to Puritanism, we believe is above y^r Excellency's comprehension as it is above ours. We should be sincerely sorry to do anything inconsistent with the Union of the States, which is and must continue to be the basis of our Liberties and Independence; on the contrary we wish it may be strengthened, confirmed, and endure for ever."

Whether Governor Hancock recognized in the subjects of this correspondence any of his old Castle Island acquaintances, does not appear; but we entertain no doubt that they were the same, or a part of the same negroes whose "pitiable" condition "with respect to cloathing," he had reported to the authorities in October, 1779. Why or how it happened that any of them were still within the jurisdiction of Massachusetts, we cannot explain. The exigencies of the war in South Carolina, which was threatened or invaded and overrun during the greater part of the intervening period (1779–83), may have prevented some of the owners from prosecuting promptly their intention to reclaim their slaves or returning with them to that State. The slaves themselves may have become familiar with their new homes, and willing or desirous to remain with their new masters in the various towns to which they had been scattered, and where they had been permitted to live under the orders of Council, and their new masters may have become warmly interested in the desire to keep them. Under such circumstances the authorities may have found it difficult to obtain a compliance with the agreement to return them when called for, without enforcing the reclamation in the courts of law. Add to all this, the disposition of some of the Supreme Court judges "to substitute an unwritten higher law, interpreted by individual conscience, for the law of the land and the decrees of human tribunals"—and we shall not be surprised at the result indicated in these imperfect memorials of the proceedings in 1783, '84.

We may expect from future researches in Massachusetts more light on this as well as other points indicated in these Notes; and we trust especially that these deficiencies may "compel a discovery" of the opinions of the Judges. They would furnish an extremely important illustration of the state and progress of anti-slavery ideas in 1783, bearing directly on the construction of the Constitution of 1780, which we have still to discuss. The only additional item we have found which may bear on this case is the following:

In the Supreme Judicial Court of the Commonwealth of Massachusetts, Suffolk, 26th August, 1783, the following named negroes were brought up on habeas corpus and discharged, the Court declaring the mittimus insufficient to hold them.

Affa Hall, wife of Prince Hall,
Quash,   Robert,

John Polly, Anthony,
Jack Phillips, Peggy, wife of said An-
George Polly, thony.
Records, 1783, *fol.* 177, 178.

VIII.

WE return again to trace the progress of public opinion on slavery in Massachusetts during the Revolution. It is indicated in part by the public press of the time. William Gordon, afterward well known as the author of a history of the Revolution, was very busy as a writer on this and kindred topics. In Letter V (of a series), dated Roxbury, September 21, 1776, he says:

" The Virginians begin their Declaration of Rights with saying, 'that *all* men are born equally free and independent, and have certain inherent natural rights, of which they cannot, by any compact, deprive themselves or their posterity; among which are the enjoyment of life and *liberty*.' The Congress declare that they 'hold these truths to be self-evident, that all men are created *equal,* that they are endowed by their Creator with certain *unalienable rights,* that among these are life, *liberty* and pursuit of happiness.' The Continent has rang with affirmations of the like import. If these, Gentlemen, are our genuine sentiments, and we are not provoking the Deity, by acting hypocritically to serve a turn, let us apply earnestly and heartily to the extirpation of slavery from among ourselves. Let the State allow of nothing beyond servitude for a stipulated number of years, and that only for seven or eight, when persons are of age, or till they are of age : and let the descendants of the Africans born among us, be viewed as free-born ; and be wholly at their own disposal when one-and-twenty, the latter part of which age will compensate for the expense of infancy, education, and so on.[1]"

In the Independent Chronicle, November 14, 1776, there is a Plan for the gradual extermination of slavery out of the Colony of Connecticut. It was sent to the publishers by Dr. Gordon, from Roxbury, Nov. 2, 1776. This plan is very severe on slaveholders, and portraying the death-bed scene of one of them, raises the query, whether he is sinner or saint ? Gordon himself says, "I shall say nothing further of the plan, than that, tho' I am well pleased, to have the absurdity of perpetuating slavery exposed, I am not for unsainting every man that through the power of prevailing prejudice and custom, is chargeable with inconsistency and absurdity: for if so, who then can be saved ?"

A "Son of Liberty" writes vigorously against slavery in the Independent Chronicle, November 28, 1776. He calls loudly for legislation, etc., "that no laws be in existence contrary to sound reason and revelation."

At this period, advertisements of slave-property were common in the newspapers. We quote a few specimens :

---

[1] The methods proposed in this letter do not give any countenance to the modern theories that slavery was illegal, and that hereditary slavery was always contrary to law in Massachusetts.

From the Independent Chronicle, October 3, 1776.

" *To be* SOLD A stout, hearty, likely NEGRO GIRL, fit for either Town or Country. Inquire of Mr. *Andrew Gillespie, Dorchester, Octo.* 1., 1776."

From the same, October 10.

" A hearty NEGRO MAN, with a small sum of Money to be given away."

From the same, November 28.

" To SELL—A Hearty likely NEGRO WENCH about 12 or 13 Years of Age, has had the Small Pox, can wash, iron, card, and spin, etc., for no other Fault but for want of Employ."

From the same, February 27, 1777.

" WANTED a NEGRO GIRL between 12 and 20 Years of Age, for which a good Price will be given, if she can be recommended."

From the Continental Journal, April 3, 1777.

" *To be* SOLD, a likely NEGRO MAN, twenty-two years old, has had the small-pox, can do any sort of business; sold for want of employment."

" *To be* SOLD, a large, commodious Dwelling House, Barn, and Outhouses, with any quantity of land from 1 to 50 acres, as the Purchaser shall choose within 5 miles of Boston. Also a smart well-tempered NEGRO BOY of 14 years old, not to go out of this State and *sold for* 15 *years only, if he continues to behave well.*"

From the Independent Chronicle, May 8, 1777.

" *To be* SOLD, for want of employ, a likely strong NEGRO GIRL, about 18 years old, understands all sorts of household business, and can be well recommended."

These and similar advertisements drew forth the following communication to the Printers from Dr. Gordon; but without any immediate effect, if we may judge from the fact that the last advertisement above was continued in the same paper in which was published

Mr. Gordon's Hint on Slavery.
Independent Chronicle, May 15, 1777.

"Messieurs Printers,

"I would hope that you are the Sons of Liberty from principle, and not merely from interest, wish you therefore to be consistent, and never more to admit the sale of negroes, whether boys or girls, to be advertised in your papers. Such advertisements in the present season are peculiarly shocking. The multiplicity of business that hath been before the General Court may apologize for their not having attended to the case of slaves, but it is to be hoped that they will have an opportunity hereafter, and will, by an Act of the State, put a final stop to the public and private sale of them, which may be some help towards eradicating slavery from among us. If God hath made of one blood, all nations of men, for to dwell on all the face of the earth, I can see no reason why a black rather than a white man should be a slave.

"Your humble Servant,
"William Gordon.

"N. B. I mean the above as a hint also to the other printers."

But although the Boston newspapers still continued to advertise slave-property, and, as we shall hereafter fee, in a manner even more shocking to the modern reader, it is to this period we are to refer the last attempt in the Legislature to put an end to slavery in Massachusetts. It is the most emphatic, if indeed it is not the only direct, attack made on that institution in all their legislation. The Legislature were also at this time beginning their first essay at constitution-making—the establishment of a new system of government for the State. The failure of this attack on slavery was as signal and complete as possible, while the method by which it was accomplished presents a curious illustration of the growth of the sentiment and principle of nationality. It is not amiss to remember, that in the first and last and only direct and formal attempt to abolish slavery in Massachusetts, the popular branch of the Legislature of that State laid the bill for that purpose on the table, with a direction "that application be made to Congress on the subject thereof."

On the 18th of March, 1777, another petition of Massachusetts slaves was presented to the Legislature, as appears from the following entry on the Journal of that date:

"A petition of Lancaster Hill, and a number of other negroes, praying the Court to take into consideration their state of bondage, and pass an act whereby they may be restored to the enjoyment of that freedom which is the natural right of all men. Read and committed to Judge Sergeant, Mr. Dalton, Mr. Appleton, Col. Brooks, and Mr. Story."

The original petition is preserved among the Archives of Massachusetts, and furnishes some additional interefting particulars. They pray for the paffage of an act, "whereby they may be reftored to the enjoyment of that freedom, which is the natural right of all men, and *their children (who were born in this land of liberty) may not be held as flaves after they arrive at the age of twenty-one years.*" The petition is figned by Lancafter Hill, Peter Befs, Brifter Slenfen, Prince Hall, Jack Pierpont (his × mark), Nero Funelo (his × mark), and Newport Sumner (his × mark). It bears date January 13th, 1777, and has the following endorfement: " Mar. 18. Judge Sergeant, Mr. Dalton, Mr. Appleton, Coll. Brooks, Mr. Story, Mr. Lowell and to confider ye matter at large Mr. Davis." *Mafs. Archives, Revolutionary Refolves, Vol.* VII., *p.* 132.

The addition of " Mr. Lowell and to confider ye matter at large Mr. Davis" indicates further proceedings, which we are unable to give, in confequence of the deficiencies in all the copies of the Journals known to us. The action of the Legiflature, however, refulted in a bill, which was probably drawn by Judge Sargent, who was the firft named of this committee.

On Monday afternoon, June 9th, 1777, " a Bill entitled an Act for preventing the Practice of holding perfons in Slavery" was " read a firft time, and ordered to be read again on Friday next, at 10 o'clock, A. M." *Journ.*, 19. On the 13th, the bill was " read a fecond time, and after Debate thereon, it was moved and feconded, That the fame lie upon the Table, and that Application be made to Congrefs on the fubject thereof; and the Queftion being put, it paffed in the Affirmative, and Mr. Speaker, Mr.

Wendell, and Col. Orne, were appointed a Committee to prepare a letter to Congrefs accordingly, and report." *Journ.*, 25. On the following day, Saturday, June 14th, " the Committee appointed to prepare a Letter to Congrefs, on the fubject of the Bill for preventing the Practice of holding Perfons in Slavery, reported." Their report was " Read and Ordered to lie." *Journ.*, 25. We find no further trace of it.

" STATE OF MASSACHUSETTS BAY. IN THE YEAR OF OUR LORD, 1777.

" An act for preventing the practice of holding perfons in Slavery.

"WHEREAS, the practice of holding Africans and the children born of them, or any other perfons, in Slavery, is unjustifiable in a civil government, at a time when they are afferting their natural freedom ; wherefore, for preventing fuch a practice for the future, and eftablifhing to every perfon refiding within the State the invaluable bleffing of liberty.

" *Be it Enacted*, by the Council and Houfe of Reprefentatives, in General Court affembled, and by the authority of the fame,—That all perfons, whether black or of other complexion, above 21 years of age, now held in Slavery, fhall, from and after the   day of   next, be free from any fubjection to any mafter or miftrefs, who have claimed their fervitude by right of purchafe, heirfhip, free gift, or otherwife, and they are hereby entitled to all the freedom, rights, privileges and immunities that do, or ought of right to belong to any of the fubjects of this State, any ufage or cuftom to the contrary notwithstanding.

" *And be it Enacted*, by the authority aforefaid, that all written deeds, bargains, fales or conveyances, or contracts without writing, whatfoever, for conveying or transferring any property in any perfon, or to the fervice and labor of any perfon whatfoever, of more than twenty-one years of age, to a third perfon, except by order of fome court of record for fome crime, that has been, or hereafter fhall be made, or by their own voluntary contract for a term not exceeding feven years, fhall be and hereby are declared null and void.

" And WHEREAS, divers perfons now have in their fervice negroes, mulattoes or others who have been deemed their flaves or property, and who are now incapable of earning their living by reafon of age or infirmities, and may be defirous of continuing in the fervice of their mafters or miftreffes,—*be it therefore Enacted*, by the authority aforefaid, that whatever negro or mulatto, who fhall be defirous of continuing in the fervice of his mafter or miftrefs, and fhall voluntarily declare the fame before two juftices of the County in which faid mafter or miftrefs refides, fhall have a right to continue in the fervice, and to a maintenance from their mafter or miftrefs, and if they are incapable of earning their living, fhall be fupported by the faid mafter or miftrefs, or their heirs, during the lives of faid fervants, anything in this act to the contrary notwithftanding.

"*Provided*, neverthelefs, that nothing in this act fhall be underftood to prevent any mafter of a veffel or other perfon from bringing into this State any perfons, not Africans, from any other part of the world, except the United States of America, and felling their fervice for a term of time not exceeding five years, if twenty-one years of age, or, if under twenty-one, not exceeding the time when he or fhe fo brought into the State fhall be twenty-fix years of age, to pay for and in confideration of the tranfportation and other charges faid mafter of veffel or other perfon may have been at, agreeable to contracts made with the perfons fo tranfported, or their parents or guardians in their behalf, before they are brought from their own country." *Mafs. Archives: Revolutionary Refolves, Vol. vii., p.* 133.

An endorfement on the bill is, "Ordered to lie till the fecond Wednefday of the next Seffion of the General Court." It was not taken up at that time, nor at any other time that we can difcover.

We have faid that Judge Sargent was probably the author of this bill. He was a very ftrong advocate of anti-flavery doctrines, and fubfequently, in his career as a Judge of the Supreme Court, had a principal agency in accomplifhing the overthrow of flavery by judicial conftruction, without the aid of legiflation in which he had failed.

There is among the archives of Maſſachuſetts the following draft of a bill, evidently the original of the preceding act, which appears to have been written by Judge Sargent on the back of a note addreſſed to him by Rev. Dr. Eliot, an eminent miniſter of Boſton who took a very prominent part in the patriotic proceedings of the Revolutionary period.

"In ye year of our Lord 1777.

"An Act for preventing ye wicked & unnatural Practice of holding Perſons in Slavery.

"Whereas ye unnatural practice in this ſtate of holding certain Perſons in Slavery, more particularly thoſe tranſported from Africa & ye children born of ſuch perſons, is contrary to ye laws of Nature, a ſcandal to profeſſors of ye Religion of Jeſus, & a diſgrace to all good Governments, more eſpecially to ſuch who are ſtruggling againſt Oppreſſion & in favour of ye natural & unalienable Rights of human nature—

"Wherefore in ſome meaſure to ſecure the bleſſings of freedom to ſuch who ſhall be hereafter born within this State—

"*Be it Enacted* by ye Council & Houſe of Repreſentatives in general court aſſembled & by ye authority of y^e ſame that all perſons who ſhall be born within ye limits of this ſtate from & after ye day of   next whether their parents be black or white, or eſteemed Bond or free, of whatſoever nation, People or condition, ſuch perſons born as aforeſ'd ſhall be & hereby are intitled to all ye freedom, Rights, Liberties, privileges & immunities that do or of right ought to belong unto free & natural born ſubjects of this State, any uſage or cuſtom to ye contrary notwithſtanding—

"And for ye effectual preventing of ye unnatural practice of ſelling promiſcuouſly and transferring a property in our fellow creatures, diſgraceful to human nature, & a ſcandal to profeſſing chriſtians—Therefore *Be it Enacted* by ye authority aforeſaid that all bargains, ſales, conveyances & other writings or contract without writing whatſoever for ye conveying or transferring of any property in our fellow creatures or of ye labour or ſervice of any perſons whatſoever of more than twenty-one years of age to a third perfon other than of fuch perfon who fhall voluntarily make himfelf a party to fuch Inftruments or writings or where he fhall be fubjected to fuch fale, or fervice by virtue of y⁰ order of fome court of Record, made after y⁰   day of   next fhall be null & void to all intents, conftructions & purpofes whatfoever, any Law, Ufage or cuftom to y⁰ contrary in any wife notwithftanding." *Mafs. Archives: Vol.* 142, 58.

On the 11th of September, 1777, a petition was read in the Houfe of Reprefentatives, from the felectmen of the town of Woburn, praying an abatement of their quota of men for the Continental Army, for *Slaves*, Idiots, Infane, Captives, &c., and thofe under age. The petitioners had leave to withdraw their petition.

A trace of the exercife of private judgment and one phafe of public opinion foon afterwards, on this fubject, may be feen in the following extract from the Journal of the Houfe of Reprefentatives, 24th September, 1777:

"A Petition of Jofeph Prout of Scarborough, fetting forth that Mr. William Vaughan lately told his two Negroes that by an Act of Court all Negroes were made free, in confequence whereof they have fince left him, and one of them has hired himfelf to faid Vaughan, who withholds him from the Petitioner, therefore praying relief. Read and difmiffed." *p.* 86.

As the efforts towards the formation of a State Conftitution gradually ftrengthened and took fhape, the fubject of flavery and the ftatus of the negro came up again and again. There was a conflict of opinions and interefts, and the newfpapers of the day bear witnefs to its progrefs. The friends of the negro did not by any means have it all their own way. The mufes were invoked on both fides. In the Independent Chronicle of the 29th Jan., 1778, nearly a column of the paper is occupied with about one hundred lines of verfe ridiculing negro equality, which was refponded to by another production in verfe in the paper of the 12th February. This brought out a rejoinder, alfo in verfe, in the following week, Feb. 19th, 1778.

The difcuffion was not confined to thefe poetical champions. As early as the 8th of January, 1778, Doctor Gordon took up one phafe of the bufinefs with an article in the Independent Chronicle, in which he faid:

" Would it not be ridiculous, inconfiftent and unjuft, to exclude *freemen* from voting for reprefentatives and fenators, though otherwife qualified, becaufe their fkins are black, tawny or reddifh? Why not difqualified for being long-nofed, fhort-faced, or higher or lower than five feet nine? A black, tawny or reddifh fkin is not fo unfavorable an hue to the genuine fon of liberty, as a tory complection. Has any other State difqualified freemen for the color of their fkin? I do not recollect any; and if not, the difqualification militates with the propofal in the Confederation, that the free inhabitants of each State fhall, upon removing into any other State, enjoy all the privileges and immunities belonging to the free citizens of fuch State."

With regard to the proceedings of the Legiflature-Convention of 1777–1778, little is known; but the draft of a Conftitution was prepared, which was debated at length, approved by the Convention, prefented to the Legiflature, and fubmitted to the people, by whom it was rejected. *Barry: History of Mass.*, II., 175.

We have been fortunate enough to recover a fragment of the debates in the Convention, which bears on our subject. It shows that there was a continued contest in that body between those who supported and those who opposed negro equality, in which the latter carried the day; and also that it was after debate—not unconsciously or without notice—that a majority of the Legislature of Massachusetts, specially instructed to frame the organic law for the new State, deliberately, in the year 1778, excluded negroes, Indians, and mulattoes from the rights of citizenship.

From the Independent Chronicle, September 23, 1779.

Mr. WILLIS.

Please to insert the following in your Independent Chronicle, and you will oblige the publick's friend and humble servant,

JOHN BACON.

Stockbridge, Sept. 10, 1779.

" *Open thy mouth, judge righteously, plead the cause of the poor and needy.*"—KING SOLOMON.

The substance of a speech delivered in the late Convention, on a motion being made for reconsidering a vote, by which this clause, "except Negroes, Indians and Mulattoes," in the twenty-third article of the report of the Committee, was inserted.

Mr. PRESIDENT:—As I have from the beginning of these debates been opposed to that clause, the erasure of which has now been moved for, I beg leave briefly to lay the reasons of my opposition before this honorable Convention.

In the first place, Mr. President, by retaining this clause in our Constitution, we make ourselves singular, or nearly so. No Constitution on the Continent, one only excepted, bears the least complexion of this kind. Say the honorable and patriotick Convention of Pennsylvania, in their Bill of Rights, Art. 7 : " all free men having a sufficient evident common interest with, and attachment to the community, have a right to elect officers, or be elected into office." The constitutions in general which have been formed of late through the Continent, breathe a like consistent and genuine spirit of liberty. But be this as it may, Sir, whether we hereby make ourselves singular or not, I have other reasons to offer for being in favor of the motion. By holding up this clause in our constitution, we sap the foundation of that liberty which we are now defending at the expense of all that blood and treasure which we so liberally part with in the prosecution of the present war with Great Britain; by holding up this clause, we contradict the fundamental principle on which we engaged in our present opposition to that power. The principle on which we engaged in this opposition, Sir, I take to be this, that representation and taxation are reciprocal,—that we, not being represented in the Parliament of Great Britain, Parliament had no right to tax us without our consent. When the Parliament of Great Britain assumed this power and plead the charter of this (then) Province to justify their claim, we in our turn, not only plead the same charter in opposition to such claim, but even contended, that on supposition the charter gave them this power, yet it was a power so inconsistent with the essential natural rights of men, that no contract whatever could, in such case, bind us. On this principle, Sir, we engaged in the present war,—on this principle we suppose ourselves justified in resisting, even to blood, that power which would thus arbitrarily exact upon us; and on the same principle, I conceive, the persons excepted in the clause now before the Convention, would be justified in making the same opposition against us which we are making against Great Britain: If not, Mr. President, let any gentleman point out the difference between the two cases; no essential difference has yet been pointed out by any gentleman who has spoke to the question, and no such difference, I presume, does in fact exist.

But I am apprised of an objection that is made by gentlemen on the opposite side. They say, "that by being protected by our laws (without any share in the representation) they secure benefits which are fully equivalent to the tax which we lay upon them." This, Sir, is the very argument by which Great Britain pretend to support their claim of taxing us; and I confess, Sir, it appears to me, in every view, as fully to justify their pretensions with respect to us, as it does ours with respect to those persons who are the subject of the present debate. So that, by retaining this clause in our constitution, we bring ourselves into this unhappy dilemma, that either in one case or the other, we must, out of our own mouth, and by our own conduct, be condemned. So far as we can justify our conduct in our present opposition to Great Britain, so far it must be condemned as it relates to those who are mentioned in the article now before us and vice versa. But this is not all, Mr. President; Who are to set a value on the privileges which these people enjoy under our government? Do we allow them a voice in the contract? By no means. We set a price upon our own commodity, and oblige them to give it whether they will or not; and this, not as to the *luxuries* of life, not as to the *necessaries* of life only, but even *life itself*. And if we may take upon us, without their consent, to set a value upon those benefits which they receive from our laws, and make them pay accordingly, we may, on the same principle, set these benefits at a higher or lower price, and so tax them in a greater or less proportion according to our own sovereign pleasure. According to our own avowed principles, if we may take from them one farthing in this way, we may by the same rule, take from them every farthing they possess. Nay more, we may subject them to perpetual servitude, as being no more than a just compensation for the benefit they receive in having their lives protected by our laws; and if this is not to establish slavery by a constitution, the foundations of which, it is pretended, are laid in the most extensive principles of liberty, I confess, Sir, I am utterly ignorant of what the terms *liberty* and *slavery* mean.

But it is further urged by gentlemen on the opposite side, "that the case now before the Convention is widely different from that between us and Great Britain,—that Great Britain assume a right to impose taxes on us of which they pay no part themselves,—that the more they lay upon us, the less they have to pay themselves,—that hence there is to them a strong inducement to bear us down by exorbitant taxation; whereas we, in taxing these people, tax ourselves at the same time." But who, Mr. President, perceives not the futility and deceit of this argument? If we are to tax them, not as members of our community, but as receiving particular benefits from our laws, what security can they have that we shall not multiply taxes upon them in proportion to the value which our caprice or covetousness may set upon these supposed benefits. And whether we tax ourselves at the same time that we tax them, or not, is wholly immaterial: They are to be taxed on quite a different footing from that on which we are taxed ourfelves; yea, as perfons who do not belong to our community, and the more we lay upon them, the lefs we fhall certainly have to pay ourfelves.

But it is ftill further urged by gentlemen on the other fide, "that thefe perfons are *foreigners*, and therefore not intitled to a voice in legiflation."

But how does this appear, Mr. Prefident? What, unlefs it be their color, conftitutes them foreigners? Are they not Americans? Were they not (moft of them at leaft) born in this country? Is it not a fact, that thofe who are not natives of America, were forced here by us, contrary, not only to their own wills, but to every principle of juftice and humanity? I wifh, Sir, thefe gentlemen would tell us what they mean by *foreigners*. Do they mean by it, fuch perfons, whofe anceftors came from fome other country? If fo, who of us is not a foreigner? Or do they mean to include under the denomination of *foreigners*, all thofe who are not born in this State, how long foever they may have lived among us, whatever property they may have acquired, whatever connexions they may have formed, or however they may have been incorporated with us by our prefent laws and conftitution? Thefe people, Sir, by our prefent conftitution, are intitled to the fame privileges with any of their fellow-fubjects; and by what authority we are now to wreft thefe rights and privileges from them, I cannot conceive, unlefs by dint of mere power. And I hope, Sir, that right, as founded in mere power, is not to receive a fanction from our conftitution.

But there is one argument more which has been urged by gentlemen on the oppofite fide, as being of great weight and importance, which is this, "That by erafing this claufe out of the conftitution, we fhall greatly offend and alarm the Southern States." Should this be the cafe, Sir, it would be furprifing indeed! But can it be fuppofed, Mr. Prefident, that any of the fifter States will be offended with us, becaufe we don't fee fit to do that which they themfelves have not done? Nay, more, will they be offended or alarmed that we do not violate thofe effential rights of human nature which they have taken the moft effectual care to eftablifh and fecure? It will not bear a fuppofition; the argument, Sir, is moft ridiculous and abfurd.

In fine, Sir, I hope we fhall not be fo inconfiftent with ourfelves, so destitute of all regard to common justice and the natural rights of men, as to suffer this form of constitution to go abroad with this exceptionable clause ; I hope the motion will obtain, and the clause be reprobated by the Convention. But should this not be the case, should it eventually appear that there is so great a want of virtue within these walls, I still hope there will be found among the people at large, virtue enough to trample under foot a form of government which thus saps the foundation of civil liberty, and tramples on the rights of men.

We have already intimated that these liberal and enlightened views did not prevail. On the contrary, the "Constitution and Form of Government for the State of Massachusetts Bay, agreed upon by the Convention of said State, February 28, 1778, to be laid before the several towns and Plantations in said State, for their Approbation or Disapprobation," has the following article:

"V. Every male inhabitant of any town in this State, being *free*, and twenty-one years of age, *excepting Negroes, Indians and molattoes*, shall be intitled to vote for a Representative or Representatives, as the case may be. . . . ," etc.[1]

This not only excludes Negroes, Indians, and Molattoes from the chief right of citizenship, but also recognizes the existence of slavery in the State; and although it was rejected by an overwhelming vote, we have seen no evidence that this feature of the instrument elicited such opposition as might be expected in a community already prepared for negro emancipation and enfranchisement. In the famous Essex Result, the ablest document on the subject now to be found—

[1] The remainder of the section relates to residence and property qualifications, etc.

an elaborate report, written by Theophilus Parfons, of a Committee appointed by the Ipfwich Convention for the exprefs purpofe of ftating the non-conformity of this Conftitution to the true principles of government applicable to the territory of the Maffachufetts Bay—the fifth article is not referred to; and the exiftence of flavery, although earneftly deprecated, is clearly recognized, as well as the impracticability of immediate emancipation.

"The opinions and confent of the majority muft be collected from perfons, delegated by every freeman of the State for that purpofe. Every freeman who hath fufficient difcretion fhould have a voice in the election of his legiflators. . . . All the members of the State are qualified to make the election, unlefs they have not fufficient difcretion, or are fo fituated as to have no wills of their own. Perfons not twenty-one years old are deemed of the former clafs. . . . Women alfo. . . . Slaves are of the latter clafs and have no wills. But are flaves members of a free government? We feel the abfurdity, and would to God, the fituation of America and the tempers of its inhabitants were fuch, that the flaveholder could not be found in the land." *Refult of the Convention, etc.*, pp. 28, 29.

Dr. Gordon continued his zealous championfhip of the colored races, and in one of his letters on the propofed Conftitution [1] attacked this Fifth Article in a moft pungent ftyle of oppofition. Gordon's rela-

[1] Letter No. II., to the Freemen of the Maffachufetts Bay, dated Roxbury, April 2d, 1778, publifhed in the Continental Journal, April 9th, 1778.

tions with the Legiflature had been moft intimate, as Chaplain to both Houfes, and he well knew how reluctantly the partifans of flavery were giving ground. We quote the paffages referred to:

"The complexion of the 5th Article is blacker than that of any African; and if not altered, will be an everlafting reproach upon the prefent inhabitants; and evidence to the world, that they mean their own rights only, and not thofe of mankind, in their cry for liberty. I remember not, that any State have been fo inconfiftent as to declare in their Conftitution, however they may practice, that a freeman fhall not have the right of voting, merely becaufe of his being a Negro, an Indian, or a Molatto. I am forry the Convention did not take the hint when given in time, and avoid this public fcandal. It hath been argued, that were Negroes admitted to vote, the Southern States would be offended, and we fhould be foon crowded with them from thence. This would be to fuppofe the Southern States as weak as the argument. Will not the Negroes be as likely to crowd into the State, if they may be free, though they are debarred the right of voting? Will any be fo hardy as to fly in the face of all the declarations through the Continent, and affert that the Negroes are made to be, and are fit for nothing but flaves? Let fuch know, that in Jamaica, there are a number of free Negroes, who, refenting the tyranny of their mafters, freed themfelves from flavery, and continued in a ftate of war for feveral years, till at length King George the IId., by letters patent, empowered two gentlemen to conclude a treaty of peace and friendfhip with them, which was done on the 1st of March, 1739, wherein they had their liberties confirmed. The exception of Indians is still more odious, their ancestors having been formerly proprietors of the country. As to Molattoes they should have been defined. We should have been told, whether it intended the offspring of a white and Negro, or also of a white and Indian; and whether the immediate offspring alone, or any of their remote descendants, so that the blood of a white being intermixed with that of a Negro or Indian, it should be contaminated to the latest posterity, and cut off the male offspring to the hundredth generation, from the right of voting in an election.

"Gentlemen, blot out the exception, and thereby wipe off from the country in general, the disgrace that has been brought upon it by the Convention in particular. If any are afraid, that the Bay inhabitants will, in consequence of it, at some distant period, become Negroes, Indians or Molattoes, let the General Court guard against it by future Acts of State."

Dr. Gordon had already become very obnoxious to the members of the Legislature, and was summarily dismissed from his office of Chaplain to both Houses, April 4th–6th, 1778, in consequence of his Letter I, published in the Independent Chronicle, April 2d, 1778, in which he was said to have "rashly reflected upon the General Court," and "misrepresented their conduct," etc.

In Boston, the subject of slavery became the source of angry contention, which grew into public disorder and riots. Thomas Kench, in Col. Craft's Regiment of Artillery, then on Castle Island, had applied to the

Legiflature for leave to raife a detachment of negroes for military fervice. This was on the third of April, 1778. On the feventh of the fame month he addrefsed a fecond letter to the Council, as follows:

"The letter I wrote before I heard of the difturbance with Col. Seares, Mr. Spear, and a number of other gentlemen, concerning the freedom of negroes, in Congrefs Street. It is a pity that riots should be committed on the occafion, as it is juftifiable that negroes fhould have their freedom, and none amongft us be held as flaves, as freedom and liberty is the grand controverfy that we are contending for; and I truft, under the fmiles of Divine Providence we fhall obtain it, if all our minds can but be united; and putting the negroes into the fervice will prevent much uneafinefs, and give more fatisfaction to thofe that are offended at the thoughts of their fervants being free.

"I will not enlarge, for fear I fhould give offence; but fubfcribe myfelf," &c. *Mafs. Arch., Vol.* 199, 80, 84.

The propofed Conftitution failed to pafs the ordeal of the popular judgment, fo far as an opinion could be gathered from the very partial returns made of the votes. A hundred and twenty towns neglected to exprefs any opinion at all; and but twelve thoufand perfons, out of the whole State, went to the polls to anfwer in any way. Two-fixths of them, however, voted in the negative. *Adams's Works:* IV., 214. Thus the Conftitution was rejected, negro claufe and all fharing the fame fate. We have no means of afcertaining the exact ftate of parties on this fubject; but there can be no doubt that there was a wide difference of opinions among the people.

From the proceedings of the town of Bofton, it does not appear that the citizens of that place objected to the negro exclufion, although they were unanimous againft the conftitution. In Cambridge it was voted down unanimoufly, all the voters prefent being Freemen, more than 21 years of age, and neither "a NEGRO, INDIAN or MOLATTO." *Independent Chronicle: June 4, 1778.*

On the contrary, the town of Dartmouth notes the inconfiftency of excluding the negroes, &c., and favors their equal recognition, but at the fame time affures the public that there is no Negro, Indian or Molatto among their voters. *Continental Journal, June,* 1778.

It is not by any means well afcertained at what period, if ever, the negro was placed on the footing of political equality with the white man in Maffachufetts. Public opinion has been juftly characterized as a power often quite as ftrong as the law itfelf. At once the great Ruler, Lawgiver, and Judge of the Anglo-Saxon race, it has held its throne and feat of judgment nowhere more firmly than in Maffachufetts. The flave was "emancipated by the force of public opinion;" and the fame authority, without the abfolute declaration and forms of law, continued to exclude the negro from actual practical equality of civil and political as well as focial rights.

A "petition of feveral poor negroes and mulattoes," who were inhabitants of the town of Dartmouth, dated at that place on the 10th of February, 1780, shows the condition they were in at that time. They humbly reprefent:

"That we being chiefly of the African extract, and

by reafon of long bondage and hard flavery, we have been deprived of enjoying the profits of our labor or the advantage of inheriting eftates from our parents, as our neighbors the white people do, having fome of us not long enjoyed our own freedom; yet of late, contrary to the invariable cuftom and practice of the country, we have been, and now are, taxed both in our polls and that fmall pittance of eftate which, through much hard labor and induftry, we have got together to fuftain ourfelves and families withall. We apprehend it, therefore, to be hard ufage, and will doubtlefs (if continued) reduce us to a ftate of beggary, whereby we fhall become a burthen to others, if not timely prevented by the interpofition of your juftice and power.

"Your petitioners further fhow, that we apprehend ourfelves to be aggrieved, in that, *while we are not allowed the privilege of freemen of the State, having no vote or influence in the election of thofe that tax us,* yet many of our color (as is well known) have cheerfully entered the field of battle in the defence of the common caufe, and that (as we conceive) againft a fimilar exertion of power (in regard to taxation), too well known to need a recital in this place.

"We moft humbly request, therefore, that you would take our unhappy cafe into your ferious confideration, and, in your wifdom and power, grant us relief from taxation, while under our prefent depreffed circumftances," &c.

This petition was addreffed "to the Honorable Council and Houfe of Reprefentatives, in General Court affembled, for the State of Maffachufetts Bay, in New England." The lofs or imperfections of the journals of this period prevent us from knowing what, if any, action was had on this petition, but a memorandum in the handwriting of the leading petitioner, on the copy from which the above was taken, tells the story:

"This is the copy of the petition which we did deliver unto the Honorable Council and Houfe, for relief from taxation in the days of our diftrefs. But we received none.   JOHN CUFFE."

Another copy of the petition was found, with the date, "January 22d, 1781," not figned, by which it would appear that they intended to renew their application to the government for relief.

The records of the town of Dartmouth alfo fhow that thefe colored inhabitants refifted the payment of taxes, and the 22d of April, 1781, they applied to the felectmen of the town, "to put a ftroke in their next warrant for calling a town-meeting, fo that it may legally be laid before faid town, by way of vote, to know the mind of faid town, *whether all free negroes and mulattoes fhall have the fame privileges in this faid town of Dartmouth as the white people have*, refpecting places of profit, choofing of officers, and the like, together with all other privileges in all cafes that fhall or may happen or be brought in this our faid Town of Dartmouth." *Nell's Colored Patriots of the Revolution, pp.* 87–90.

It has been ftated that thefe proceedings refulted in eftablifhing the right of the colored man to the elective franchife in Maffachufetts, and that a law was enacted by the legiflature granting him all the privileges belonging to other citizens. *Ibid.*, *pp.* 90, 77. But we can find no evidence to corroborate this statement, which is also entirely inconsistent with subsequent legislation.

As late as 1795, the political status of the negro in Massachusetts was by no means definitely determined. Dr. Belknap gave, as the result of his inquiries on the subject, the statement that they were "equally under the protection of the laws as other people. Some gentlemen (says he) whom I have consulted, are of opinion, that they cannot elect, nor be elected, to the offices of government; others are of a different opinion." Mr. Thomas Pemberton was one of the persons referred to by Dr. Belknap, and in his letter of March 12, 1795, says expressly that "the qualifications required by the Massachusetts Constitution prevents the people of colour from their being electors or elected to any public office."

Dr. Belknap continues, "For my own part, I see nothing in the constitution which disqualifies them either from electing or being elected, if they have the other qualifications required; which may be obtained by blacks as well as by whites. Some of them certainly *do* vote in the choice of officers for the state and federal governments, and no person has appeared to contest their right. Instances of the election of a black to any publick office are very rare. I knew of but one, and he was a town-clerk in one of our country towns. He was a man of good sense and morals, and had a school education. If I remember right, one of his parents was black and the other either a white or mulatto. He is now dead." *M. H. S. Coll.*, i., iv., 208.

The queſtion muſt have been regarded as of little practical importance, for the relative number of negroes was ſmall; and of thoſe all but a very inſignificant fraction were excluded by the property qualification. Had it been regarded with intereſt enough to call for an authoritative deciſion, there is little room for doubt what it would have been.

IX.

WE come now to the Conſtitution of 1780, the inſtrument by which it is alleged that ſlavery was aboliſhed in Maſſachuſetts. In the illuſtration of our ſubject, its hiſtory is very important, and demands careful and accurate criticism.

After the failure of the attempt in 1778, a convention of delegates choſen for the purpoſe was decided upon to form a conſtitution of government. They were elected in the ſummer of 1779, and met at Cambridge on the 1ſt of September of that year. On the 3d they reſolved to prepare a Declaration of Rights of the people of the Maſſachuſetts Bay, and alſo to proceed to the framing a new Conſtitution of Government. On the next day, Sept. 4th, a Committee of thirty perſons was choſen to prepare a Declaration of Rights and the form of a Conſtitution. On the 6th September, the Convention adjourned until the 28th October, for the purpoſe of giving the Committee time to prepare a report. Immediately upon the adjournment, the General Committee met in Boſton, and delegated the duty of preparing a draught of a

Conftitution to a fub-committee of three members—James Bowdoin, Samuel Adams, and John Adams. By this fub-committee the tafk was committed to John Adams, who performed it. The preparation of a Declaration of Rights was intrufted by the General Committee to Mr. Adams alone. His own ftatement with regard to it is, "The Declaration of Rights was drawn by John Adams; but the article refpecting religion, was referred to fome of the clergy or older and graver perfons than myfelf, who would be more likely to hit the tafte of the public." *MS. Letter of John Adams to William D. Williamfon*, 25 February, 1812, quoted in *Williamfon's Maine*, II, 483, note. *Adams's Works:* IV., 215-16.

The firft Article of the Declaration of Rights, as reported to the Convention, was as follows:

"ART. I. All men are born equally free and independent, and have certain natural, effential and unalienable rights: among which may be reckoned the right of enjoying and defending their lives and liberties; that of acquiring, poffeffing, and protecting their property; in fine; that of feeking and obtaining their fafety and happinefs." *Report, p.* 7.

This article, as reported, met with no oppofition, elicited little or no difcuffion, and was accepted with but flight and unimportant verbal amendments. *Journal, p.* 37. It ftands thus in the Conftitution of Maffachufetts:

"ART. I. All men are born free and equal, and have certain natural, effential, and unalienable rights; among which may be reckoned the right of enjoying, and defending their lives and liberties; that of acquiring, poffeffing, and protecting property; in fine, that of feeking and obtaining their fafety and happinefs." *Conftitution, p.* 7.

Its language is nearly the fame with that of the firft article of the Bill of Rights of Virginia, written by George Mafon, and adopted by her Convention on the 12th of June, 1776, when "Virginia proclaimed the Rights of Man." *Bancroft,* viii., 381. The fame language, common in thofe days, became more familiar in the Declaration of Independence, on the 4th of July, 1776, and in the Pennfylvania Declaration of Rights, July 15th—September 28th, 1776; and this affirmation of natural and even unalienable rights had long ceafed to be a novelty before Maffachufetts repeated it in her Convention of 1779–80. The Conftitution was fubmitted to the people in March, adopted by a popular vote in June, and the new government went into operation on the 25th of October, 1780.

It is a remarkable ftatement for a Maffachufetts writer to make, but it is undoubtedly true, that " much intereft has been felt of late years to know when, and under what circumftances, flavery ceafed to exift in Maffachufetts." *M. H. S. Coll.,* iv., iv., 333. The fact that Daniel Webfter had not been able a few years before his death to determine this queftion fatisfactorily, is pretty good evidence that it was doubtful; and will go far to juftify a good degree of caution in its decifion. In 1836, Chief-Juftice Shaw made an interefting ftatement on this point:

" How or by what act particularly, flavery was abolifhed in Maffachufetts, whether by the adoption of the opinion in Somerset's cafe, as a declaration and modification of the common law, or by the Declaration of Independence, or by the Conftitution of 1780, it is not now very eafy to determine, and it is rather a matter of curiofity than utility ; it being agreed on all hands, that if not abolifhed before, it was fo by the Declaration of Rights." *Commonwealth* v. *Aves*, 18 *Pickering*, 209.

Few perfons can now be found hardy enough to date the abolition of flavery in Maffachufetts from Lord Mansfield's decifion in the Somerfet cafe, or the Declaration of Independence. But the received opinion in Maffachufetts is, that the firft article of the Declaration of Rights was not fimply the declaration of an abftract principle or dogma, which might be wrought out into a practical fyftem by fubfequent legiflation, but was *intended* to have the active force and conclufive authority of law ; to diveft the title of the mafter, to break the bonds of the flave, to annul the condition of fervitude, and to emancipate and fet free by its own force and efficacy, without awaiting the enforcement of its principles by judicial decifion. *Compare* 7 *Gray*, 478. 5 *Leigh*, 623.

We have made diligent inquiry, fearch, and examination, without difcovering the flighteft trace of pofitive contemporary evidence to fhow that this opinion is well founded. The family traditions which have defignated the elder John Lowell as the author of the Declaration, and affigned the intention to abolifh flavery as the exprefs motive for its origin, will not ftand the teft of hiftorical criticifm. The truth is, that the bold judicial conftruction by which it was afterwards made the inftrument of virtual abolition, was only gradually reached and fuftained by public opinion—the Court having advanced many fteps further than was intended by the Convention or underftood by the people, in their decifion on this fubject. If it were poffible that fuch a purpofe could have been avowed in the Convention and wrought into their work, without oppofition, it certainly could not have paffed abfolutely without notice. Such a converfion would be too fudden to be genuine; and if we follow the facts in their natural chronological order, the actual refult will fall into its due place and pofition without force or violation of the truth of hiftory.

Now there is no evidence of oppofition, either in the Convention or out of it. Not even a notice of this important revolution, in the newfpapers of the day or elfewhere, has rewarded our earneft and careful fearch. John Adams, the author of the Bill of Rights, was not in favor of immediate emancipation (*see ante*, *p.* 110). The moft ftrenuous anti-flavery men were unconfcious of any fuch intention or refult for a long time afterward; and the newfpapers continued to advertife the fales of negroes as before. There is nothing to fhow that fo great a change was contemplated or realized, and thofe who maintain it would have us believe that the people of Maffachufetts, like the Romans on another memorable occafion, fuddenly became quite another people.[1]

The addrefs of the Convention, on fubmitting the refult of their labors to their conftituents, makes no

[1] "Ad primum nuntium cladis Pompeianæ populus Romanus repente factus eft alius."

allufion whatever to this fubject. No one can read it
—fetting forth as it does the principal features of the
new plan of government, the grounds and reafons
upon which they had formed it, with their explana-
tions of the principal parts of the fyftem—and retain
the belief that they had confcioufly, deliberately, and
intentionally adopted the firft claufe in the Declaration of Rights for the exprefs purpofe of abolifhing
flavery in Maffachufetts. The fame Bill of Rights
provided that "no part of the property of any individual, can, with juftice, be taken from him, or applied
to public ufes, without his own confent, or that of the
reprefentative body of the people," and, in another
claufe, that "no fubject fhall be . . . deprived of his
property but by the judgment of his peers, or the law
of the land." *Conftitution*, *p.* 10, 11. Did the members
of that Convention intend deliberately to diveft the
recognized title to property of their fellow-citizens,
amounting to not lefs than half a million of dollars,
without a word of explanation of the high grounds of
juftice or public policy on which they bafed their
action? If any further evidence is needed in this connection, it may be found in the fubfequent fuits, with
the entire proceedings and arguments of counfel, by
which the refult of virtual abolition was finally fecured;
as well as in the legiflative proceedings which followed
—all utterly inconfiftent with the theory of a direct
and intentional abolition by the Convention and
People. Compare *Wafhburn*, in *M. H. S. Coll.*, IV.,
iv., 333—346.

We have faid that earneft anti-flavery men at that
time were not aware of the alleged intention of the

Convention to abolish slavery by the declaration in the Bill of Rights. We have previously referred to the earnest efforts of Deacon Colman, of Newbury, against slavery as early as 1774–'75. A controversy between him and his conservative minister, as shown in the Church Records from 1780 to 1785, demonstrates this fact. The minister was the father of Theophilus Parsons, afterwards so well known in the State of Massachusetts as Chief Justice—the "Giant of the Law." In the Deacon's Testimony and Declaration, he says:

"The slaves in this State have petitioned for Liberty and Freedom from Bondage, since our Troubles began, in the most importunate and humble manner; *yet they are not set free in a general way*. . . . Magistrates, Ministers and common people have had a hand in this Iniquitous Trade. . . . . Should you plead, Sir, the Law of the Land, or the practice of the people, as an excuse in your favour; I answer, that neither the law of the land, nor the commonness of the people's practice in this affair, alters the nature of the Crime at all: for that which is Wrong in its own nature, can never be made right by any law or practice of men." *Coffin's Newbury:* 342–50.

This was written November 7th, 1780, after the establishment of the new government, and months after the Convention had completed their work and submitted it to the people.

The records of the church at Byfield contain a long account of the controversy between Mr. Parsons and his zealous anti-slavery deacon—neither of whom appears to have been aware that slavery, which was the fubject of their difpute, had been abolifhed, either "virtually" or otherwife.

As late as the 3d of November, 1783, the deacon, *who had been fufpended from communion on account of the violence of his zeal againft the inftitution*, addreffed the brethren by a communication, in which he declared that they had fhut him out of their communion "for bearing Teftimony againft the deteftable practice of Slave keeping, and making merchandife of human people." He adds, "you can't but be fenfible the practice of Slave keeping is Reprobated, and Abhorr'd by the moft Godly people through this State," etc. All seem to be utterly ignorant of the abolition intention of the firft claufe in the Declaration of Rights. See *Coffin's Newbury: pp. 342 et seqq.*

Let us turn again to the newfpapers. Have the advertifements, which provoked the indignation of Doctor Gordon in 1776, difappeared before the new Conftitution and the firft article of the Bill of Rights? Let the following felections anfwer the query! They are from papers publifhed during the continuance of the Convention, and the year following, until six months after the new government went into operation.

From the Continental Journal, November 25, 1779.

"*To be* SOLD A likely NEGRO GIRL, 16 years of Age, for no fault, but want of employ."

From the fame, December 16th, 1779.

"*To be* SOLD, A Strong likely NEGRO GIRL," &c.

From the Independent Chronicle, March 9th, 1780.

"*To be* SOLD, for want of employment, an exceeding likely NEGRO GIRL, aged fixteen."

From the fame, March 30th and April 6th, 1780.

"*To be* SOLD, very Cheap, for no other Reafon than for want of Employ, an exceeding Active NEGRO BOY, aged fifteen. Alfo, a likely NEGRO GIRL, aged feventeen."

From the Continental Journal, Auguft 17, 1780.

"*To be* SOLD, a likely NEGRO BOY."

From the fame, Auguft 24th and September 7th.

"*To be* SOLD or LETT, for a term of years, a ftrong, hearty, likely NEGRO GIRL."

From the fame, Oct. 19th and 26th, and Nov. 2d.

"*To be* SOLD, a likely NEGRO BOY, about eighteen years of Age, fit for to ferve a Gentleman, to tend horfes or to work in the Country."

From the fame, October 26th, 1780.

"*To be* SOLD, a likely NEGRO BOY, about 13 years old, well calculated to wait on a Gentleman. Inquire of the Printer."

"*To be* SOLD, a likely young Cow and CALF. Inquire of the Printer."

Independent Chronicle, Dec. 14th, 21ft, 28th, 1780.

"A NEGRO CHILD, *foon expected, of a good breed,* may be owned by any Perfon inclining to take it, and Money with it."

Continental Journal, Dec. 21, 1780, and Jan. 4, 1781.

"*To be* SOLD, a hearty, ftrong NEGRO WENCH, about 29 years of age, fit for town or country."

The terms of the following announcement indicate the fact that "notions of Freedom" were beginning to find their way into other heads befides thofe of mafters and miftreffes.

Slavery in Maſſachuſetts.

From the Continental Journal, March 1, 1781.

"To be SOLD, an extraordinary likely NEGRO WENCH, 17 years old, ſhe can be warranted to be ſtrong, healthy and good-natured, *has no notion of Freedom*, has been always uſed to a Farmer's Kitchen and dairy, and is not known to have any failing, but being with Child, which is the only cauſe of her being ſold."[1]

This advertiſement, which was repeated for two weeks after in the papers of the 8th and 15th March, muſt cloſe our quotations of this ſort. If it was not the laſt publiſhed in Maſſachuſetts, it ought to have been! It brings us in point of time to the period in which ſuits growing out of the relations of maſter and ſlave were brought in the courts of law, which ultimately reſulted in extending the Declaration in the Bill of Rights to enſlaved Indians and Negroes— preaching deliverance to the captives, and ſetting at liberty them that were bruiſed—the virtual abolition of ſlavery.

No contemporaneous report appears to be extant, of the deciſions by which the general queſtion of the legality of ſlavery in Maſſachuſetts was determined. Chief-Juſtice Parſons, in 1806, in the caſe ſo frequently quoted before, ſtated that, "in the firſt action involving the right of the maſter, which came before

[1] This reminds us of the period in Britiſh hiſtory when Ireland was the greateſt mart for Engliſh ſlaves. In thoſe days, when any one had more children or ſervants than he could keep, he took them to the ready market of Briſtol, and there found Iriſh merchants, ready to purchaſe. Malmesbury affirms, that it was no uncommon thing to behold young girls, expoſed to ſale there, in a ſtate of pregnancy, which raiſed their value *Bridge's Jamaica:* II., *Notes*, 455–6.

the Supreme Judicial Court after the eftablifhment of the Conftitution, the judges declared that, by virtue of the firft article of the Declaration of Rights, flavery in this State was no more." IV. *Mafs. Reports,* 128. The report does not ftate what cafe was here referred to, and there has been a confiderable difference of opinion among thofe who have referred to the fubject. The accounts are various and inconfiftent, agreeing only in one refpect, that a determination gradually grew up to *confider flavery as abolifhed,* notwithftanding the failure of every attempt to deftroy it by legiflation.

The cafe of Elizabeth Freeman, better known as "Mum Bet," has been ftated by fome as the turning-point of legal decifion; in which Judge Theodore Sedgwick defended the flave, who was pronounced free. The biographer of Mr. Sedgwick in the New American Cyclopædia fays: "This, it is believed, was the firft fruit of the declaration in the Maffachufetts Bill of Rights that 'all men are born free and equal,' and led to the end of flavery in Maffachufetts."[1]

The Duke de la Rochefoucault Liancourt gives an account of the termination of flavery in Maffachufetts, which is the more interefting that it may have been derived from Mr. Sedgwick himfelf, with whom he was acquainted at Philadelphia, and whofe hofpitality he enjoyed in Maffachufetts. He fays: "In 1781, fome negroes, prompted by private fuggeftion,

---

[1] A writer in the Edinburgh Review, for January, 1864, reprefents this cafe as having occurred in 1772, and the refult of the Maffachufetts Conftitution of 1780!

maintained that they were not flaves: they found advocates, among whom was Mr. Sedgwick, now a member of the Senate of the United States; and the caufe was carried before the Supreme Court. Their counfel pleaded, 1º. That no antecedent law had eftablifhed flavery, and that the laws which feemed to fuppofe it were the offspring of error in the legiflators, who had no authority to enact them:—2º. That fuch laws, even if they had exifted, were annulled by the new Conftitution. They gained the caufe under both afpects: and the folution of this firft queftion that was brought forward fet the negroes entirely at liberty, and at the fame time precluded their pretended owners from all claim to indemnification, fince they were proved to have poffeffed and held them in flavery without any right. As there were only a few flaves in Maffachufetts, the decifion paffed without oppofition, and banifhed all further idea of flavery." *Travels, etc.*, II., 166, 212–13.

John Quincy Adams, in reply to a queftion put by John C. Spencer, ftated that "a note had been given for the price of a flave in 1787. This note was fued, and the Court ruled that the maker had received no confideration, as man could not be fold. From that time forward, flavery died in the Old Bay State." *Nell's Colored Patriots*, 59.

There is now, however, little room for doubt that the leading cafes were thofe concerning a flave named Quork Walker, belonging to Nathaniel Jennifon, a farmer of the town of Barre, in Worcefter County. The flave deferted his mafter, and was received and employed as a fervant by John Caldwell, a neighbor, alfo a farmer.¹ The flave had been beaten and imprifoned, and otherwife maltreated by his mafter, whether before or after his defertion, or both, does not appear. Out of thefe principal facts grew the feries of actions in the Courts which we are now briefly to fketch. Two of them were commenced in the Inferior Court of Common Pleas for the County of Worcefter, at the June Term in 1781. They were entitled, *Nathaniel Jennifon* vs. *John and Seth Caldwell*, and *Quork Walker* vs. *Nathaniel Jennifon*.

The firft was a fuit for damages for enticing away the flave from his mafter, etc., which refulted in a verdict againft the friends of the flave, and an affefsment of damages at twenty-five pounds (25*l*.) in lawful gold or filver, or bills of public credit equivalent thereto, and cofts of fuit at ² in like money, in favor of the mafter. From this judgment the friends of the flave appealed.

The fecond was a fuit for damages for affault and beating, etc., which refulted in a verdict againft the mafter. The jury found that the faid Quork was a freeman, and not the proper negro flave of the defendant, and affeffed damages for the plaintiff in the fum of fifty pounds (50*l*.) in lawful gold or filver, or bills of public credit equivalent thereto. The cofts were taxed at 6*l*. 11*s*. 7*d*, like money. From this judgment the mafter appealed.

Both appeals came on at the next Term of the Su-

---

¹ Jennifon's wife was a Caldwell, and he acquired poffeffion of this flave, in right of his wife, who owned him before marriage. It may be that this controverfy originated in fome family quarrel.

² The amount of cofts is not ftated in the record.

perior Court, held at Worcefter on the third Tuefday (18th) of September, 1781, before Judges Sargent, Sewall, and Sullivan.

In the firſt cafe, *Nathaniel Jennifon, App^t.*, vs. *Quork Walker*, the recorded refult was—"And now the Appellant being called comes into Court, but does not produce and give into Court attefted copies of the writ, Judgment, or of the Evidences filed in the Inferior Court, as the law directs, wherefore it is ordered that his default be recorded." *Docket September Term*, 1781, *in Worcefter. Records*, 1781, *fol.* 79. In his fubfequent attempts to procure a re-entry of this caufe, Jennifon grounded his petition to the Legiflature on the allegation that he had "confided in his Council to produce the papers from the Court of Common Pleas, which papers the faid Council failed to produce, by means whereof he became defaulted, and judgment was rendered againſt him." *Maſs. Refolves,* 1782, *p.* 182.

Quork Walker, Comp^t., vs. *Nathaniel Jennifon*, accordingly obtained an affirmation of the judgment. As recorded in the Superior Court, it is a "Judgment for 50*l*. Gold or Silver, or Bills of public Credit of the new Emiſſion equivalent 1 7-8th for one Silver Dollar. Damage and coſts taxed at 9*l.* 10*s.* 7*d.* Exon. iffued Feb. 6th, 1782." The Legiſlature granted a ſtay of execution by their refolve of March 5th, 1782. *Refolves, p.* 182. The legiſlative proceedings on this fubject will be noticed hereafter.

In the appeal of the fecond cafe, *John Caldwell et al. App^{ts}.* vs. *Nathaniel Jennifon*, the Jury found "the Appellants not guilty in manner and form as the

Appellee in his Declaration has alleged;" and they accordingly had Judgment for Cofts. *Records,* 1781, *fol.* 79, 80.

The array of counfel in this cafe was diftinguifhed, being, for the Appellants, Caleb Strong and Levi Lincoln ; and for the Appellee, Simeon Strong, John Sprague, and William Stearns. Mr. Wafhburn, in his paper on " the Extinction of Slavery in Maffachufetts," gives an interefting account of thefe fuits, and prints " the *fubftance* " of Mr. Lincoln's brief, which is fo important as to provoke our fincere regret that he did not print it entire and without modification. *M. H. S. Coll.,* iv., iv., 340–44.

The refult of the civil actions encouraged the friends of the flave to proceed ftill further; and an indictment was found at the fame Term of the Court (September, 1781) againft the mafter " for affault and battery, and falfe imprifonment." It was not tried until nearly two years later, April Term, 1783, when the defendant was found guilty and fentenced to be fined 40s., pay cofts of profecution, and ftand committed till fentence be performed. *Records,* 1783, *fol.* 85.

Dr. Belknap wrote and printed, in the year 1795, a notice of this trial, which we copy.

" In 1781, at the Court in Worcefter County, an indictment was found againft a white man for affaulting, beating, and imprifoning a black. He was tried at the Supreme Judicial Court in 1783. His defence was, that the black was his flave, and that the beating, etc., was the neceffary reftraint and correction of the mafter. This was anfwered by citing the aforefaid clause in the declaration of rights. The judges and jury were of opinion that he had no right to imprison or beat the negro. He was found guilty and fined 40 shillings. This decision was a mortal wound to slavery in Massachusetts." *M. H. S. Coll.*, 1., iv., 203.

When owners of slaves found that under the new régime they were to be held liable in damages for correction of their slaves, they were not slow to see the necessary consequences, and at once appealed to the Legislature, if they approved the judgment of the Court, to release them from the statute obligations growing out of their relations under the law of slavery in Massachusetts. Nor did their anxiety diminish when fine and imprisonment for criminal breach of the peace were added to civil damages for the same offence. Had the members of the Convention entertained the opinions which have since been ascribed to them, there would have been no room left for doubtful construction of general principles, for all the laws which sustained slavery would have been expressly repealed, by the very first legislatures under the Constitution, in which many of the same men were present. But the Legislature considered, hesitated, and did nothing. Their proceedings would seem to have been governed by caprice, if we did not recognize the difficulties under which they labored, and the various and conflicting elements which controlled them.

The first movement in the Legislature was made at about the same time the suits were begun at Worcester. In the House of Representatives, on the 9th of June, 1781, it was "*Ordered*, that Mr. Lowell, Col. Ashley, and Mr. Robbins be a Committee with such as the honorable Senate shall join, to consider a Remonstrance of a number of persons *owning negro servants*, and to report what may be proper to be done thereon." Mr. Lowell promptly declined to serve on this committee, for the next entry is, "Mr. Lowell is excused, and Dr. Dunsmore is put on in his room." *Journal, Vol.* ii., *p. 50*. The order was sent up for concurrence, and we find on the same day, in the Senate, a concurrence in the appointment of "Doct. Densmore in the room of Mr. Lowell resigned, excused by the House." *Journal*, ii., 24. On the 12th of June, the Senate refused to concur in the "Order of the House on the Remonstrance and petition of Nathan Jennison and others *owning Negro Servants*." *Ibid.*, 28.

We have been unable to find this memorial, in which other slaveholders besides Jennison joined, apparently with a remonstrance against the very first steps in those proceedings whose results they had no difficulty in foretelling. In all the subsequent applications for legislative relief, Jennison appears alone.

In the House of Representatives, on the 28th of January, 1782, a petition was read from Nathaniel Jennison, praying for leave to re-enter an appeal of an action against Quock Walker, which had been defaulted through the neglect of his counsel, at the Supreme Judicial Court next to be holden at Worcester. It was referred to Mr. Metcalf, Mr. Smead, and Mr. Chamberlain, who reported the same day a resolve granting his prayer, which was read and accepted, and sent up for concurrence. *Journal, Vol.* ii., 487, 492. The Senate, on the 14th of February, refused to concur, *Journal, Vol.* II., 263, but on the 5th of March paſſed a reſolve directing, on the petition of Jenniſon, that the petitioner ſerve the adverſe party with an atteſted copy of the Petition, and to ſhow cauſe. This reſolve was concurred in by the Houſe. *Ibid.*, 300. It is printed in the book of reſolves, March, 1782, *p.* 182.

On the 18th of April, 1782, this matter came up again in the Senate, Jenniſon having complied with the previous reſolve; and his petition, together with the anſwer of Quock Walker, was read. It was then "ordered, that Iſrael Nichols, Eſq., with ſuch as the Houſe ſhould join be a Committee to conſider this Petition and the Anſwer, hear the parties and report." On the following day, the Houſe concurred and appointed Meſſrs. Feſſenden and White upon the joint Committee. This committee of both Houſes preſented their report on the 29th of April, on which it was "Ordered that the Petition lie till ſufficient evidence be produced that the petitioner loſt his Law." *Senate Journal*, II., 344, 363. *Houſe Journal*, II., 676.

The next movement opens a wider view of the whole affair. In the Houſe of Repreſentatives, on the 18th of June, a new petition was preſented from Nathaniel Jenniſon, "ſetting forth that he was deprived of ten Negro Servants by a judgment of the Supreme Judicial Court on the following clauſe of the Conſtitution, 'That all men are born free and equal,' and praying that if ſaid judgment is approved of, he may be freed from his obligations to ſupport ſaid negroes." *Journal*, III., 99.

Jenniſon's original memorial, of which the notice

on the Journal is an abstract, is still preserved. He respectfully "shows that by the Bill of Rights prefixed to the Constitution of Government, it is among other things declared 'that all men are born free and equal,'—*which clause in the said Constitution has been the subject of much altercation and dispute—that the Judges of the Supreme Judicial Court have so construed the same as to deprive your memorialist of a great part of his property*, to which he thought his title good, not only by ancient and established usage, but by the Laws of the Land. That your Memorialist having been possessed of Ten Negro Servants, most of whom were born in his family, some of them young and helpless, others old and infirm, is now informed that by *the determination of the Supreme Judicial Court, the said Clause in the Bill of Rights is so to be construed, as to operate to the total discharge and manumission of all Negro Servants whatsoever*. What the true meaning of said Clause in the Constitution is, your Memorialist will not undertake to say, but it appears to him the operation thereof in manner aforementioned, is *very different from what the People apprehended at the time the same was established.*"

He argues that "they could not mean to offend the Southern States in so capital a point *with them*, and thereby to endanger the Union, and what is more, they could not mean to establish a doctrine repugnant and contradictory to the revealed word of God." He enforces the latter argument by abundant quotation from the 25th chapter of Leviticus; and concludes his memorial with an earnest appeal to the Legislature, that if servants are to be made free, their masters may also be emancipated—regarding the statute obligation to provide for the freedmen whenever they ſhould be in want, as a ſpecies of ſlavery alſo inconſiſtent with the Bill of Rights.

Jenniſon's Memorial was at once "committed to Colonel Pope, Mr. Stow, and Dr. Manning." *Journal*, III., 99. We find no further direct trace of it, but, three days afterward, a bill was introduced into the Houſe, entitled "an Act repealing an Act entitled an Act relating to Molatto and Negro ſlaves;" which was read a firſt time and referred to the next ſeſſion of the General Court. *Journal*, III., 418. The act thus propoſed to be repealed was the old Province Law of 1703, Chap. 2, whoſe proviſions in reſtraint of emancipation, etc., we have previouſly noticed (*ante, pp.* 53-4); and whoſe repeal would be in accordance with the alternative propoſition in the memorial of Jenniſon.

Whether they were ſtimulated by the new views of the ſubject in the Houſe, or "ſufficient evidence had been produced" to ſatisfy them that Jenniſon had "loſt his law," we cannot ſay; but on the 3d of July, 1782, the Senate paſſed another resolve, "on the petition of Nathaniel Jenniſon, permitting him to re-enter his appeal, etc., at the Supreme Judicial Court at Worceſter." They ſent it down for concurrence, but, this time, the Houſe refuſed to concur. *Senate Journal*, III., 109.

Having taken the initiative towards repealing the old laws concerning the rights and obligations of maſters and ſlaves, they may have thought it unneceſſary to promote judicial action, until the new ſyſtem ſhould be perfected. Nearly three months afterward, on the 26th of September, 1782, they sent a message to the Senate to request that the petition (and resolve thereon) of Mr. Nathaniel Jennison, "on the files of the Senate, might be sent down to the House, which was done. *House Journal,* III., 203. *Senate Journal,* III., 151. We find no further action of either branch of the Legislature on this petition.[1]

At the next session of the General Court, on the 7th of February, 1783, the bill for repealing the Act of 1703, which had been so referred, was brought up and read, and "Saturday, 10 o'clock, assigned for the second reading thereof." *House Journal,* III., 436. On the 8th, "the bill was taken up and debated. Whereupon it was ordered that Mr. Sedgwick, Gen. Ward, Mr. Dwight, Mr. Dane, and Mr. Cranch, be a Committee to bring in a bill upon the following principles:

    1st. Declaring that there never were legal slaves in this Government.

    2d. Indemnifying all Masters who have held slaves *in fact.*

    3d. To make such provisions for the support of Negroes and Molattoes as the Committee may find most expedient." *Ibid.*, 444.

---

[1] Nathaniel Jennison appears again with a petition in the House, on the 29th of May, 1784, praying that a judgment obtained against him in a court of law might be set aside. It was referred to a committee, who reported, on the 2d of June, 1784, a resolve granting its prayer. Debate ensued, and the resolve was re-committed. On the 4th of June, the committee reported another resolve for staying the execution therein mentioned in part, and granting a new trial. This was accepted and sent up for concurrence. *Journal*, v., 19–20, 30, 37. We have been unable to ascertain whether the judgment and execution referred to have any connection with the slave cases.

On the 28th of February, "a Bill intituled an Act refpecting Negroes and Molattoes was read the firft time, and Saturday, 10 o'clock, affigned for the fecond reading thereof." *Ibid.*, 529. It was read a fecond time on the firft of March; and, on the 4th, was read a third time, paffed to be engroffed, and fent up for concurrence. *Ibid.*, 537. In the Senate, on the 7th of March, "a Bill entitled 'An Act refpecting Negroes and Molattoes' was read the firft time, and ten o'clock to-morrow is affigned for the fecond reading." *Senate Journal*, III., 413.

But it never had that fecond reading; and this laft attempt in the legiflative annals of Maffachufetts, to provide, at the fame time, for the hiftory and law of flavery within her own borders, came to an untimely end, like all its predeceffors.

If the bill fhould be found, and its hiftory more fully explained, efpecially the caufes of its failure, much additional light may be thrown upon the ftate of public opinion in Maffachufetts on this fubject in 1783. As to the propofed declaration, that there never were *legal* flaves in Maffachufetts, we need only fay, that its authors could hardly have been familiar with all the facts of that hiftory which they thus determined to fum up in a contradiction. Neither that, nor the propofition to indemnify mafters for their loffes by emancipation from this illegal and illufive flavery, which never had any lawful exiftence, was ever heard of again in that day and generation. But the failure to make fuitable provifion for the fupport of Negroes and Mulattoes, led to ferious difficulties, great embarraffment in the law-courts and

Legiflature, conftant and continued litigation, in which the State authorities, towns, and individuals continued ftruggling until the last pauper Indian, negro, or mulatto, who had been a flave, relieved himfelf and the community by dying off.[1] It is a humiliating fact, which fhould not be omitted here, that the moft diftinct and permanent evidence of fervice of the colored patriots of the Revolution, belonging to Maffachufetts (moft of whom were or had been flaves), has been found in the reports of the law courts in pauper cafes.

Upon a comparifon of the condition of the negro in Maffachufetts, before and after emancipation, Dr. Belknap faid that, "unlefs *liberty* be reckoned as a compenfation for many inconveniencies and hard-

[1] Many petitions were prefented to the Legiflature concerning the support of pauper negroes. The committee on the revision of the laws were inftructed to report who was refponsible. *Journals*, IX., 85, 125. In 1790, the Houfe were requefted to decide whether they were chargeable to the State or Towns. *Ib.*, X., 230. In 1793, on the 8th of March, "a Bill determining Indians, Negroes, and Mulattoes, who are objects of charity, to be the poor of this commonwealth," was read in the Houfe, and committed to Mr. Sewall, Mr. Thompson, and Mr. Smead. *Mafs. Spy, March* 21, 1793. Dr. Belknap ftated, in 1795, that the queftion had not then been decided, either in the Legiflature or by the courts. M. H. S. *Coll.*, I., iv., 208. In the cafe of *Shelburne* vs. *Greenfield*, in Hampfhire, 1795, the court decided that certain flaves had gained a fettlement where their masters were fettled, and therefore were not chargeable on the commonwealth as State paupers. They gave no opinion on the point, whether they were to be the charge of the town, or of their late mafters; nor was this point decided when James Sullivan communicated the report of this cafe, with others, for publication in 1798. M. H. S. *Coll.*, I., v., 46, 47. In the cafe of *The Inhabitants of Shelburne* vs. *The Inhabitants of Greenfield*, 1795, the children of two negro flaves were confidered to have their fettlement in the latter town, becaufe their parents had a fettlement there under their mafter; although the parents were married, and their children born, in Shelburne. MS. *referred to in Andover* vs. *Canton*, 13 *Mafs. Reports*, 552.

ships, the former condition" was in moſt caſes preferable. This was in 1795. In 1846 a Maſſachuſetts author wrote as follows reſpecting their deſcendants remaining in the State:

"A prejudice has exiſted in the community, and ſtill exiſts againſt them on account of their color, and on account of their being the deſcendants of ſlaves. They cannot obtain employment on equal terms with the whites, and wherever they go a ſneer is paſſed upon them, as if this ſportive inhumanity were an act of merit. They have been, and are, moſtly ſervants, or doomed to accept ſuch menial employment as the whites decline. They have been, and are, ſcattered over the Commonwealth, one or more in over two thirds of all the towns; they continue poor, with ſmall means and opportunities for enjoying the ſocial comforts and advantages which are ſo much at the command of the whites. Thus, though their legal rights are the ſame as thoſe of the whites, their condition is one of degradation and dependence, and renders exiſtence leſs valuable, and impairs the duration of life itſelf. . . . Owing to their color and the prejudice againſt them, they can hardly be ſaid to receive . . . even ſo cordial a ſympathy as would be ſhown to them in a *ſlave* ſtate, owing to their different poſition in ſociety." *Chickering's Statistical View*, *p.* 156. In view of theſe facts, it will hardly be deemed ſtrange, that the ſame writer calmly contemplated their extinction as a race, comforting himſelf with the reflection, that "many inſtances of ſimilar diſplacement are to be found in hiſtory." *Ibid., pp.* 159–60.

X.

We have ſtill to notice two acts of legiſlation in Maſſachuſetts, which were paſſed in the year 1788— eight years after the alleged termination of ſlavery in that State by the adoption of the Conſtitution. Theſe acts were paſſed juſt after the adoption of the Federal Conſtitution by the State Convention.

The firſt is the only one directly and poſitively hoſtile to ſlavery to be found among all their ſtatutes. It is a very remarkable fact that the reluctance of the Legiſlature to meet the ſubject fairly and fully in front ſhould have left their ſtatute-book in ſo queſtionable a ſhape. With Portia, glowing with delight at the unſucceſsful choice of her ſable ſuitor, they ſeem to have wiſhed to ſay,

> "A gentle riddance: draw the curtains; go—
> Let all of his complexion chuſe me ſo."
> *Merchant of Venice*, Act II., Sc. VIII.

But neither the cupidity of their ſlave-trading merchants, nor the peculiar improvidence of the negro —the one ſharpened by ſucceſsful gain, the other hardened into hopeleſs acquieſcence with pauperiſm— would permit this "gentle riddance," and although the "curtains" have been "drawn" over theſe disagreeable features for nearly a century, the hiſtorian of ſlavery muſt let in the light upon them.

As early as 1785, the Legiſlature inſtituted an inquiry as to the meaſures proper to be adopted by them to diſcountenance and prevent any inhabitant of the Commonwealth being concerned in the ſlave-trade. A joint committee was appointed on the subject, Jan. 25th, 1785—William Heath and John Lowell on the part of the Senate, and Mr. Reed, Mr. Hofmer, and Mr. Sprague, of the Houfe. The inquiry was alfo extended to the condition of negroes then in the Commonwealth, or who might thereafter come or be brought into it. *H. of R. Journals,* v., 222. Bills were prepared and referred to the Committee on the Revifion of the Laws, with inftruction to revife all the laws refpecting negroes and mulattoes, and report at the next fitting of the General Court. *Ib.*, 342.

In the following year, March 1, 1786, a joint order was made for a committee to report meafures for preventing negroes coming into the Commonwealth from other States. *H. of R. Journals,* vi., 463. Another similar order was made by the Houfe of Reprefentatives in 1787. *Journals,* vii., 524.

Earlier in the fame year, February 4, 1787, a number of African blacks petitioned the Legiflature for aid to enable them to return to their native country. *Ib.*, vii., 381. A Quaker petition againft the flave-trade was read in the Senate, June 20, 1787, and not accepted, but referred to the Revifing Committee, who were directed to report a bill upon "the fubject matter of negroes in this Commonwealth at large." *Senate, Vol.* viii., 81. *H. of R., Vol.* viii., 88.

The prohibition of the flave-trade by Maffachufetts was at laft effected in 1788. A moft flagrant and outrageous cafe of kidnapping occurred in Bofton in the month of February, in that year. *M. H. S. Coll.*, I., iv., 204. Additional particulars may be found by reference to the newfpapers of the day. Efpecially

The N. Y. Packet, Feb. 26 and *Aug.* 29, 1788. This infamous tranfaction aroufed the public indignation, and all claffes united in urging upon the Legiflature the paffage of effectual laws to prevent the further profecution of the traffic, and protect the inhabitants of the State againft the repetition of fimilar outrages.

Rev. Dr. Jeremy Belknap was one of the foremoft in promoting the paffage of this act. He confulted fome of his friends as to the practicability of improving the occafion to effect the abolition of flavery in the State. His brother-in-law, Mr. Samuel Eliot, agreed with him that the time was moft opportune, but faid the difficulty in fuch cafes was, who fhould ftep forward,—and recommended him to fuggeft to the Affociation of minifters, at their next meeting, a petition to the General Court, whofe feffion was then about to commence; if he failed to gain the co-operation of the minifters, to apply to the Humane Society, and at all events to have a petition drafted.

Mr. Belknap drew up a petition, which his friends pronounced "incapable of amendment," gained the fupport of the Affociation, and of a large number of citizens befides. The blacks alfo prefented a petition,[1] written by Prince Hall, one of their number, and there was alfo that of the Quakers in 1787, already noticed, before the Legiflature. *Life of Belknap*, 159, 160.

The movement was fuccefsful, and on the 26th of March, 1788, the Legiflature of Maffachufetts paffed

---

[1] The petition of the negroes, 27th February, 1788, is in the Maffachufetts Spy, 24th April, 1788.

"*An Act to prevent the Slave-Trade, and for granting Relief to the Families of such unhappy Persons as may be Kidnapped or decoyed away from this Commonwealth.*" By this law it was enacted "that no citizen of this Commonwealth, or other person residing within the same," shall import, transport, buy, or sell any of the inhabitants of Africa as slaves or servants for term of years, on penalty of fifty pounds for every person so misused, and two hundred pounds for every vessel fitted out and employed in the traffic. All insurance made on such vessels to be void, and of no effect. And to meet the case of kidnapping, when inhabitants were carried off, actions of damage might be brought by their friends—the latter giving bonds to apply the moneys recovered to the use and maintenance of the family of the injured party.

A proviso was added, "*That this act do not extend to vessels which have already sailed, their owners, factors, or commanders, for, and during their present voyage, or to any insurance that shall have been made, previous to the passing of the same.*" How far this proviso may be justly held to be a legislative sanction of the traffic, we leave the reader to decide. It is obvious that the "public sentiment" of Massachusetts in 1788 was not strong enough against the slave-trade, even under the atrocious provocation of kidnapping in the streets of Boston, to treat the pirates, who had already sailed, as they deserved. Rome was not built in a day,— neither could the modern Athens rejoice in an anti-slavery Minerva, fresh in an instant from the brain of the almighty "public sentiment" of Massachusetts.

This act, as we have seen, passed on the 25th of March, 1788. It was accompanied by another act, passed on the following day, hardly less hostile to the negro than this was to slavery—the pioneer of a series of similar acts (though less severe) which have subjected the new States to most unsparing censure.

The Massachusetts Law, entitled "*An act for suppressing and punishing of Rogues, Vagabonds, common Beggars, and other idle, disorderly, and lewd Persons,*" was presented in the Senate on the 6th of March, 1788. It went through the usual stages of legislation, with various amendments, and was finally passed on the 26th of March, 1788. It contains the following very remarkable provision :

"V. *Be it further enacted by the authority aforesaid* [the Senate and House of Representatives in General Court assembled], that no person being an African or Negro, other than a subject of the Emperor of Morocco, or a citizen of some one of the United States (to be evidenced by a certificate from the Secretary of the State of which he shall be a citizen), shall tarry within this Commonwealth, for a longer time than two months, and upon complaint made to any Justice of the Peace within this Commonwealth, that any such person has been within the same more than two months, the said Justice shall order the said person to depart out of this Commonwealth, and in case that the said African or Negro shall not depart as aforesaid, any Justice of the Peace within this Commonwealth, upon complaint and proof made that such person has continued within this Commonwealth ten days after notice given him or her to depart as aforesaid, shall commit the said person to any house of correction within the county, there to be kept to hard labour, agreeable to the rules and orders of the said house, until the Sessions of the Peace, next to be holden within and for the said county; and the master of the said house of correction is hereby required and directed to transmit an attested copy of the warrant of commitment to the said Court on the first day of their said session, and if upon trial at the said Court, it shall be made to appear that the said person has thus continued within the Commonwealth, contrary to the tenor of this act, he or she shall be whipped not exceeding ten stripes, and ordered to depart out of this Commonwealth within ten days; and if he or she shall not so depart, the same process shall be had and punishment inflicted, and so *toties quoties*." [1]

The edition from which we copy is the earliest classified edition of "The Perpetual Laws of the Commonwealth of Massachusetts," and is not to be found in Part I. among those relating to "The Publick and Private Rights of Persons," nor among the "Miscellaneous" Statutes, but in "Part IV.," concerning "*Criminal* Matters." We doubt if anything in human legislation can be found which comes nearer branding color as a crime!

By this law, it will be observed that all negroes,

---

[1] The old provincial statute, from which this law was mainly copied, provided for the correction by whipping, etc., of the rogues and vagabonds (without distinction of color) for whose benefit the original law was designed; but in the progress of this law through the Legislature, this feature was stricken out of that portion of the bill, but the "African or Negro" gained what the "rogue and vagabond" lost by the change. Compare *Mass. Prov. Laws of* 1699, *Chap.* VI., and *Journal of H. of R.*, VIII., 500.

refident in Maffachufetts, not citizens of fome one of the States, were required to depart in two months, on penalty of being apprehended, whipped, and ordered to depart. The procefs and punifhment could be renewed every two months. The only contemporary explanation of the defign of the law which we have met with is to the effect that it was intended to prevent fugitive flaves from reforting to that State, in hopes to obtain freedom, and then being thrown as a deadweight upon that community. *Belknap*, 1795. A recent writer ftates that this "enactment was faid to have been the work of her [Maffachufetts] leading lawyers, who were fufficiently fagacious to forefee the dangerous confequences of that conftitutional provision which, on reftoring fugitives from labor, not only threatened to difturb the public peace, but the ftability of the fyftem." *Amory's Life of Sullivan*, I., 226, *note*. We give this illuftration of legal fagacity in Maffachufetts for what it is worth, although we are fatisfied that the ftatute itfelf clearly illuftrates the intention of thofe who framed it. *Expofitio contemporanea eft optima.*

Realizing the "deadweight" already refting upon them in the body of their own free negroes (though comparatively fmall in number), they evidently thought it "fagacious" to prevent any addition to it. Future refearch muft afcertain who were "citizens" of Maffachufetts in 1788, before we can fafely declare that even Maffachufetts Negroes, Indians, and Mulattoes, were exempted from the alternative of exile or the penalties of this ftatute. The reader will not fail to notice below, the arbitrary and illegal extenfion of the ftatute, in its application to "people of color, commonly called Mulattoes, *prefumed* to come within the *intention* " of the law.

We have met with one example of the enforcement of this law, which is almoft as "fingular" as the ftatute itfelf. In the *Maffachufetts Mercury, Boston, printed by Young and Minns, Printers to the Honorable the General Court, September* 16, 1800, *No.* 22, *Vol.* XVI., the following notice occupies a confpicuous place, filling a column of the paper:

NOTICE TO BLACKS.

THE Officers of Police having made return to the Subfcriber of the names of the following perfons, who are Africans or Negroes, not fubjects of the Emperor of *Morocco* nor citizens of the *United States,* the fame are hereby warned and directed to depart out of this Commonwealth before the 10th day of October next, as they would avoid the pains and penalties of the law in that cafe provided, which was paffed by the Legislature, March 26, 1788.

CHARLES BULFINCH,
Superintendant.
By order and direction of the Selectmen.

OF PORTSMOUTH.

Prince Patterson,	Eliza Cotton,
Flora Nafh.	

RHODE ISLAND.

Thomas Nichols and	Philis Nichols,
Hannah Champlin,	Plato Alderfon,
Raney Scott,	Jack Jeffers,
Thomas Gardner,	Julius Holden,
Violet Freeman,	Cuffy Buffum,
Sylvia Gardner,	Hagar Blackburn,
Dolly Peach,	Polly Gardner,
Sally Alexander,	Philis Taylor.

PROVIDENCE.

Dinah Miller, Silvia Hendrick,
Rhode Allen, Nancy Hall,
Richard Freeman, Elizabeth Freeman,
Nancy Gardner, Margaret Harrison.

CONNECTICUT.

Bristol Morandy, John Cooper,
Scipio Kent, Margaret Russell,
Phœbe Seamore, Phœbe Johnson,
Jack Billings.

NEW LONDON.

John Denny, Thomas Burdine,
Hannah Burdine.

NEW YORK.

Sally Evens, Sally Freeman,
Cæsar West and Hannah West,
Thomas Peterson, Thomas Santon,
Henry Sanderson, Henry Wilson,
Robert Willet, Edward Cole,
Mary Atkins, Polly Brown,
Amey Spalding, John Johnson,
Rebecca Johnson, George Homes,
Prince Kilsbury, Abraham Fitch,
Joseph Hicks, Abraham Francis,
Elizabeth Francis, Sally Williams,
William Williams, Rachel Pewinck,
David Dove, Esther Dove,
Peter Bayle, Thomas Bostick,
Katy Bostick, Prince Hayes,
Margaret Bean, Nancy Hamik,
Samuel Benjamin, Peggy Ocamum,
Primus Hutchinson.

PHILADELPHIA.

Mary Smith, Richard Allen,
Simon Jeffers, Samuel Posey,
Peter Francies, Prince Wales,
Elizabeth Branch, Peter Gust,
William Brown, Butterfield Scotland,

Clariſſa Scotland,   Cuffy Cummings,
John Gardner,   Sally Gardner,
Fortune Gorden,   Samuel Stevens.

BALTIMORE.

Peter Larkin and   Jenny Larkin,
Stepney Johnſon,   Anne Melville.

VIRGINIA.

James Scott,   John Evens,
Jane Jackſon,   Cuffey Cook,
Oliver Naſh,   Robert Woodſon,
Thomas Thompſon.

NORTH CAROLINA.

James Jurden,   Polly Johnſon,
Janus Crage.

SOUTH CAROLINA.

Anthony George,   Peter Cane.

HALIFAX.

Catherine Gould,   Charlotte Gould,
Cato Small,   Philis Cole,
Richard M'Coy.

WEST INDIES.

James Morfut and   Hannah, his wife,
Mary Davis,   George Powell,
Peter Lewis,   Charles Sharp,
Peter Hendrick,   William Shoppo and
Mary Shoppo,   Iſaac Johnſon,
John Pearce,   Charles Eſings,
Peter Branch,   Newell Symonds,
Roſanna Symonds,   Peter George,
Lewis Victor,   Lewis Sylveſter,
John Laco,   Thomas Foſter,
Peter Jeſemy,   Rebecca Jeſemy,
David Bartlet,   Thomas Grant,
Joſeph Lewis,   Hamet Lewis,
John Harriſon,   Mary Brown,
Boſton Alexander.

CAPE FRANCOIS.

Caſme Franciſco and Nancy, his wife,
Mary Fraceway.

AUX CAYES.
Sufannah Rofs.
PORT AU PRINCE.
John Short.
JAMAICA.
Charlotte Morris,   John Robinfon.
BERMUDA.
Thomas Williams.
NEW PROVIDENCE.
Henry Taylor.
LIVERPOOL.
John Mumford.

AFRICA.
Francis Thompfon,   John Brown,
Mary Jofeph,   James Melvile,
Samuel Bean,   Hamlet Earl,
Calo Gardner,   Charles Mitchel,
Sophia Mitchel,   Samuel Frazier,
Samuel Blackburn,   Timothy Philips,
Jofeph Ocamum.

FRANCE.
Jofeph ———
ISLE OF FRANCE.
Jofeph Lovering.

List of INDIANS and MULATTOES.

The following perfons from feveral of the *United States*, being people of colour, commonly called Mulattoes, are prefumed to come within the intention of the fame law; and are accordingly warned and directed to depart out of the Commonwealth before the 10th day of October next.

RHODE ISLAND.
Peter Badger,   Kelurah Allen,
Waley Green,   Silvia Babcock.
PROVIDENCE.
Polly Adams,   Paul Jones.

Slavery in Massachusetts.

CONNECTICUT.

John Brown,
John Way and
Peter Virginia,
Lucinda Orange,
Britton Doras,
Frank Francies.

Polly Holland,
Nancy Way,
Leville Steward,
Anna Sprague,
Amos Willis,

NEW-LONDON.
Hannah Potter.

NEW-YORK.

Jacob and Nelly Cummings,
John Schumagger,
Peggy Willouby,
Mary Reading,
John Miles,
Betſy Harris,
Suſannah Foſter,
Mary Thomſon,
Lucy Glapcion,
Eliza Williams,
Cæſar and Sylvia Caton,
William Guin.

James and Rebecca Smith,
Judith Chew,
Thomas Willouby,
John Reading,
Charles Brown,
Hannah Williams,
Duglaſs Brown,
Thomas Burros,
James and Freelove Buck,
Lucy Lewis,
Diana Bayle,
—— Thompſon,

ALBANY.

Elone Virginia,
Lydia Reed,
Rebecca Reed and

Abijah Reed and
Abijah Reed, Jr.,
Betſy Reed.

NEW-JERSEY.

Stephen Boadley,
Hannah Victor.

PHILADELPHIA.

Polly Boadley,
Hannah Murray,
Nancy Principeſo,
George Jackſon,
Moſes Long.

James Long,
Jeremiah Green,
David Johnſon,
William Coak,

MARYLAND.
Nancy Guſt.

BALTIMORE.

John Clark,	Sally Johnſon.

VIRGINIA.

Sally Hacker,	Richard,
John Johnſon,	Thomas Steward,
Anthony Paine,	Mary Burk,
William Hacker,	Polly Loſours,
Betſy Guin,	Lucy Brown.

AFRICA.

Nancy Doras.[1]

This notice muſt have been generally publiſhed in Boſton, and was copied in other cities without the liſt of names. We have met with it in the Commercial Advertiſer of the 20th September, 1800, and the Daily Advertiſer, 22d September, 1800, both in New York. Alſo in the Gazette of the United States and Daily Advertiſer of 23d September, 1800, in Philadelphia.

The only comments of the Boſton preſs on the ſubject which we have ſeen indicate that it was simply carrying out the original deſign of the act, to abate pauperiſm;[2] but references to it in the New York and Philadelphia papers hint at another probable cauſe

---

[1] Mr. Nell, in his work on the Colored Patriots of the American Revolution, notices (pp. 96-97), an African Benevolent Society, inſtituted at Boſton, in 1796. He ſays, its benevolent objects were ſet forth in the preamble, which alſo expressed its loyalty as follows: " Behaving ourſelves, at the ſame time, as true and faithful citizens of the Commonwealth in which we live, and that we take no one into the Society who ſhall commit any injuſtice or outrage againſt the laws of their country." He adds a liſt of the members of the " African Society." A compariſon of this liſt with that above ſhows that one fourth of the members were driven out of the Commonwealth in 1800.

[2] See " Africanus," in The Independent Chronicle and the Univerſal Advertiſer, Boſton, September 25, 1800.

of this ftringent and fweeping application of the ftatute.

In the year 1800, the whole country was excited by the difcovery of an alleged plot for a general infurrection of negroes at the South. Gabriel, the negro-general, was the "hero," though not the only victim. The affair affumed at once a very ferious afpect, and the alarm was "awful" in Virginia and South Carolina. The party violence of the day was not flow to make ufe of it, and it was doubtlefs true, that the principles of Liberty and Equality had been in fome degree infufed into the minds of the negroes, and that the incautious and intemperate ufe of thefe words by the "fierce democracie" of that day in Virginia may have infpired them with hopes of fuccefs.

But the alarm was not confined to Virginia. Even in Bofton, fears were expreffed and meafures of prevention adopted. *N. Y. Advertifer, Sept.* 26, 1800. The Gazette of the United States and Daily Advertifer, by C. P. Wayne, Vol. xviii., No. 2493, Philadelphia, September 23, 1800, copies the "Notice" with thefe remarks:

" The following notice has been publifhed in the Bofton papers: It feems probable, from the nature of the notice, that fome fufpicions of the defign of the negroes are entertained, and we regret to fay there is too much caufe."

Such was the act, and fuch was one of its applications. Additional acts were paffed in 1798 and 1802, but this portion was neither modified nor repealed. It appears in the revifed edition of 1807, without change. In 1821, the Legiflature of Maffachufetts, alarmed by "the increafe of a fpecies of population, which threatened to become both injurious and burdenfome," and, fully alive to "the neceffity of checking" it, appointed a committee to report a bill concerning the admiffion into the State of free Negroes and Mulattoes.

In the Houfe of Reprefentatives, June 7, 1821, it was "Ordered, that Meffrs. Lyman of Bofton, Bridgeman of Belchertown, Chandler of Lexington, be a Committee to take into confideration the expediency of making any alterations in the laws of this Commonwealth concerning the admiffion into a refidence in this State of Negroes and Mulattoes, with leave to report by bill or otherwife." *Journals, Vol.* XLII., 62. On the 14th of June, the journal notes a Report on the Free Negroes, detailing a ftatement of facts, and authorizing the appointment of a committee to report a bill at the next feffion. Read and accepted, and the fame gentlemen were appointed. *Ibid.*, 121. On the next day, the Houfe refufed to reconfider the vote for a committee, etc. *Ibid.*, 129.

At the next feffion, on the 15th of January, 1822, a "report of the Committee appointed at the laft feffion concerning the admiffion into this State of Free Negroes, praying to be difcharged from that fubject, was read, and the fame was ordered to lie on the table. The fame was afterwards accepted." *Ibid.*, 174.

This report, written by Theodore Lyman, Jr., chairman of the Committee, was printed. It juftifies the motive which induced the appointment of the Committee by the following ftatements: "that the black convicts in the State Prison, on the first of January, 1821, formed 146½ part of the black population of the State, while the white convicts, at the same time, formed but 2140 part of the white population. It is believed that a similar proportion will be found to exist in all public establishments of this State; as well Prisons as Poor-Houses." The Committee, however, "found it impossible, after all the research and deliberation in their power to bestow on the subject, to accomplish that duty which they undertook by the direction of the House of Representatives. They have not succeeded in preparing a bill, *the provisions of which they could conscientiously vindicate to this House. They have already found in the Statute Books of this Commonwealth, a law passed in* 1788, *regulating the residence in this State of certain persons of color—they believe that this law has never been enforced, and, ineffectual as it has proved, they would never have been the authors of placing among the Statutes, a law so arbitrary in its principles, and in its operation so little accordant with the institutions, feelings, and practices of the people of this Commonwealth.* The History of that law has well convinced the Committee that no measure (which they could devise) would be attended with the smallest good consequence. That it would have been matter of satisfaction and congratulation to the Committee if they had succeeded in framing a law, which should have received the approbation of this Legislature, and should have promised to check and finally to overcome an evil upon which they have never been able to look with unconcern. But a law, which should produce that effect, would entirely depart from that love of humanity, that respect for hospitality and for the just rights of all classes of men, in the constant and successful exercise of which, the inhabitants of Massachusetts have been singularly conspicuous."[1]

The committee, however, did not recommend a repeal of the act of 1788. Is it possible to avoid the inference that the true reason of their failure to report a new bill, such as they were instructed to prepare, was that they considered the State amply protected by the old law?

It appears again in the revised laws of 1823. Another additional act was passed in 1825, but without alteration of the provision against negroes; and this statute, "so arbitrary in its principle, and in its operation so little accordant with the institutions, feelings and practices of the people of the Commonwealth," continued to disgrace the Statute-Book of Massachusetts until the first day of April, 1834, after which time

---

[1] Although this committee did not accomplish their assigned task, they did achieve a further report, by way of addition, which deserves notice. They agreed that "it does not comport with the dignity of this State, to withhold that brief statement of facts, to be found in its annals, concerning the abolition of this trade in Massachusetts—a statement which will prove both highly honorable, and in perfect accordance with that remarkable spirit of wholesome and rational liberty, by which this Commonwealth has been greatly distinguished from the earliest period. But to the clear understanding and better elucidation of this subject, the committee think it useful to introduce the following short account of the existence of Slavery in Massachusetts." In the elaborate statement which follows, there are no important facts which are not already familiar to the reader of these notes; but there is one idea which has, at least, the merit of novelty. After giving the general statistics of the slave population, down to the time of the Revolution, they say, "These slaves were procured in several ways—*either from the Dutch, in New York,* from the Southern provinces in North America . . . Few came by a direct trade," etc.

its undiftinguifhed repeal, (in the general repealing fection of an act of March 29th, 1834, for the regulation of Gaols and Houfes of Correction,) no longer left "public opinion" to regulate its enforcement.

And here we reft. With the exception of the repeal, already mentioned, *ante*, *p.* 59, of the law prohibiting the intermarriage of whites with Indians, Negroes, or Mulattoes, and the obfcure ftatute of 1863, which terminated the long exclufion of the latter from the ranks of the State militia, and perhaps obliterated the laft veftige of the formal legiflation of Maffachufetts againft them, there is nothing in the fubfequent hiftory or politics of the State relating to the fubject of thefe Notes. The anti-flavery agitations of the laft thirty years, in which Maffachufetts has borne fo confpicuous a part, have little if any hiftorical connection with the exiftence of Slavery in that Commonwealth. As "agreed on all hands," it was undoubtedly "confidered as abolifhed;" and during thefe ftormy and portentous contefts which have changed the hiftory of the nation, it has been "put afide and covered," and "remembered only as forgotten."

The reader of thefe Notes cannot fail to notice the ftrong refemblance in the mode of the extinction of flavery in Maffachufetts and that of villenage in

England. Of the latter Lord Mansfield faid, in 1785, that "villains in grofs may in point of law fubfift at this day. But the change of manners and cuftoms has effectually abolifhed them in point of fact." *Ante*, p. 115, *note*. If the parallel may be continued, it could be faid with equal juftice that flavery, having never been formally prohibited by legiflation in Maffachufetts, continued to "fubfift in point of law" until the year 1866, when the grand Conftitutional Amendment terminated it forever throughout the limits of the United States. It would be not the leaft remarkable of the circumftances connected with this ftrange and eventful hiftory, that, although *virtually* abolifhed before, the actual prohibition of flavery in Maffachufetts as well as Kentucky, fhould be accomplifhed by the votes of South Carolina and Georgia.

APPENDIX.

A. The Military Employment of Negroes in Massachusetts.

The neceffities of the fituation, for a few years after the firft fettlements, made everybody a foldier; indeed, put arms in the hands of women and children.

The General Court made an order on the 27th of May, 1652, "that all Scotfmen, Negeres and Indians inhabiting with or fervants to the Englifh from the age of fixteen to fixty years, fhal be lifted, and are hereby enjoyned to attend traynings as well as the Englifh." At the feffion in May, 1656, however, this order was repealed, fo far as it related to negroes and Indians, as follows :

" For the better ordering and fettling of feverall cafes in the military companyes within this jurifdiction, which, upon experience, are found either wanting or inconvenient, it is ordered and declared by this Court and the authoritie thereof, that henceforth no negroes or Indians, although fervants to the Englifh, fhal be armed or permitted to trayne, and y^t no other perfon fhall be exempted from trayning but fuch as fome law doth priviledge, or fome of the county courts or courts of affiftants, after notice of the partyes defires, to the officers of each company to which they belonge, upon juft caufe, fhal difmifs."

The law, as printed in 1660, required "every perfon above the age of fixteen years," to "duely attend all Military Exercife and fervice," with certain exceptions. Neither Indians, Negroes, or Slaves are among thofe exempted; but it is reafonably certain that they were at no time permitted to bear arms during the period from 1656 down to the commencement of the Revolution. Gov. Bradftreet, in May, 1680, expreffly ftates, in anfwer to an inquiry from the Committee for Trade and Plantations as to the number of men able to bear arms—

" We account all generally from fixteen to fixty that are healthfull and strong bodys, both Housholders and Servants fit to bear Armes, *except Negros and Slaves, whom wee arme not." M. H. S. Coll.,* III., viii., 336.

The next enactment on the subject was in the brief administration of Sir Edmund Andros. The Act for settling the militia, enacted by this very unpopular Governor and his Council for his Majesty's territory and dominion of New England, March 24, 1687, provided " that no person whatsoever above sixteen years of age remain unlisted by themselves, masters, mistresses or employers." Negroes and Indians are not exempted by any provision of this act; but it is extremely doubtful whether it ever went into practical operation. One of the most obnoxious of his measures was his attempt to control the militia in New England. This is, however, not very important; for after the English Revolution and the establishment of the new Province charter, among the earliest of the laws was the act for regulating the militia— 1693—by which Indians and negroes were exempted from all trainings. In Sewall's tract against slavery in 1700 (*ante, p.* 84), he says, " As many Negro Men as there are among us, so many empty places are there in our Train Bands." A later publication in the Boston News Letter, June 10th, 1706, shows that " Negroes do not carry Arms to defend the Country as Whites do," and further, that they could not be employed as substitutes for whites who were impressed or drafted, (*ante, p.* 107.)

A subsequent act for the regulating of free negroes, &c.,—1707— illustrates their exact position more clearly. The recital in the preamble is that

" Whereas, in the several towns and precincts within this province, there are several free negroes, and mulattoes able of body, and fit for labor ; who are not charged with trainings, watches, and other services required of her Majestie's subjects ; whereof they have share in the benefit," &c.

The act, therefore, provided that they should do service equivalent to trainings, &c., each able-bodied free negro or mulatto so many days' work yearly in repairing of the highways, cleansing the streets, or other service for the common benefit of the place. See *ante, pp.* 60, 61.

In common with all able to bear arms, they were required to make their appearance at parade in cases of sudden alarms, where they were to attend such service as the first commissioned officer of the military company of their precinct should direct, during the time the company continued in arms. This obviously points to menial service, or, at any rate, a service different from that of the enrolled militia.

This state of things continued down to the commencement of the war of the Revolution, and the first contemporary act shows that negroes could not be legally enrolled at that time. The general militia act of 1775, in providing for the enrolment, excepts "Negroes, Indians, and mulattoes." The act of May, 1776, providing for a reinforcement to the American army, provides that "Indians, negroes, and mulattoes, shall not be held to take up arms or procure any person to do it in their room." The act of November 14, 1776, to provide reinforcements to the American army, excepts "Negroes, Indians, and mulattoes," and the explanatory resolve passed on the 29th of the same month also excepts "Indians, negroes, mulattoes, &c." The resolve in the same year for taking the number of all male inhabitants above sixteen years of age excepts "Indians, negroes, and mulattoes." This census was doubtless taken with a view to the approaching necessity for a draft, and even here they are excluded, although they were apparently included in the poll-lists at the same time—being rateable polls, if not free citizens.

It was only when the pressure of the terrible reverses of the winter of 1776-7 came that they were included in the number of persons liable to draft. The resolve, January 6, 1777, was "for raising every seventh man to complete our quota," and "without any exceptions, save the people called Quakers"—one seventh of all male persons of sixteen years old and upwards. A resolve in August of the same year was similar in its object and character. But this proceeding was not allowed to pass without remonstrance, not by the negroes, but the white men. In the Massachusetts Legislature, March 5, 1778, a petition of Benjamin Goddard in behalf of the selectmen, committee of safety, and militia officers of the town of Grafton, praying that they may be excused from raising a seventh part of the blacks in said town, they being exempt from military duty and free occupants on their own estate, was read, and the petitioner had leave to withdraw his petition.

During the remainder of the war the law appears to have regarded as liable to military duty "any person living or residing in any town or plantation within this State the term of three months together;" but at the same time, although they had the benefit of the example of

Rhode Ifland in the organization of their famous regiment of negro flaves, an attempt in Maffachufetts to authorize the formation of a fimilar corps "does not appear to have been deemed advifable at the time."

The war came to an end, and, foon after, the very firft general militia act, paffed March 10, 1785, revived the old feature, and continued the exemption of "negroes, Indians, and mulattoes" from both train-band and alarm-lift. In the time of the infurrection in 1786, negroes offered their fervices to Governor Bowdoin, to go againft the infurgents, to the number of feven hundred; but the Council did not advife fending them.

The fubftance of the next law is the fame, although they changed the "way of putting it" by adopting the language of the United States law, in which negroes do not appear among the exempts, but are excluded in the enrolment.

The militia law of June 22, 1793, authorizes the enrolment of "each and every free, able-bodied white male citizen of this, or any other of the United States, refiding within this Commonwealth," between the ages of eighteen and forty-five years, fave as excepted.

This exclufion from military employment, and the privilege of bearing arms, continued apparently without change until the year 1863, when, by Chapter 193 of the Acts of that year, approved April 27, 1863, the Maffachufetts laws were made to conform to thofe of the United States, which had already recognized and accepted the negro as a foldier.

B. Additional Notes, Etc.

1. *Page* 21. On the 9th of November, 1716, P. M., was prefented to the Houfe of Reprefentatives of Maffachufetts "a Petition of *William Brown*, fon of a Freeman, by a Servant Woman, and has been fold as a flave, and is at prefent owned by Mr. *Andrew Boardman*, fhowing that his faid Mafter will fet him at liberty, and make him Free, if this Court will indemnify him from the Law relating to the Manumiffion of Negroes, as to maintaining of him in cafe of Age, Difability etc., Praying the Court to indemnify him."

On the following day, this Petition was "further confidered, and the following Vote paffed thereon, viz.: Inafmuch as the Petitioner is a young able-bodied Man, and it cannot be fuppofed, that he is Manumitted, by his Master, to avoid charge in supporting him, *Ordered*, that the Prayer of the Petitioner be Granted. And that the Petitioner be deemed Free, when set at liberty by his Master, although no security be given to indemnify the Town where he dwells from charge by him, and in case the Petitioner shall hereafter want Support, his said Master shall not be obliged to be at the charge thereof, any Law, Usage, or Custom to the contrary notwithstanding." This order was sent up for concurrence, concurred in and consented to by the Governor on the same day, November 10th, 1716. *Journal H. of R.*, *p.* 36. *General Court Records*, x., *p.* 108.

2. *Page* 51. Massachusetts has enjoyed the distinction of appearing in the first Census of the United States without any slaves among her population.

" The following anecdote connected with this subject, it is believed, has never been made public. In 1790 a census was ordered by the General Government then newly established, and the Marshal of the Massachusetts district had the care of making the survey. When he inquired for *slaves*, most people answered none : if any one said that he had one, the marshal would ask him if he meant to be singular, and would tell him that no other person had given in any. The answer then was, "If none are given in, I will not be singular;" and thus the list was completed without any number in the column for slaves." *Life of Belknap, pp.* 164–5.

Dr. Belknap's own account of this census, written and published in 1795, is as follows :

"In 1790, a census of the United States was made by order of the federal government; the schedule sent out on that occasion contained three columns for free whites of several descriptions, which, in the State of Massachusetts and district of Maine, amounted to 469,326; a fourth for "all other free persons," and a fifth for " slaves." There being none put into the last column, it became necessary to put the *blacks*, with the *Indians*, into the fourth column, and the amount was 6001. Of this number, I suppose the blacks were upwards of 4000; and of the remaining 2000, many were a mixed breed, between Indians and blacks . . . . In the same census, as hath been before observed, no slaves are set down to Massachusetts. This return, made by the marshal of the district, may be considered as the formal evidence of the *abolition of slavery* in Massachusetts, especially as no person has appeared to conteſt the legality of the return." *M. H. S. Coll.*, i., iv., 199, 204.

3. *Page* 53. In 1718, a committee of both Houſes prepared a bill entitled "An Act for the Encouraging the Importation of White Male Servants, and the preventing the Clandeſtine bringing in of Negroes and Molattoes." It was read in Council a firſt time on the 16th of June, and "ſent down recommended" to the Houſe, where it was alſo read a firſt time on the ſame day. The next day it was read a ſecond time, and "on the queſtion for a third reading, decided in the negative." *Journal H. of R.*, 15, 16. *General Court Records*, x., 282.

4. *Pages* 54, 90. The Act of 1705, Chapter 6, underwent ſome changes in the Council, after it had paſſed in the Houſe. It was read in Council on Monday the 3d of December, 1705, a firſt time, "as paſſ'd in the Houſe of Repreſentatives." The next day it was read a ſecond and third time "with ſome Amendments and Additions agreed to." On the 5th it was "Read and Voted to be paſſed into an Act." *General Court Records*, viii., 187, 188, 190.

5. *Page* 61. A draft of Governor Dudley's letter "concerning Indian Captives from Carolina," was preſented and approved in the Houſe of Repreſentatives on the 15th of June, 1715. *Journal*, 28.

6. *Page* 65. A recent examination of the collection of Tax-Acts in the poſſeſſion of Ellis Ames, Eſq., of Canton, Maſſachuſetts, enables us to add that Indian, Negro, and Mulatto ſervants were eſtimated proportionably as other perſonal eſtate, according to the ſound judgment and diſcretion of the Aſſeſſors in each and every year from 1727 to 1775, excepting 1730, 1731, 1749, 1750. The acts for theſe years we have not ſeen, but it is reaſonably certain that the proviſion was the ſame as in all the others. That of 1776 was probably ſimilar to that of 1777, in which the Poll-Tax is levied on Male Polls above 16 years of age, including Negroes and Mulattoes, and ſuch of them that are under the government of a Maſter or Miſtreſs, to be taxed to the ſaid Maſter or Miſtreſs reſpectively, in the ſame manner as Minors and Apprentices are taxed. This method continued to 1791. The act of 1793 omits the mention of Negroes and Mulattoes, taxing "minors, apprentices and ſervants" *as above*. In 1803, ſuch as are under "the *immediate* government" of a maſter, etc. In 1805, the ſervants are omitted, and there is a ſeparate ſection concerning minors.

Appendix. 249

7. Page 94, *and note.* With reference to the flave's "right to Religion," we fhould have added a word refpecting the peculiar "feparation" of the religious people of Maffachufetts and their well-known "fear of polluting the ordinances;" to which was afcribed, in this very connection, that neglect of "proper means to make men godly," which became "the mifery of New England." *Stoddard's Anfwer to fome Cafes of Confcience, etc.,* 1722, *p.* 12. It was the opinion of this writer that "if they (fervants) had proper Helps, they might be as forward in Religion, as the *Englifh." Ibid.*

8. *Pages* 97, 101. Inftructions fimilar to thofe given to Andros in 1688 (*ante, pp.* 51-2, 96) were repeated to fubfequent governors of the various colonies. We have found no act paffed in accordance with thefe inftructions in Maffachufetts, or any other colony or province excepting New Hampfhire; where fuch a law was enacted, in which the diftinction noted in the text between the *Chriftian* fervants or flaves, and the *Indians and Negroes,* is emphatically illuftrated. The Province Law of 1718, Chap. 70, is as follows (*Edit.* 1771, *p.* 101):

An Act for reftraining Inhuman Severities.

§ 1. BE IT ENACTED *by His* EXCELLENCY *the* GOVERNOR, COUNCIL, *and* REPRESENTATIVES, *convened in* GENERAL ASSEMBLY, *and it is hereby* ENACTED *by the* AUTHORITY *of the fame,* That for the prevention and reftraining inhuman feverities, which by evil mafters or overfeers may be ufed towards their Chriftian fervants, that from and after the publication hereof, if any man fmite out the eye or tooth of his man-fervant or maid-fervant, or otherwife maim or disfigure them much, unlefs it be by meer cafualty, he fhall let him or her go free from his fervice, and fhall allow fuch further recompence as the court of quarter feffions fhall adjudge him.

§ 2. AND IT IS *further* ENACTED, *and* ORDAINED *by the* AUTHORITY *aforefaid,* That if any perfon or perfons whatever within this province fhall wilfully kill his *indian* or *negro* fervant or fervants, he fhall be punifhed with death.

It is true, that Chriftian fervants were protected in Maffachufetts by the earlieft law refpecting the "liberties of fervants" from which the provifions of the firft fection of the foregoing law were copied; but the relations of the Indian and Negro flaves and their mafters were ftill regulated in accordance with the contemporary standards of opinion concerning what was morally required by "the law of God established in Israel," or what may be described as the New-English-Hebrew-Christian common or customary law. The familiar phrase—"treated worse than a negro"—is historical in Massachusetts. *Sewall's Diary, October* 20*th*, 1701, quoted in *Quincy's Harv. Coll.*, I., 490.

9. *Pages* 126–28. On the 25th of June, 1766, a petition was presented in the House of Representatives, from Ezekiel Wood, the representative for the town of Uxbridge, setting forth that there were in said town two aged and infirm negroes not belonging there, etc. On the 28th, this petition was dismissed, and a Committee was appointed to bring in a bill at the next session for preventing Fraud in the sale of Negroes. On the 1st of November, in the same year, "a Bill intituled An Act to prevent Frauds in the sale of Negroes" was "read a first time and ordered a second reading on Tuesday next at Ten o'clock." On the 4th, it was read a second time and recommitted for amendment.

The draft of the bill is preserved, as well as the report of the committee. *Mass. Archives, Domestic Relations,* 1643–1774, *Vol.* 9, 449, 450. It was intended to prevent fraudulent sales made by the original purchasers or owners to persons of no responsibility. Under its provisions, the towns were authorized to bring actions against the next vendor of ability, and each and every vendor from the original purchaser or owner was made liable. In this way the maintenance of the pauper negroes was to be provided for without charge to the towns.

We find no further proceedings on the subject until the 4th of June, 1767, when the "Bill to prevent Fraud in the sale of Negroes and to provide for their maintenance" was read, and the Secretary was ordered to "lay on the Table the Act for laying a duty of Impost on the Importation of Negro or other Slaves into this Province," which he accordingly did. The latter bill, as we have seen, had fallen between the two houses in March previous. Whether it was proposed, at this time, by bringing them together to devise some new movement on the subject of either or both, we cannot ascertain, having found no trace of further action upon them.

C. Judge Saffin's Reply to Judge Sewall, 1701.

WHILE thefe fheets are paffing through the prefs, we are kindly favored with the opportunity to make ufe of this extremely rare and valuable, if not unique tract, from which we copy below. We are indebted to the generous and liberal courtefy of GEORGE BRINLEY, Efq., of Hartford, Connecticut, for this moft interefting and important addition to our work. Compare *ante, pp.* 83–88.

"A Brief and Candid Anfwer to a late Printed Sheet, Entituled, The Selling of Jofeph.

"THAT Honourable and Learned Gentleman, the Author of a Sheet, Entituled, *The Selling of Jofeph, A* Memorial, feems from thence to draw this conclufion, that becaufe the Sons of *Jacob* did very ill in felling their Brother *Jofeph* to the *Ifhmaelites*, who were Heathens, therefore it is utterly unlawful to Buy and Sell Negroes, though among Chriftians; which Conclufion I prefume is not well drawn from the Premifes, nor is the cafe parallel; for it was unlawful for the *Israelites* to Sell their Brethren upon any account, or pretence whatfoever during life. But it was not unlawful for the Seed of *Abraham* to have Bond men, and Bond women either born in their Houfe, or bought with their Money, as it is written of *Abraham, Gen.* 14. 14. & 21. 10. & *Exod.* 21. 16. & *Levit.* 25. 44. 45, 46 *v.* After the giving of the Law: And in *Jofh.* 9. 23. That famous Example of the *Gibeonites* is a fufficient proof where there no other.

"To fpeak a little to the Gentlemans firft Affertion: *That none ought to part with their Liberty themfelves, or deprive others of it but upon mature confideration;* a prudent exception, in which he grants, that upon fome confideration a man may be deprived of his Liberty. And then prefently in his next Pofition or Affertion he denies it, *viz.: It is moft certain, that all men as they are the Sons of* Adam *are Coheirs, and have equal right to Liberty, and all other Comforts of Life,* which he would prove out of *Psal.* 115. 16. *The Earth hath he given to the Children of Men.* True, but what is all this to the purpofe, to prove that all men have equal right to Liberty, and all outward comforts of this life; which Pofition feems to invert the Order that God hath set in the World, who hath Ordained different degrees and orders of men, some to be High and Honourable, some to be Low and Despicable; some to be Monarchs, Kings, Princes and Governours, Masters and Commanders, others to be Subjects, and to be Commanded; Servants of sundry sorts and degrees, bound to obey; yea, some to be born Slaves, and so to remain during their lives, as hath been proved. Otherwise there would be a meer parity among men, contrary to that of the Apostle, 1 *Cor.* 12 *from the* 13 *to the* 26 *verse,* where he sets forth (by way of comparison) the different sorts and offices of the Members of the Body, indigitating that they are all of use, but not equal, and of like dignity. So God hath set different Orders and Degrees of Men in the World, both in Church and Common weal. Now, if this Position of parity should be true, it would then follow that the ordinary Course of Divine Providence of God in the World should be wrong, and unjust, (which we must not dare to think, much less to affirm) and all the sacred Rules, Precepts and Commands of the Almighty which he hath given the Son of Men to observe and keep in their respective Places, Orders and Degrees, would be to no purpose; which unaccountably derogate from the Divine Wisdom of the most High, who hath made nothing in vain, but hath Holy Ends in all his Dispensations to the Children of men.

"In the next place, this worthy Gentleman makes a large Discourse concerning the Utility and Conveniency to keep the one, and inconveniency of the other; respecting white and black Servants, which conduceth most to the welfare and benefit of this Province: which he concludes to be white men, who are in many respects to be preferred before Blacks; who doubts that? doth it therefore follow, that it is altogether unlawful for Christians to buy and keep Negro Servants (for this is the Thesis) but that those that have them ought in Conscience to set them free, and so lose all the money they cost (for we must not live in any known sin) this seems to be his opinion; but it is a Question whether it ever was the Gentleman's practice? But if he could perswade the General Assembly to make an Act, That all that have Negroes, and do set them free, shall be Re imbursed out of the Publick Treasury, and that there shall be no more Negroes brought into the Country; 'tis probable there would be more of his opinion; yet he would find it a hard task to bring the Country to consent thereto; for

Appendix. 253

then the Negroes muft be all fent out of the Country, or elfe the remedy would be worfe than the Difeafe; and it is to be feared that thofe Negroes that are free, if there be not fome ftrict courfe taken with them by Authority, they will be a plague to this Country.

"*Again*, If it fhould be unlawful to deprive them that are lawful Captives, or Bondmen of their Liberty for Life being Heathens; it feems to be more unlawful to deprive our Brethren, of our own or other Chriftian Nations of the Liberty, (though but for a time) by binding them to Serve fome Seven, Ten, Fifteen, and fome Twenty Years, which oft times proves for their whole Life, as many have been; which in effect is the fame in Nature, though different in the time, yet this was allow'd among the *Jews* by the Law of God; and is the conftant practice of our own and other Chriftian Nations in the World: the which our Author by his Dogmatical Affertions doth condemn as Irreligious; which is Diametrically contrary to the Rules and Precepts which God hath given the diverfity of men to obferve in their refpective Stations, Callings, and Conditions of Life, as hath been obferved.

"And to illuftrate his Affertion our Author brings in by way of Comparifon the Law of God againft man Stealing, on pain of Death: Intimating thereby, that Buying and Selling of Negro's is a breach of that Law, and fo deferves Death: A fevere Sentence: But herein he begs the Queftion with a *Caveat Emptor*. For, in that very Chapter there is a Difpenfation to the People of *Israel*, to have Bond men, Women and Children, even of their own Nation in fome cafe; and Rules given therein to be obferved concerning them; Verfe the 4*th*. And in the before cited place, *Levit*. 25. 44, 45, 46. Though the *Israelites* were forbidden (ordinarily) to make Bond men and Women of their own Nation, but of Strangers they might: the words run thus, verse 44. *Both thy Bond men, and thy Bond maids which thou fhalt have fhall be of the Heathen, that are round about you: of them fhall you Buy Bond men and Bond maids*, &c. See also, 1 *Cor*. 12. 13. Whether we be Bond or Free, which fhows that in the times of the New Teftament, there were Bond men alfo, *&c*.

"*In fine*, The fum of this long Haurange, is no other, than to compare the Buying and Selling of Negro's unto the Stealing of Men, and the Selling of *Jofeph* by his Brethren, which bears no proportion therewith, nor is there any congruiety therein, as appears by the foregoing Texts.

"Our Author doth further proceed to anfwer fome Objections of his own framing, which he fuppofes fome might raife.

"Object. 1. *That thefe Blackamores are of the Posterity of* Cham, *and therefore under the Curfe of Slavery.* Gen. 9. 25, 26, 27. The which the Gentleman feems to deny, faying, *they ware the Seed of Canaan that were Curfed, &c.*

"*Anfw.* Whether they were fo or not, we fhall not difpute: this may fuffice, that not only the feed of *Cham* or *Canaan*, but any lawful Captives of other Heathen Nations may be made Bond men as hath been proved.

"Obj. 2. *That the Negroes are brought out of Pagan Countreys into places where the Gofpel is Preached.* To which he Replies, *that we muft not doe Evil that Good may come of it.*

"*Anf.* To which we anfwer, That it is no Evil thing to bring them out of their own Heathenish Country, where they may have the Knowledge of the True God, be Converted and Eternally faved.

"Obj. 3. *The* Africans *have Wars one with another;* our Ships bring lawful Captives taken in thofe Wars.

"To which our Author anfwers Conjecturally, and Doubtfully, *for ought we know*, that which may or may not be; which is infignificant, and proves nothing. He alfo compares the Negroes Wars, one Nation with another, with the Wars between *Jofeph* and his Brethren. But where doth he read of any fuch War? We read indeed of a Domeftick Quarrel they had with him, they envyed and hated *Jofeph;* but by what is Recorded, he was meerly paffive and meek as a Lamb. This Gentleman farther adds, *That there is not any War but is unjuft on one fide, &c.* Be it fo, what doth that fignify: We read of lawful Captives taken in the Wars, and lawful to be Bought and Sold without contracting the guilt of the *Agreffors;* for which we have the example of *Abraham* before quoted; but if we muft ftay while both parties Warring are in the right, there would be no lawful Captives at all to be Bought; which feems to be rediculous to imagine, and contrary to the tenour of Scripture, and all Humane Hiftories on that fubject.

"Obj. 4. *Abraham had Servants bought with his Money, and born in his Houfe.* Gen. 14. 14. To which our worthy Author anfwers, *until the Circumftances of Abraham's purchafe be recorded, no Argument can be drawn from it.*

Appendix. 255

"*Anf.* To which we Reply, this is alfo Dogmatical, and proves nothing. He farther adds, *In the mean time Charity Obliges us to conclude, that he knew it was lawful and good.* Here the gentleman yields the cafe; for if we are in Charity bound to believe *Abrahams* practice, in buying and keeping *Slaves* in his houfe to be lawful and good: then it follows, that our Imitation of him in this his Moral Action, is as warrantable as that of his Faith; *who is the Father of all them that believe.* Rom. 4. 16.

"In the clofe of all, Our Author Quotes two more places of Scripture, *viz.*; *Levit.* 25. 46, and *Jer.* 34, from the 8. to the 22. v. To prove that the people of Ifrael were strictly forbidden the Buying and Selling one another for *Slaves:* who queftions that? and what is that to the cafe in hand? What a ftrange piece of Logick is this? Tis unlawful for Chriftians to Buy and Sell one another for flaves. *Ergo,* It is unlawful to Buy and Sell Negroes that are lawful Captiv'd Heathens.

"And after a Serious Exhortation to us all to Love one another according to the Command of Christ. *Math.* 5, 43, 44. This worthy Gentleman concludes with this Affertion, *That thefe Ethiopeans as Black as they are, feeing they are the Sons and Daughters of the firft* Adam; *the Brethren and Sifters of the Second* Adam, *and the Offspring of God; we ought to treat them with a refpect agreeable.*

"*Ans.* We grant it for a certain and undeniable verity, That all Mankind are the Sons and Daughters of *Adam,* and the Creatures of God: But it doth not therefore follow that we are bound to love and refpect all men alike; this under favour we muft take leave to deny; we ought in charity, if we fee our Neighbour in want, to relieve them in a regular way, but we are not bound to give them fo much of our Eftates, as to make them equal with our felves, because they are our Brethren, the Sons of *Adam,* no, not our own natural Kinfmen: We are Exhorted *to do good unto all, but efpecially to them who are of the Houfhold of Faith, Gal.* 6. 10. And we are to love, honour and refpect all men according to the gift of God that is in them: I may love my Servant well, but my Son better; Charity begins at home, it would be a violation of common prudence, and a breach of good manners, to treat a Prince like a Peafant. And this worthy Gentleman would deem himſelf much neglected, if we ſhould ſhow him no more Defference than to an ordinary Porter : And therefore theſe florid expreſſions, the Sons and Daughters of the Firſt *Adam*, the Brethren and Siſters of the Second *Adam*, and the Offspring of God, ſeem to be miſapplied to import and inſinuate, that we ought to tender Pagan Negroes with all love, kindneſs, and equal reſpect as to the beſt of men.

"By all which it doth evidently appear both by Scripture and Reaſon, the practice of the People of God in all Ages, both before and after the giving of the Law, and in the times of the Goſpel, that there were Bond men, Women and Children commonly kept by holy and good men, and improved in Service; and therefore by the Command of God, *Lev.* 25, 44, and their venerable Example, we may keep Bond men, and uſe them in our Service ſtill; yet with all candour, moderation and Chriſtian prudence, according to their ſtate and condition conſonant to the Word of God.

"The Negroes Character.

" *Cowardly and cruel are thoſe* Blacks *Innate,*
Prone to Revenge, Imp of inveterate hate.
He that exaſperates them, ſoon eſpies
Miſchief and Murder in their very eyes.
Libidinous, Deceitful, Falſe and Rude,
The ſpume Iſſue of Ingratitude.
The Premiſes conſider'd, all may tell,
How near good Joſeph *they are parallel.*"

By the same Writer:

THE TREASON OF LEE.

"Mr. Lee's Plan—March 29, 1777." The Treaſon of Charles Lee, Major-General, Second in Command in the American Army of the Revolution. By GEORGE H. MOORE, Librarian of the New York Hiſtorical Society. 1 vol., 8vo, cloth. Two Steel Portraits, and Two Lithograph Fac-ſimiles of Documents. *Three dollars.*

"It is a clear and most interesting development of one of the strangest events in the history of the Revolution. It is as important as it is curious, for the acts and motives of a man who held so high a rank in the army and in the public estimation should be known. They affect the character of others, and throw light on transactions which could not otherwise be explained."

JARED SPARKS.

"Your paper was certainly the most instructive one ever presented (within my observation) to any one of our Historical Societies.

"The work does you great credit; it is full of interest, of facts collected from far and near. The story is well told, the criticism careful and discriminating. I feel certain it will bring you much reputation for its completeness and manner of execution. * * * Go on; and you will win honor for yourself, while you will assist to make American History what it ought to be."

GEORGE BANCROFT.

"I have read it with great interest. It is a curious, valuable, and conclusively argued contribution to our Revolutionary history."

GULIAN C. VERPLANCK.

"I am greatly indebted to you for a copy of your beautiful monograph. * * * I rejoice that you have found the means (and made such good use of them) of putting his worthlessness beyond all question."

EDWARD EVERETT.

"You have done a good service to history. I ran it through with the greatest interest."

ROBERT C. WINTHROP.

"Many thanks for 'Lee's Treason.' * * * Moore has made out the case against him."

W. F. DE SAUSSURE (of S. C.)

"The Treason of Lee is placed beyond doubt, and the original documents establishing it are published in the recent highly valuable monograph of G. H. Moore Esq., on that subject."—*Everett's Life of Washington.*

" We commend Mr. Moore's work as the most valuable contribution to our Revolutionary history that has appeared for many a day, and assure our readers that the perusal of its elegant and eloquent pages cannot but repay the few hours that it will require."—*Historical Magazine.*

" We commend this essay to the attention of historical students, admiring the simplicity and lucidity of its style."—*Express.*

" A work which we have read with great pleasure, * * * well worthy the attention of our readers, and we take great pleasure in recommending it to them."— *Boston Post.*

" This beautifully printed volume is an important contribution to the history of the war of the Revolution. It establishes beyond a question the treason of one of the most distinguished generals of that war, who was second in command to Washington."—*Providence Journal.*

" The researches of Mr. Moore reflect great credit on his industry and penetration as a historical student, and we unite with those better capable of judging than ourselves, that he has brought to light important facts, which tend more to clear up obscure points in our Revolutionary history than any thing that has appeared since the events alluded to took place."—*Providence Journal.*

" The volume abounds with curious details, and will be read with great interest by the student of American history."—*N. Y. Tribune.*

No student of American history can afford to be without this book."—*R. I. Schoolmaster.*

" One of the most valuable contributions to our Revolutionary history that has ever been published. * * * Mr. Moore's carefulness and completeness of research are fine qualities of the historian, happily exhibited in this volume."—*Christian Intelligencer.*

" Sound judgment, thorough research, just appreciation of character, an acute perception of the logical connection of events chronologically disjoined, and a ready command of clear, precise, and appropriate language, have enabled Mr. Moore to make a volume, which, taken in all its bearings, may unhesitatingly be pronounced the most important monograph ever contributed to the history of the War of Independence."—*New York Times.*

" Crammed with the valuable results of original investigations. Many of the documents never before published, and throwing a new and unexpected light on a very interesting episode of the Revolution."—*Evening Post.*

Also:

HISTORICAL NOTES ON THE EMPLOYMENT
of Negroes in the American Army of the Revolution. Pamphlet. 8vo. 24 pages. *Fifty cents.*

[*PROSPECTUS.*]

THE
STATUTES AT LARGE OF NEW-YORK
1664–1691.

"*The laws of a nation form the most instructive portion of its history.*"

I propose to publish the STATUTES AT LARGE OF NEW YORK from 1664 to 1691. The first English Laws were established in the Province immediately after the reduction of the Dutch in New-Netherland, by the authority of Letters Patent granted by King Charles II. to his brother, James, Duke of York, March 12th, 1664. These laws, since known as "the Duke's Laws," were altered, explained, and amended by the same authority during the succeeding years until 1683, when the first Representative Assembly met in New-York. Laws were enacted by this Assembly in that and the following year, and a second Assembly met and enacted others in the year 1685, after the accession of James II. to the throne. This, however, was the only meeting of an Assembly in New-York during his reign—for in 1686 he abolished the Assembly, and made his Governor and Council the legislature of the Province. Several acts were passed by this body in the years 1687 and 1688; and these, with the acts of the Assembly summoned by Leisler during the troubles which attended the Revolution, complete the Body of Laws which it is now proposed to publish.

Of all these statutes, fragments only are accessible to the student either of Law or History. It is well known that no printing-press was established in New-York until after the era of the English Revolution of 1688; and the laws were published in manuscript, many being preserved only in the public records; and the Acts of the first Assemblies were so neglected, that the historian, also one of the principal lawyers of the time, declared more than a century ago, that they were "for the most part rotten, defaced, or lost."

In the first volume of the Collections of the New-York Historical Society there is a copy of the East Hampton Book of Laws, and in the Appendix to the Revised Laws of 1813 are imperfect copies of three of the Acts of the First Assembly, while in one instance (and but one, I believe), another Act of the same Assembly is recited in an enactment of a subsequent legislature. The printed laws of New-York begin with the year 1691, and, with the exceptions just mentioned, the whole body of laws of the first twenty-six years of the English government of New-York exists only in scattered, obscure, and fast perishing manuscripts.

Their importance to the lawyer as well as the historian is obvious, for they are the basis of all subsequent legislation in respect to the subjects to which they relate.

They "tend to show the progressive state of our laws, with the various changes they have undergone from the commencement, and serve to throw great light on the historical transactions" of the colonial period. Instances have not been wanting, and may yet occur, in which, "though they do not govern, they may be found proper to guide."

The volume will comprise the Nicolls Code as originally promulgated in 1665; the Alterations, Additions, and Amendments of 1665 and 1666; the "Duke's Laws," as approved and established in 1667–'68; the Orders of the General Court of Assizes and the Governor and Council, from 1667 to 1683; the Acts of Assembly of 1683, 1684, and 1685; the Acts of the Governor and Council from 1686 to 1689; and the Acts of the Assembly summoned by Leisler in 1690.

Various illustrative documents will be given, with a Historical Introduction and Notes, among which will be found biographical notices of the English Governors of New-York from 1664 to 1691. I propose to add fac-similes of various acts of approval, and the volume will be completed by a full and thorough analytical index.

It will be printed in the best manner, in large octavo form, and will make a volume of not less than three hundred pages.

PRICE, FIVE DOLLARS, payable on delivery.

GEORGE H. MOORE,
Librarian of the New-York Historical Society.

NEW-YORK, *October*, 1862.

☞ If sufficient encouragement is given to warrant the undertaking, the work will be continued through the remainder of the Colonial period—1691–1775. Of nearly two thousand statutes enacted during these years by thirty-two different Assemblies, not one-third have been printed in the various collected and revised editions, and all are long since out of print.

www.ingramcontent.com/pod-product-compliance
Lightning Source LLC
Chambersburg PA
CBHW031348230426
43670CB00006B/467